"Pick up this book, open it anywhere, read it for two minutes, and take one lesson as a suggestion. Your testing, test planning, test management, or thinking about testing will improve dramatically."

Johanna Rothman, Rothman Consulting Group, Inc.

"If you test software, or depend on people who do, then read this book. Each page bubbles with hard-won advice for handling the practical problems you encounter every day."

Sam Guckenheimer
Senior Director of Automated Testing Technology
Rational Software Corporation

"Definitely a book worth reading and keeping around. Smart, practical, insightful and thought-provoking."

Ross Collard, Collard & Company

"These three distinguished test professionals have written a precisely-stated and thought-provoking book that offers a distinctive and important perspective on testing and test project management."

Rex Black, Author of Managing the Testing Process *and* Critical Testing Processes

"This is the book the testing community has been looking for and didn't realize it. A must read for any test engineer or manager."

George Hamblen Jr., Director of Software Quality Assurance
for a large financial services company

"This isn't textbook stuff. It's better. It's real life under discussion and observation. I'm excited to see so many aspects of testing being brought together into one book. I expect great discussions to be had because of this book."

Steve Tolman, Manager of Software Quality, PowerQuest

"These lessons contain wonderful insights about software testing in the real world, from the leading practical experts on software testing. Whether you test software, or work with people who do, this book is great stuff."

Alan Myrvold

"Clear and succinct. It has brought clarity to many of my own learning experiences and provoked a lot of new thoughts."

Fran McKain
Software Test Manager
Hewlett-Packard Company

"Reviewing this book was one of my greatest learning experiences. I warmly recommend this as a must-have for any testing professional."

Hans Buwalda, Author of Integrated Test Design and Automation

"The book is packed with nuggets of gold derived from years of practical experience. The chapter on test automation alone is more useful than any of the books I've seen on test automation. The chapter on techniques has powerful ideas, simply stated!"

Doug Hoffman, Consultant, Software Quality Methods, LLC

"*Lessons Learned in Software Testing* is a must read for the beginner who needs tried and true tips and for the mature test manager who is looking for more refinements for his or her organization."

Chris DeNardis, Supervisor of Software Engineering, Rockwell Automation

" . . . offers an invaluable collection of real world practices based on years of experience shared by the authors collectively and many of their colleagues . . . an absolute must for anyone who has a serious interest in software testing."

Hung Q. Nguyen, President and CEO, LogiGear Corporation
Author of Testing Applications on the Web

"The lessons format is simple and succinct, just the thing for us to use in late night test planning sessions. Where other books have been long on theory and are great for study, this is long on reality, practicality, and immediate usefulness."

Mary Romero Sweeney, Author of Visual Basic for Testers

"This is an excellent book. I have had similar experiences as documented in this book, without being able to learn the lessons whilst in the middle of the problem."

Ståle Amland, Amland Consulting, Norway

Lessons Learned in Software Testing

A Context-Driven Approach

Cem Kaner

James Bach

Bret Pettichord

Wiley Computer Publishing

John Wiley & Sons, Inc.

NEW YORK • CHICHESTER • WEINHEIM • BRISBANE • SINGAPORE • TORONTO

Publisher: Robert Ipsen
Editor: Margaret Eldridge
Assistant Editor: Adaobi Obi
Managing Editor: Micheline Frederick
Text Design & Composition: D&G Limited, LLC

This book is printed on acid-free paper. ∞

This publication is designed to provide accurate and authoritative information in regard to the subject matter covered. It is sold with the understanding that the publisher is not engaged in professional services. If professional advice or other expert assistance is required, the services of a competent professional person should be sought.

Library of Congress Cataloging-in-Publication Data:

Kaner, Cem.
    Lessons learned in software testing : a context-driven approach / Cem Kaner, James Bach, Bret Pettichord.
      p. cm.
    "Wiley Computer Publishing."
    Includes bibliographical references and index.
    ISBN 0-471-08112-4 (pbk. : alk. paper)
      1. Computer software—Testing. I. Bach, James. II. Pettichord, Bret. III. Title.

  QA76.76.T48 K34 2001
  005.1'4—dc21   2001046886

Printed in the United States of America.

10 9 8 7 6 5 4 3 2 1

To Brian Marick and Sam Guckenheimer, who set the spark for this book.

To Dave Gelperin, who believed in us and built a community.

To Jerry Weinberg, whose life and work embodies the highest ideals of an expert tester.

In memoriam, Anna Allison, colleague and friend, September 30, 1952–September 11, 2001.

CONTENTS

Chapter 3   Testing Techniques

Chapter 4   Bug Advocacy

Chapter 5   Automating Testing

Chapter 6   Documenting Testing

Chapter 7   Interacting with Programmers

Chapter 8   Managing the Testing Project

Chapter 10   Your Career in Software Testing

Chapter 11   Planning the Testing Strategy

Imagine that you are holding a bottle of 50-year-old port. There is a way to drink port. It is not the only way, but most folks who have enjoyed port for many years have found some guidelines that help them maximize their port-drinking experience. Here are just a few:

Lesson 1: Don't drink straight from the bottle. If you have no glass, nor any other possible containers available, pour a tiny amount of port into the palm of your hand and sip from there. The port aroma should be smelled as you sip. Let the port swirl over your tongue. Don't gulp down the port.

Lesson 2: Don't drink the entire bottle. If you are drinking because you are thirsty, put down the port and drink a big glass of water. A small amount of port each time maximizes the enjoyment of the entire bottle.

Lesson 3: Don't pollute the port. If someone tells you that you ought to try a new cocktail made with orange juice, seawater, and port, politely refuse. With a big smile, say, "But I would enjoy a glass of port."

Lesson 4: Don't covet the port. Hoarding your port means that you will never have the pleasure of gentle conversation while sipping. Port is best shared with friends who also enjoy a glass. Remember, they have a bottle somewhere, too.

You are not holding a bottle of port in your hands. You are holding *Lessons Learned in Software Testing*, a very valuable book about software testing. This book has been ripening to perfection throughout the 50 work-years of the authors' experiences. While port is for your taste buds, this book is for your brain. I think that you will find any other differences to be marginal. I have savored this book and offer you this advice to maximize your reading experience.

Lesson 1. Don't drink straight from the bottle. Bring your own vessel to the reading of this book. That is, bring all of your experiences in software development and testing. If you have never participated in a serious software effort, this book will be too heady for you. It will leave you confused and unable to operate heavy machinery for some time. If you are experienced, savor the book's contents in the context of your own projects.

Lesson 2. Don't drink the entire bottle. Don't read this book in one sitting. Read a lesson or two, close the book, and decide how you respond to the words of Messrs. Kaner, Bach, and Pettichord. As you will discover, they call their approach to testing "context-driven." Only you know the context of your own work. You must determine where there is a fit between a given lesson and your particular work.

Lesson 3. Don't pollute the port. Somebody out there is going to make a list of the titles of the 293 lessons contained in this book. Please don't let it be you. The heart of the book is the explanation attached to each of the lessons. Be warned as well that someone else will immediately try to ISO-ify or CMM-ummify the contents. I can see the article title now, "Getting to CMM Level 293 using the 293 Lessons of *Lessons Learned in Software Testing*." Argh! As the authors explain, " . . . we don't believe in 'best practices.' We believe some practices are more useful than others under some circumstances." Written by pros, those statements represent the quintessence of attaining the state of Master-crafter of Software Testing.

Lesson 4. Don't covet the port. If there ever is a book to be read with your colleagues, this is it. Buy a carton-load and hand a copy out to everyone who tests and to everyone who thinks that she or he manages testers. Read a few selected lessons at a time and get together to talk about them over coffee, lunch, even port! Read, ruminate, enjoy. Cheers!

Tim Lister
August 17, 2001
lister@acm.org
The Atlantic Systems Guild, Inc.
New York City

The *Software Engineering Body of Knowledge* (SWEBOK) is being proposed as a suitable foundation for government licensing, for the regulation of software engineers, and for the development of university curricula in software engineering. The SWEBOK document claims to be consensus-based. One would expect such a document to carry the accumulated knowledge and wisdom (the accumulated *lessons*) of the field.

Here is everything that SWEBOK has to say about exploratory testing:

> Perhaps the most widely practiced technique remains ad hoc testing: tests are derived relying on the tester skill and intuition ("exploratory" testing), and on his/her experience with similar programs. While a more systematic approach is advised, ad hoc testing might be useful (but only if the tester is really expert!) to identify special tests, not easily "captured" by formalized techniques. Moreover it must be reminded that this technique may yield largely varying degrees of effectiveness. (SWEBOK 0.95, 2001, 5-9)

How does SWEBOK treat what it acknowledges is the field's most widely practiced technique? Nothing about how to practice the technique well. Only a statement that exploration should be done only by *real experts*, that other approaches are advised, and the suggestion that other, formalized techniques will yield less varying degrees of effectiveness.

Hah!

We *don't* pretend to offer a consensus document that describes our field's alleged *body of knowledge*, but *we do have a lot more* to say about our field's most common practices. Rather than dismissing exploratory testing, this book shows you what testing looks like through the eyes of people who use exploratory methods (and many other methods) in a drive to achieve excellent testing under real-life conditions.

Welcome to *Lessons Learned in Software Testing*

This book is about software development as we've experienced it. We've had a combined total of 50 to 60 years of development experience (depending on how you count). We've been at this for a while. We've seen a lot of great work and a lot of not-so-great work.

This book is not about how software engineering might be in a tidier and more controlled world. We're writing about the world as we've worked in it.

In our world, software development teams often work under ambitious deadlines, discovering what needs to be done at the same time as they're discovering how to do it. Sometimes their approaches are more formal, sometimes less. It depends on a wide range of circumstances.

We follow the *context-driven approach* in software testing. We expect that a method that works wonderfully under some circumstances will not work under others. Rather than talk about best practices, we talk about practices that are well-suited to the context at hand. We discuss the context-driven approach at the end of the book, but in essence, context-driven testing looks at the "what" of testing (the techniques, tools, strategies, and so on) in terms of "who," "when," "where," "why," and "what if."

Our goal is to match our selection of practices to the circumstances at hand in a way that achieves excellent testing. We don't expect to achieve great testing by taking over the project, nor by stamping our feet and telling the project manager (or executives) how Real Professionals would run the project. We don't expect to achieve great testing by intimidating programmers, nor by being obsequious to them. We don't expect to do great testing by filling out thousands of little pieces of paper (or comparable electronic records), nor by wasting everyone else's time on unnecessary processes.

We don't have a political or a bureaucratic or a formal-methods recipe for great testing.

That recipe doesn't exist!

We think great testing involves skillful technical work (searching for defects) and accurate, persuasive communication.

The skilled search is always exploratory. There's an infinite amount of testing to do, and a tiny amount of time in which to do just a little bit of that infinity. Every test we do, every document we write, every meeting we attend takes time away from running other tests that could expose a key defect. Facing that constraint, we optimize our testing processes so that they take advantage of our ever-growing knowledge of the product, its market, its applications, and its weaknesses. What we learn today gets reflected in more powerful tests tomorrow.

Even if:

- the product is well specified, and
- the specification accurately reflects a requirements document, and
- the requirements document accurately represents the actual needs of the product's stakeholders

(have you *ever* been on a project where all these "even if's" were true?); we will still learn a lot about how to test the product while we are testing it. In particular, as we discover errors, we learn how this group of programmers can go wrong. The specifications tell us about how the program is supposed to work when it is coded correctly. They don't tell us what mistakes to anticipate, nor how to design tests to find them. At that task, our key task, we get better from the start to the end of the project, on every project.

No matter what it looks like from the outside, whenever we are testing with our brains engaged, our work is exploratory.

Who This Book Is For

This book is for anyone who tests software, anyone who manages testers, and anyone who has to deal with testers in their software development projects. That includes project managers and executives.

The primary reader that we have in mind, the "you" in this book, has been testing for a few years and might recently have been promoted to a supervisory role. We hope that you'll see a lot in this book that matches your experience, that you'll gain new insights from our lessons, that you'll find lessons that are useful for quoting to your manager, that you'll like a few of our statements so much that you'll photocopy them and stick them on the outside of your cubicle, and maybe that you'll react to at least one statement so strongly that you'll stick a copy on the middle of your dart board. (We want to stimulate thought, not only agreement.)

Newcomers to testing (and those of you who are just applying for a testing job) won't have as many occasions to feel that you've already experienced what we're writing about. For you, this book might provide some early insights and warnings, giving you a good taste of what issues testers face.

Hint: If you are absolutely new to testing and you are looking for a book to study from in order to prepare for a job interview, this is the wrong book. If this is the only book available to you, pay your most careful attention to the chapters on "Testing Techniques" and "Your Career in Software Testing." If you have a choice of books, we suggest the first five chapters of *Testing Computer Software* (Kaner *et al.*, 1993).

Programmers, project managers, and executives who have to work with testers will find this book a useful source of ideas for setting your expectations of the testing group. We hope that it will help you evaluate and discuss your concerns with the testing group if you disagree with their policies or feel that they are spending their time unwisely.

What This Book Is About

Over the years, we've learned many useful practices and helpful ways of evaluating situations. Our conclusions are based on experience. We summarize much of our experience in this book, in a series of short, readable descriptions of a few hundred *lessons*.

We adopted several criteria for including a lesson in this book. They are:

- The lesson should be useful or should provide insight.

- The lesson should pass the 90-minutes-thinking-alone test. A lesson is not worth including in the book if almost anyone who thought about testing for 90 minutes of undistracted time could come up with it.

- The lesson must be based on our actual experience. At least one of us (preferably all three of us) had to have successfully applied the advice we give. At least two of us had to have been burned by attempting to follow a practice we criticize. (*Note:* Sometimes, we come to different conclusions, based on different experiences. Occasionally, you'll see that we choose to provide two viewpoints rather than one. Even if only one view is presented, you cannot assume that all three of us fully agree with it—in the event of disagreement, we are likely, among the three of us, to defer to the one or two who have the most extensive experience with a given situation.)

- Lessons should be tempered by the experiences of our colleagues. We've been collecting detailed experience reports at the Los Altos Workshops on Software Testing, the Software Test Managers Round Tables, the Workshops on Heuristic and Exploratory Techniques, the Austin Workshops on Test Automation, the Patterns of Software Testing Workshops, the Workshop on Model-Based Automated Testing, Systems Effectiveness Management Groups, at dozens of software testing conferences, and at less formal peer cross-trainings (such as the annual Consultants' Camps in Crested Butte).

- The lesson should be brief and to the point but easily understood.

- A lesson can be longer, but only to the extent needed to explain how to do something or to provide a useful tool. Long descriptions and detailed background information are for the textbooks.

- Lessons should be self-contained. You should be able to start reading anywhere in the book.

- The collection of lessons should give you a feel for how we do and think about testing.

What This Book Is Not

This book is not a comprehensive guide to software testing.

This book is not a collection of lessons that are always true. These are *our* lessons, based on *our* experiences. We believe these are broadly applicable, but some lessons that have been useful and important in our careers may not work for you. You have to use your own judgment. As a particular limiter on the generality of this work, we should note that we've worked more on the development of software for the mass market and on contract-specified software than we have on software developed for in-house use. Our experience with life-critical software and embedded software is limited.

This book is not a collection of best practices. In fact, we don't believe in "best practices." We believe some practices are more useful than others under some circumstances. We are concerned that many things sold as best practices are pushed (and applied) uncritically, to situations that aren't appropriate to them.

How to Use This Book

We structured this book to make it easy for you to skim it or flip through it, rather than trying to read it from start to finish. At some point (we hope), you'll find a nugget, an idea that is very appealing to you. We cannot recommend that you apply this idea uncritically. (Our lessons are not best practices.) Instead, we urge you to evaluate the lesson in terms of its appropriateness to your situation.

Here are some questions that might help you perform that evaluation:

- Under what circumstances would an application of this lesson work in your company?

- Under what circumstances would the application not work?

- Has anyone you know tried anything like this lesson before? What happened? Why? What's different about your current project from that person's project? Should that difference matter?

- Who is most likely to benefit from the attempt to apply this lesson?

- Who is most likely to be disadvantaged as a result of an attempt to apply the lesson?

- What will you learn from attempting to apply this lesson?

- Trying anything new adds risk. Does it make sense to see how well this lesson would apply to your company by running a pilot study, a situation in which you try out the lesson without committing yourself to it, or under a situation of low risk? Is it feasible to conduct a pilot study in your company, on (or in the service of) your current project?

- How will you know whether your application of this lesson worked? If it did work, how will you know whether the success came more from the intrinsic value of the lesson, which will last as you keep applying it, than from your enthusiasm in trying out the idea?

- What are the best and worst things that could happen to you as a result of trying to apply this lesson?

- What are the best and worst things that could happen to another stakeholder, such as a user or another member of the development team?

- What if a key person in your company disagrees with a lesson that you want to follow? How will you overcome their objections and then sell it to them?

We Hope This Book Stimulates Conversations and Debates

This book draws sharp contrasts between our views and some others. We think that clarity will help fuel debates that the field should be having. We don't believe there is an accepted paradigm in software testing or in software engineering as a whole. That's why we're not among the folks pushing government licensing and regulation of software engineers after standardization on a *body of knowledge*. In our experience, there are remarkably different, credible views as to the best ways to proceed.

We want to be very clear about this. We often critique the work of people we respect highly. In many cases, we refer to work done by good friends of ours. Don't mistake an attack on an idea with an attack on the proponent or clearest author of that idea.

We think the field will benefit by head-on comparisons and contrasts of those views. It's important for our field to have conversations about our methods. We advocate the further development of skilled practices within every one of the main approaches. Eventually, we will all learn the circumstances under which the different approaches are the best. Until then, let the thousand flowers bloom.

A Few Notes on Vocabulary

Here are some of the key words in this book, and how we use them:

We. The authors.

You. The reader.

A *fault* is an error, a mistake in the implementation or design of the program.

As we use the term, an *error* is a fault.

A *failure* is the misbehavior of the program, resulting from the program encountering a fault.

Failures occur under *conditions*. For example, a program will crash when it attempts to divide by zero. The fault in this case is in the code that allows division by zero. The failure is the crash. But you don't see a failure unless the critical variable in the division has the value zero. That variable, having a value of zero, is the critical condition that must be met for the failure to occur.

A *symptom* is like a failure but less serious. For example, if the program has a memory leak, it might start slowing down long before it fails with an out-of-memory error message. The slowdown is a symptom of an underlying problem (memory shortage) that is not directly visible.

The word *bug* is a catch-all term. It could refer to anything wrong with the software. Someone reporting a bug might describe a fault, a failure, or a limitation of the program that makes it less valuable to a stakeholder.

If we define *quality* as value to some person (Weinberg, 1998, 2.i.), a *bug report* is a statement that some person considers the product less valuable because of the thing being described as a bug.

The word *defect* carries a legal charge. It means Something Is Definitely Wrong With The Product. Some companies don't allow the words *defect* or *defective* to appear in their bug tracking systems or bug-related memos.

Some companies prefer to say *anomaly, problem,* or *issue* instead of *bug.*

After you report a bug, the programmers (or the Change Control Board) will fix it or decide not to fix it. They will mark the bug *resolved* (fixed, deferred, not reproducible, works as designed, and so on).

Black box testing. Testing the external behavior of the program, by feeding the program inputs and examining the outputs. In typical black box testing, the tester has no knowledge of the internals of the code and is instead more familiar with the explicit and implicit product requirements, such as the ways the program will be used, the types of data likely to be fed to the program, any regulatory issues associated with the problem the software is attempting to solve or help solve, and the hardware and software environments in which the software will run.

Behavioral testing. Testing the external behavior of the program, similar to black box testing, but using as much knowledge of the internals of the program as is available to the tester and relevant to the test.

Functional testing. Black box or behavioral testing.

White box or glass box testing. Testing with knowledge of the internals of the program.

Structural testing. White box testing that is focused on the internal structure of the program, such as the flow of control from one decision or action to the next.

Smoke testing or *build verification testing.* A standard suite of tests applied to a new build. The tests look for fundamental instability or key things missing or broken. If the build fails these tests, you do not test it any further. Instead, you keep testing the old build or wait for the next one.

Project manager. The person who is accountable for shipping the right product on time and within budget. Some companies split the work that we ascribe to the project manager between a program manager and a development manager.

MaxInt. The largest integer possible on the user's platform or the programmer's development language. A number larger than MaxInt cannot be stored as an integer.

Client. Someone whose interests it is your job to serve. This probably includes everyone on the project to some extent, as well as the ultimate users of the product.

ACKNOWLEDGMENTS

This book would not have been possible without the support and assistance of a great many people. We thank Lenore Bach, Jon Bach, Becky Fiedler, Leslie Smart, and Zach Pettichord for support, understanding, and assistance while three frantic men thought of nothing but their book. We thank Pat McGee for providing research assistance at a crucial time.

We benefited from detailed and thoughtful reviews of early drafts. We've added several of our reviewers' examples and descriptions of alternative perspectives to the book. We thank Ståle Amland, Rex Black, Jeffrey Bleiberg, Hans Buwalda, Ross Collard, Lisa Crispin, Chris DeNardis, Marge Farrell, Dorothy Graham, Erick Griffin, Rocky Grober, Sam Guckenheimer, George Hamblen, Elisabeth Hendrickson, Doug Hoffman, Kathy Iberle, Bob Johnson, Karen Johnson, Ginny Kaner, Barton Layne, Pat McGee, Fran McKain, Pat McQuaid, Brian Marick, Alan Myrvold, Hung Nguyen, Noel Nyman, Erik Petersen, Johanna Rothman, Jane Stepak, Melora Svoboda, Mary Romero Sweeney, Paul Szymkowiak, Andy Tinkham, Steve Tolman, and Tamar Yaron.

This book has benefited enormously from numerous discussions we've had at the Los Altos Workshops on Test Automation, the Workshops on Heuristic & Exploratory Techniques, the Software Test Managers' Roundtable, the Austin Workshops on Test Automation, the Patterns of Software Testing Workshops, and at many other workshops, conferences, classes, and worksites with so many people who have put their hearts into finding better ways to test software. We thank you all.

CHAPTER 1

The Role of the Tester

What are testers supposed to do for a project? That's the question we address in this chapter. Like many things about testing, the answer may seem obvious or trivial at first glance, but it's not.

A role is a relationship. That means you don't control your role, but you can negotiate it. People expect things from you that might not be reasonable. When you find yourself blamed for a low-quality product (and that will happen), whoever is blaming you probably suffers from role confusion. Maybe they think your job is to beat the product with the Magic Mallet of Quality before it ships, and they think you didn't hit it hard enough.

When you're clear about your role—when you have negotiated it—you have a foundation for setting expectations in any situation that may arise. However, even a clear and appropriate testing role is a demanding one.

You are the headlights of the project.

A project is like a road trip. Some projects are simple and routine, like driving to the store in broad daylight. But most projects worth doing are more like driving a truck off-road, in the mountains, at night. Those projects need headlights. As the tester, *you light the way.* You illuminate the road ahead so the programmers and managers, however they bicker over the map, can at least see where they are, what they're about to run over, and how close they are to the cliff. The detailed mission of the testing group varies from company to company. Behind those details, though, is a common factor.

Testing is done to find information. Critical decisions about the project or the product are made on the basis of that information.

Lesson 2

Your mission drives everything you do.

Your mission might depend on your industry, company, project, or the personalities on the team. Test projects vary greatly from place to place. A challenge for the evolution of testing as a craft has been the difficulty of creating a conversation about test practices that will span the cultural and technical differences among us. Many of these differences amount to different missions for the test team. For instance, in some testing organizations, a test plan is just a tool to help the testers. It could be written on a napkin and still be effective. Other organizations create test plans as products that must be delivered along with the software. Their test plans may have to follow strict format and content guidelines.

Any of the following requirements might define your mission. Which ones are expected of you?

- Find important bugs fast.
- Provide a general assessment of the quality of the product.
- Certify that the product meets a particular standard.
- Help your clients improve product quality and testability.
- Assure that the test process meets accountability standards.
- Educate your clients about testing and how to work with testers.
- Follow a particular set of methods or rules.
- Help predict and control the costs of support.
- Help your clients improve their processes.
- Perform your work in a manner that minimizes cost, time, or undesirable side effects.
- Do whatever is necessary to satisfy particular clients.

If you spend time and effort on requirements that your clients don't care about, you risk being treated as irrelevant or counterproductive. Negotiate your mission with your manager. Clarify it. If you can't come to agreement on the mission, you won't have a good foundation for anything you do.

What should you do when you don't know what to do? One answer is review your mission. It identifies the core problems that you own. When you're clear on your testing mission, you can defend your work and determine specifically what to do next. You can also explain your role to other people, in simple terms. If you can't work toward your mission for some reason, take the matter to management right away.

What should you do when you know exactly what to do? Once in a while, revisit your mission to make sure that your clear plan hasn't focused you so much on one part of the testing problem that you've forgotten about the rest.

You serve many clients.

Testing is a service role. Feel good about that. The service you provide is vital. Service implies *clients*—the people you serve. Your success is measured primarily by how well you serve your clients' desires and best interests. That might not be so hard, except that testing has *many* clients. They all have their own needs, and their collective needs don't necessarily align:

- *The project manager.* Project managers are entitled to know your process and influence it. You serve the project manager by reporting your status on demand, reporting important problems fast, and not being a bottleneck to the project. It's the project manager's prerogative to direct the project. It's your job to tell him what you are able to do, what you can't do, and what the impact on testing will be of any given decision or condition on the project.

- *The programmer.* You make the programmer's job easier by providing good bug reports, as soon as possible. Strive to know your craft and know the product so you don't waste the programmer's time with mistaken or frivolous reports. If you can do that, you'll have a lot more credibility, and that will translate into support and influence.

- *The technical writer.* Like you, the people who write the manuals and the online help get incomplete information about the product. You can help them understand how the product really works, and you can alert them to errors in the documentation. Writers can help you, too. As they do their research on the product and how the people who have to read the documentation will use the product, they will learn things that you don't know. If you have a good relationship with the writers, they'll alert you to new features, new uses, holes in your test plan, and to the bugs they find. Some of those bugs would never be reported unless a particular writer knows that a particular tester cares.

- *Technical support.* Whatever problems are left in the product become a burden for the people who provide technical support. You serve the support group by alerting them to aspects of the product that may trouble the user. If you work with them during development, sometimes the support staff will help you make the case that a bug should be fixed. You should also offer to help investigate difficult problems found in the field. Doing so will bring you into closer contact with support people and, therefore, with the customer.

- *Marketing.* Marketing needs to know whether anything in the product is inconsistent with the key benefits the product is supposed to provide to customers. A bug that seems minor to programmers might be critical to marketers. They might recognize that the bug makes it harder for the customer to do an important task. Also, by reviewing planned marketing documents or statements, you can help marketing promote an accurate account of the product's capabilities.

- *Top management and stockholders.* You serve the business. That's why you must be careful not to sound or act like a quality fanatic instead of a reasonable person. Especially near the end of the project, perform your work in a way that takes into account the short-term and long-term interests of the company. Express test status reports in crisp, operational terms, so that executives feel they have a basis on which to make decisions.

- *The user.* In your heart, you serve the people who will make use of the product. Their satisfaction is in the best interests of your project, of course. But there is also a special satisfaction that goes with being the primary user advocate on the project team.

This list is in no particular order, but your project may have a pecking order, so look into it. Find out who matters on your project. Discover whom you serve. This is the first step to great testing.

You discover things that will "bug" someone whose opinion matters.

Your group's mission includes (or should include) informing clients about *anything* that threatens the value of the product, according to your clients' definition(s) of value. If you can show that the product will not be valued even if it works as intended, it's your duty to report your concerns. If your clients choose to dismiss the report, that's their prerogative.

Find important bugs fast.

Most likely, your mission includes finding bugs that are important (as opposed to insignificant) and finding them quickly. If so, what does this mean in terms of the tests you run?

- Test *things that are changed* before things that are the same. Fixes and updates mean fresh risk.

- Test *core functions* before contributing functions. Test the critical and the popular things that the product does. Test the functions that make the product what it is.

- Test *capability* before reliability. Test whether each function can work *at all* before going deep into the examination of how any one function performs under many different conditions.

- Test *common situations* before esoteric situations. Use popular data and scenarios of use.

- Test *common threats* before exotic threats. Test with the most likely stress and error situations.

- Test for *high-impact problems* before low-impact problems. Test the parts of the product that would do a lot of damage in case of failure.

- Test the *most wanted areas* before areas not requested. Test any areas and for any problems that are of special interest to someone else on the team.

You will also find important problems sooner if you know more about the product, the software and hardware it must interact with, and the people who will use it. Study these well.

Run with the programmers.

Supporting the programmers is probably a key part of your mission. When you test the things that the programmers are building right now, or have most recently built, your feedback will help them work more efficiently. When they deliver it, you test it. When they make a change, you test the change. Aim for the shortest, quickest feedback loop you can. While the programmers are chewing on the bugs you've just found, you are off finding more bugs. The ideal situation (for testers) is one in which they're so busy fixing the problems you've found that they, not you, are the bottleneck of the project.

Question everything, but not necessarily out loud.

It's possible to test without questioning, but it's not possible to test *well*. Questions are fundamental to your role on the project. If you do not question, your testing will be aimless and mechanical. However, explicit questions can be provocative. They often put people on the defensive.

Questions can be like strong medicine—best asked in low doses or taken with a meal (*i.e.*, other kinds of communication). Fortunately, the value of questions is not limited to those that are asked out loud. Any question that occurs to you may help provoke your own thoughts in directions that lead to vital insights.

If you ever find yourself testing and realize that you have no questions about the product, take a break.

You focus on failure, so your clients can focus on success.

Testing is the only role on the project that does not directly focus on success. Everyone else creates something or creatively guides its creation. But testers are *negative*. This can be a depressing job, almost like a parody of a Greek myth: "On the island of the testers, they were doomed forever to search for what could not and should not exist, knowing that to succeed would bring misery to the Gods."

It would be a mistake to redefine your mission more *positively*, as someone who verifies that the program works. Even if "verify that the program works" is handed to you as your mission, advise your client that such verification is impossible. It's hideously expensive. Unless you run every possible test, you can't prove the product works. The best you could say is "For the tests I performed, I didn't notice that the product didn't work." The opposite, however, is marvelously economical: With as little as one test, you can show that the product doesn't work.

Testers focus on failure because it improves their chances of finding it. Look for key problems in the product with all your creativity and skill. If you don't find them, they can't be fixed, and then the users may find them for you. By finding what's there to find in the product, you help the project team learn more about their own skills and the product's risks, and you help them make the product better, more supportable, and probably more successful in the marketplace.

You will not find all the bugs.

It's your job to find and report significant bugs. But you won't find all of them. To find all of them, you'd have to look everywhere there could be a bug, you'd have to look there under every different situation that could arise, and you'd need a foolproof way of recognizing every different kind of bug when it occurred. If you think you can do that, you have either a very simple product or a very limited imagination.

You have to make choices about how to spend your time, knowing and accepting that you can't do everything.

Beware of testing "completely."

Some testers who agree they can't know they've found all the bugs in a product still talk loosely about what it means to be finished testing. Saying "it will take me five days to test that" can be interpreted to mean that you think you will have *completely* tested that part of the product in five calendar days. And that might be taken to mean you will find every bug in five days. *Completeness* is more often implied than stated. Either way, it's a concept you must treat with great care. Think about what complete testing might mean:

- Completed the discovery of every bug in the product.
- Completely examined every aspect of the product.
- Completed the testing that you believe is useful and cost-effective to perform at this time.
- Completely fulfilled the stated objectives of the project to the best of your ability.
- Completed the agreed-upon tests.
- Completed everything humanly possible to test, under the circumstances.
- Completed everything you knew how to do.
- Completed your part of the testing, regardless of anyone else's part.
- Completed a broad, but not deep, pass of testing on the product.
- Completed one kind of testing on the product.
- Completed the time period assigned to testing.

If you take care to clarify what you mean and don't mean by "complete" or "finished" or "done," then you're probably safe. You're less likely to be blamed for not doing your job and better able to defend yourself if you are blamed. Be aware that the definition of "complete" is not the kind of thing that can be settled conclusively at the start of the project. You have to reconsider it as the test project evolves and as new test tasks crop up.

To cope with the general problem of miscommunication about completeness, share some of the details of your test process with your clients. Summarize the testing you do and why that testing is worthwhile, and tell your clients about other worthwhile testing you are *not* doing and why you aren't doing those tests.

You don't *assure* quality by testing.

It's all too easy to think of yourself as the guardian of quality. But you don't create quality, and you don't take it away. You may talk as if you "break the product"; the truth is it came to you already broken. Quality comes from the people who build the product, and that is sometimes a heavy burden for them to bear. A big part of your mission is to help them deal with that burden more effectively. You can't do that as well if you give the impression that you think you're the only one on the project who cares about shipping a good product.

Your team may be called "quality assurance." Don't let that go to your head. Your test results and bug reports provide information that facilitates the assurance of quality on the project, but that assurance results from the effort of the entire team.

Never be the gatekeeper!

Some testers dream of having veto control over the release of the product. They deserve to be punished by having their wish granted. The problem is that when testers control the release, they also must bear the full responsibility for the quality of the product. The rest of the team will relax a little bit, or maybe a lot. If any bug sneaks by the testers and out the gate, the rest of the team can (and will) shrug and blame the testers. After all, why did the testers ship such a buggy product? On the other hand, if the testers delay the release, they bear intense scrutiny and pressure for being such quality fanatics.

Ultimately, it's the people who control the project who are best equipped to bear the responsibility to release the product. However, most highly effective projects we've seen use some kind of consensus approach. If you're ever given authority to control the release, we recommend immediately insisting on sharing that authority with the other roles on the team.

Beware of the not-my-job theory of testing.

Testing is so complex and so interconnected with other project activities that you may be tempted to get a better handle on it by adopting a narrow view of the testing mission. Some testers feel that their mission is simply to find variances between the product and the specifications. Anything beyond that—such as usability problems, requirements problems, data quality, and supportability concerns—are "not my job." We urge you to take a more expansive view. All other things being equal, your mission should be to inform the team, to the best of your ability, about any problems that could adversely impact the value of the product. For this reason, excellent test teams include a diverse group of people who collectively understand the whole equation of the product: how it will be designed, manufactured, marketed, sold, used, serviced, and upgraded.

Another temptation to say "not my job" comes when you're placed in a difficult testing situation. Your colleagues on the programming side may write crummy specs. They may deliver their code so late that you don't have time for a reasonable test process. They may claim that an important problem you've found is actually a figment of your imagination. It's tempting to refuse to test under those circumstances. You could say it's not your job to interpret ambiguous specifications or to test something in such a rush. In severe cases, that may well be the right thing to do, but consider first whether your expectations are realistic and consider whether there's an alternative way to get what you need. If you adopt the philosophy that it's your job to make a reasonable effort to adapt and improvise, the programmers are more likely to consider you a boon instead of a burden. That, in turn, encourages them to make it *their* job to help *you*.

Beware of becoming a process improvement group.

Sometimes you get tired of *finding* problems, and you wonder whether it might be better to *prevent* problems. Maybe there would be fewer problems if the programmers did their work more carefully. This makes good sense, as far as it goes. But then again, it also makes sense to helpfully tell the ones you love how to live their lives better. If you've tried that, you know that good advice is not always sensibly received. Sensibility is not the issue; feelings are. No matter what else it's about, process improvement is always about feelings.

Even if you have strong management support for testing to drive a quality improvement initiative, there are many ways that the rest of the team can simultaneously foil your efforts and make you look incompetent. Yes, you can successfully participate in process improvement efforts and be successful if it's *a whole team effort*, but we urge you to resist any temptation to "elevate" the test team into a process criticism society. That way lies madness.

Don't expect anyone to understand testing, or what you need to do it well.

You are reading this book. Don't expect anyone else to read it. It's up to you to let your clients know what you need in order to do your job effectively. You are profoundly affected by the choices made by management and programmers. If they're unclear about their plans, or they design a product that's hard to test, your test project could be crippled. You may not get everything you want, but give them a chance to help you.

It's not that they don't care about testing or quality. They probably just don't understand the impact their actions have on the test process. An important part of the role of testing is to explain testing to our clients. Your explanations are like a flu vaccine—healthy and not that painful, but the effect wears off, so you have to do it over and over again.

CHAPTER 2

Thinking Like a Tester

Testers come from many backgrounds. They are a diverse bunch, but most people agree: Testers think differently. How do they think differently? Some say testers are "negative" thinkers. Testers complain, they like to break things, they take a special thrill in delivering bad news. This is a common view. We propose an alternative view. Testers don't complain; they offer evidence. Testers don't like to break things; they like to dispel the illusion that things work. Testers don't enjoy giving bad news; they enjoy freeing their clients from the thrall of false belief. Our view is that thinking like a tester means practicing epistemology. Testing is applied epistemology, not grumpistics or whinography.

This chapter is an agenda for developing your mind into a fine-tuned reasoning instrument. Just remember: Use your mental powers for good, never evil.

Lesson 16 — Testing is applied epistemology.

Hey, come back! We're not talking about a new religion for movie stars, here. Trust us on this. Epistemology is a branch of philosophy that *helps you test better*.

Epistemology is the study of how you know what you know. It's the study of evidence and reasoning. It establishes the foundations of scientific practice. Epistemology is studied by scientists, educators, and philosophers—and elite software testers. Students of epistemology study science, philosophy, and psychology with the goal of learning how we all can improve our thinking. We use the term more broadly than it's classically defined so that we can take advantage of much of the recent work in critical thinking. Applied to software testing, epistemology asks questions like the following:

- How do you know the software is good enough?
- How would you know if it wasn't good enough?
- How do you know you've tested enough?

Socrates advocated and embodied the critical examination of belief 2400 years ago. We, therefore, see him as an early epistemologist. Philosophers, scientists, and psychologists have continued the study of epistemology up to the present day. As a tester, this is your heritage.

Studying epistemology helps you test better.

Topics in Epistemology that relate directly to software testing include:

- How to gather and assess evidence.
- How to make valid inferences.
- How to use different forms of logic.
- What it means to have a justified belief.
- Differences between formal and informal reasoning.
- Common fallacies in informal reasoning.
- Meaning and ambiguity in natural language.
- How to make a good decision.

Lots of people who never studied these subjects have done good testing. But if you want to be *better* than good, learn this stuff. Studying epistemology will help you devise effective testing strategies, better recognize mistakes in your work, know what your testing does and does not prove, and construct defensible test reports.

Here are three very readable books to get you started:

- *Tools of Critical Thinking: Metathoughts for Psychology* (Levy 1997). This book is aimed at psychotherapists, but it's great for testers, too. Each chapter is a different idea about thinking better. You don't have to commit to reading it all, just pick any chapter and ignore the others.

- *Thinking and Deciding* (Baron 1994). This is a general textbook covering the world of thinking in a very readable way. It's a great introduction to the subject.

- *The Craft of Research* (Booth, Colomb, and Williams 1995). Intended for college students, this is a nice little book on critical reading and writing, including how to construct persuasive arguments.

Testing is grounded in cognitive psychology.

If epistemology tells us about how we *should* think, cognitive psychology tells us about how we *do* think. Some of its topics relating to testing include:

- Reliability of your senses and memory.
- Where beliefs come from.
- How your beliefs affect your behavior.
- Biases and short cuts you use to make decisions.
- How you learn and share what you know.
- How you think about complex things.
- How you think under pressure.
- How you recognize patterns.
- How you sort ideas and things into categories.
- How you notice differences between things.
- Distortions in remembered events.
- How you reconstruct partially remembered events (such as nonreproducible bugs).

Lots of people who never studied these subjects have done good testing. If you want to be better than good, studying cognitive psychology will help you understand the factors that affect your performance as a tester, as well as the factors that affect how people interpret your work.

To get started with this, look no further than *Cognition in the Wild* (Hutchins 1995). Hutchins studies naval navigation teams and how they work together. Much of his book is relevant to software projects and test teams, too.

A useful book about the psychology of thinking is *Theory and Evidence: The Development of Scientific Reasoning* (Koslowski 1996). In this book, Koslowski investigates how people use causal theories to reason about systems. This explains how testing is more than simply looking at external behavior and checking it against simple expectations.

Testing is in your head.

The difference between excellent testing and mediocre testing is how you think: your test design choices, your ability to interpret what you observe, and your ability to tell a compelling story about it. The rest of testing is ordinary office work, for the most part. If you see two testers working, side-by-side, you can't necessarily tell whether one is testing better than the other. The visible part of their work looks the same, which has two implications:

- Many people think testing is easy, because they can easily copy the visible behavior of a good tester, and they have no other standard for good testing.

- If you want to be a good tester, learn to think like one, not look like one.

Testing requires inference, not just comparison of output to expected results.

There's a popular view that testers just execute test cases and compare what happens against expected results. This view makes testing seems like a straightforward comparison activity and ignores the fact that some clever person must *design* the tests and *determine* the expectations. Guess what? That test designer almost never has access to an authoritative guide to what should be tested, let alone what should be expected. And what guides are available are subject to interpretation. In real life, most test design is based on inferences or taken from experience that the tester infers is relevant. Moreover, these inferences change over time. To think like a tester is to be adept at the art of exploratory inference.

Exploratory inference may sound like a strange idea. It means one idea leading to another and another in ways you can't predict in advance. For a great introduction to exploratory inference, see *Proofs and Refutations: The Logic of Mathematical Discovery* (Lakatos 1976). The great thing about this book is how Lakatos shows that the process of mathematical and scientific reasoning is exploratory, not scripted. Even mathematicians reason actively and searchingly, rather than through the application of dull formulae. They think like testers!

Good testers think technically, creatively, critically, and practically.

All kinds of thinking figure into the practice of testing. But we believe four major categories of thinking are worth highlighting:

- *Technical thinking.* The ability to model technology and understand causes and effects. This includes things like knowledge of relevant technical facts and the ability to use tools and predict the behavior of systems.
- *Creative thinking.* The ability to generate ideas and see possibilities. You will test only in ways that you can imagine testing. You will look only for problems that you imagine can exist.
- *Critical thinking.* The ability to evaluate ideas and make inferences. This includes the ability to detect and eliminate errors from your thinking, to relate product observations to quality criteria, and to build a compelling case for a particular belief or suggested course of action.
- *Practical thinking.* The ability to put ideas into practice. This ability includes such skills as applying test tools and making test techniques and effort fit within the scope of the project.

Overall, thinking like a tester leads you to believe that things may not be as they seem. However things are, they could be different. We find that when the test process fails in the most damaging ways, the root cause is most likely to be tunnel vision. In other words, it's not that we ran 10,000 tests and should have run 10,001. It's that we failed to imagine an entire category of test; testing we wouldn't have performed even if we had twice the time and resources.

Black box testing is not ignorance-based testing.

Black box testing means that knowledge of the internals of the product doesn't play a significant part in your testing. Most testers are black box testers. To do black box testing well, learn about the user, her expectations and needs, the technology, the configurations the software will run on, the other software that this software will interact with, the data the software must manage, the development process, and so on. The advantage of black box testing is that you probably think differently than the programmer, and, thus, are likely to anticipate risks that the programmer missed.

The black box emphasis on knowledge of the software's user and environment is not to everyone's liking. We've even heard this described as *ignorance-based testing* because the tester is and stays ignorant of the underlying code. We think that reflects a fundamental misunderstanding of the role of the testing group. We don't object to a tester learning about how a product works. The more you learn about a product, and the more ways in which you know it, the better you will be able to test it. But if your primary focus is on the source code and tests you can derive from the source code, you will be covering ground the programmer has probably covered already, and with less knowledge of that code than she had.

A tester is more than a tourist.

Lots of things you do with a product that aren't tests can help you learn about it. You can tour the product, see what it's made of and how it works. This is invaluable, but it's not quite testing. The difference between a tester and a tourist is that a tester's efforts are devoted to evaluating the product, not merely witnessing it. Although it's not necessary to predict *in advance* how the software should behave, an activity that puts the product through its paces doesn't become a test unless and until you apply some principle or process that will identify some kind of problem if one exists.

All tests are an attempt to answer some question.

All tests are experiments performed to answer a question about the relationship between what a product is and what it should be. Sometimes you aren't entirely aware of the questions you're asking. That might be fine if you're looking for only the *obvious* problems. In many cases, though, bugs don't jump out at you with a "report me" sign in flashing neon. A product could misbehave in ways that the user will find obvious, even if you (the tester) are oblivious. In any test activity, ask yourself what questions should drive your evaluation strategy. Otherwise, you're more tourist than tester.

All testing is based on models.

You may have a mental picture in your mind when you design tests. Or, you may be working with a list of features or a diagram of some kind. You have some concept of who the users are and what they care about. All of these are models. No matter what, your tests will be based primarily on your models of the product, not the actual product. A flawed model results in flawed tests. Learning a new way to model a product is like learning a new way to see it.

Study modeling. You will test better as you become more skillful in the art of modeling. Textbooks and classes about requirements analysis and software architecture can help. A wonderful way to gain skill in all kinds of modeling is to study systems thinking. See *An Introduction to General Systems Thinking: Silver Anniversary Edition.* (Weinberg 2001).

Intuition is a fine beginning, but a lousy conclusion.

You may be tempted to use particular test data or to judge a particular output based on your intuition—that's the "gut feel" you have that you *know*, even if you can't articulate reasons to justify your knowledge. We think this is a helpful sense, but more as a starting point than a resting point.

Apart from the fact that intuition is often strongly biased, the real trouble comes when you try to get other people, such as programmers and managers, to take your bug reports and quality assessments seriously. Unless your findings are based on intuition that all parties share, your work is liable to be dismissed.

Therefore, we recommend using intuition as a guide, but not a *justification*. When you are tempted to think "this is a bug because it's obviously a bug" consider reframing that to "this is a bug because I observe that the product behaves in a way that violates requirements X, Y, and Z, and those requirements are valued by my clients."

To test, you must explore.

To test something well, you have to work with it. You must get *into* it. This is an exploratory process, even if you have a perfect description of the product.

Until you explore that specification, either in your mind's eye or by working with the product itself, the tests you conceive will be superficial. Even after you explore enough of the product to understand it deeply, there is still the matter of exploring for problems. Because all testing is sampling, and your sample can never be complete, exploratory thinking has a role throughout the test project as you seek to maximize the value of testing.

By exploration, we mean purposeful wandering: navigating through a space with a general mission, but without a prescribed route. Exploration involves continuous learning and experimenting. There's a lot of backtracking, repetition, and other processes that look like waste to the untrained eye. Perhaps for that reason, the importance of exploration to testing, and for that matter software engineering, is often downplayed and even derided by writers and consultants in our field.

It's beyond the scope of this book to prove our assertion about the central importance of exploration. One way you can experience it vividly is to watch yourself solve a complicated jigsaw puzzle without looking at the picture on the box or play a game of Twenty Questions or Mastermind. Notice how much more difficult it would be to succeed in these activities, and how much less rewarding, with strictly pre-scripted behavior.

For a look at how disciplined exploration is used in another field much like testing, sociology, see *The Discovery of Grounded Theory: Strategies for Qualitative Research* (Glaser and Strauss 1999), and *Basics of Qualitative Research, 2nd Edition* (Strauss, Anselm, and Corbin 1998). If you like statistics, try *Exploratory Data Analysis* (Tukey 1977).

Exploring involves a lot of thinking.

Exploring is detective work. It's an open-ended search. Think of exploration as moving through a space. It involves forward, backward, and lateral thinking:

- *Forward thinking.* Work from what you know to what you don't know; what you see toward what you haven't yet seen. Seek ramifications and side effects. Example: I see a print menu item. I'll click on it and see what happens.

- *Backward thinking.* Work from what you suspect or imagine back toward what you know, trying to confirm or refute your conjectures. Example: I wonder if there's a way to print this document? I'll look through the menus and see whether there's a print item. (Solow 1990)

- *Lateral thinking.* Let your work be distracted by ideas that pop into your head, exploring tangents then returning to the main thread (de Bono 1970). Example: That's an interesting graphic. Hey, I think I'll print some complex graphics and see what happens.

The exploratory process works even if you don't have a product to test. You can explore a set of documents or interview a programmer, using the same thought processes. You make progress by building richer, better mental models of the product. These models then allow you to design effective tests.

Use the logic of abductive inference to discover conjectures.

Abductive inference, also known as hypothetical induction, is a fancy term for a vital form of reasoning that testers use every day: *reasoning to the best explanation.* It goes like this:

1. You gather some data and want to make sense of it.

2. You construct a variety of explanations that might account for the data.

3. You seek more data that will help you corroborate or refute each of the explanations.

4. You choose the *most coherent* explanation that accounts for *all the important data* from among your options, or if there is not enough evidence to justify any conclusion, continue the search.

Abductive inference is a basic method of science and of testing. Doctors use it when diagnosing illness. Testers use it when making judgments about what a product is and is not and how it should or should not work. If you want to make better abductive inferences:

- Gather more data.

- Gather more important data.

- Gather more reliable data.

- Understand the causes and effects that apply to the data.

- Identify more and better explanations that could account for the data.

- Gather more data that would refute each explanation.

- Gather more data that would differentiate among explanations.

- Don't settle on an explanation unless it accounts for all the important data and is clearly better supported than the others.

Abduction is a systematic method for finding good explanations. Although the abductive inference process does not provide absolute certainty, it's the best technique we have in most situations.

Use the logic of conjecture and refutation to evaluate a product.

The philosopher Karl Popper introduced the method of conjecture and refutation early in the 20th century (Popper 1989), while working on the problem of how to distinguish religion from science. The method is based on the premise that a scientist can never be absolutely certain of any particular fact or theory about nature. Everything is a conjecture. Some conjectures, like the existence of gravity, are very strong. What makes them conjecture, instead of absolutely certain fact, is that it's possible to imagine new information that, if it existed, would cause us to reject the conjecture. Popper noticed that though we can't prove that a conjecture is true, it *may* be possible to prove that it's false. Therefore, he suggested that the only confidence a given conjecture deserves would come from trying hard to refute it and not being able to do so.

This method of making conjectures and trying to refute them applies to testing in three important ways:

- It's more powerful to test for the purpose of showing that the product *fails*, than it is to show that it works. When you want to know whether a product works well, find ways to *refute* that it works well, and your testing will probably be better.

- A well-formed belief about the software (how it behaves, how good it is, and so on) should be *falsifiable*. That means we should be able to imagine new information that would contradict our belief. Otherwise, our belief is nothing more than faith. Faith is fine in private life but is poisonous for testing.

- Beware of tests that purport to validate or certify a product in a way that goes beyond the specific tests you ran. No amount of testing provides *certainty* about the quality of the product.

A *requirement* is a quality or condition that matters to someone who matters.

You can choose from many definitions of "requirement." This definition works well for testers. As you test, you must become aware of whose opinion about quality matters (not everyone matters equally). Then learn what they want in the product and what they don't want. This view of requirements makes no distinction between software engineering "requirements" (a set of statements published in a "requirements document" and approved by people with approval authority) and any other kind of specification. For the purposes of testing, any quality or condition that the product should exhibit or fulfill is a requirement.

Different clients want different things from the product, they don't necessarily know what they want, and what they want changes over time. This makes our job more interesting. Welcome to testing.

You discover requirements by conference, inference, and reference.

If you expect to receive requirements on a sheaf of parchment, stamped with the seal of universal truth, find another line of work. In the *best cases* we've experienced, requirements documentation (which includes any and all kinds of product specifications, use cases, vision documents, and so on) has been incomplete and ambiguous, even though it was informative and helpful. In the worst cases we've seen, the documentation was incomplete, ambiguous, *un*informative, and *un*helpful.

A tester who treats project documentation (explicit specifications of the product) as the *sole* source of requirements is crippling his test process. In any test team we were managing, insistence on such behavior would be a firing offense.

Requirements information comes to us primarily in three ways:

- *Conference.* Confer with someone whose opinion about quality matters and learn what matters to them.
- *Inference.* Determine what requirements matter by extrapolating from other things you know about the project and product.
- *Reference.* Discover implicit as well as explicit specifications and base your testing on them.

In many projects, most requirements that good testers use come either from inference or from references in the form of implicit specifications. It's your job to ferret out the information you need to test.

A great book about this is *Exploring Requirements: Quality Before Design* (Gause and Weinberg 1989).

Use implicit as well as explicit specifications.

Not all references that contain important information on which to base your tests are explicitly presented to you:

- An *explicit specification* is a useful source of requirements information, *acknowledged as authoritative* by your clients. ("Yes, that's the spec. That's a description of the product.")

- An *implicit specification* is a useful source of requirements information that is *not* acknowledged as authoritative by your clients. ("That's not the spec, but it makes sense.")

The authority of an implicit spec comes from the persuasiveness and credibility of its content, not from the blessing of your clients. In most cases, only part of an implicit spec relates to the product at hand. Implicit specs take many forms:

- Competing products
- Related products
- Older versions of the same product
- Email discussions within the project
- Comments by customers
- Magazine articles (for instance, reviews of old versions of your product)
- Textbooks on related subjects (An accounting book may pertain to an accounting application.)
- Graphic user interface (GUI) style guides
- Operating system (O/S) compatibility requirements.
- Your own well-founded experience

When a product violates an explicit spec, you have a relatively easy reporting task: "It violates the spec, therefore the product is probably wrong." When an implicit spec is violated, you have to make more of a case: "In Microsoft Office, F4 is bound to the *repeat* command. Unless we do the same, we may confuse our users, who also use Office in their daily work." Although no one would say that Microsoft Office is *the* specification for *your* product, your clients may agree that aligning the user interface to Office would improve usability. If so, Office is an implicit spec for your product.

Some testers wonder why designers don't just put everything useful into the explicit specifications so they don't have to discern specs from implicit resources. The answer to that is simple: Although it would be convenient for testers, it's expensive and unnecessary. Our clients trust us to use whatever references are required to find important problems fast.

"It works" really means it appears to meet some requirement to some degree.

Any time you hear someone say "I tried it and it worked," "I'm sure it works," or "It's working better now," we recommend that you translate "it works" into "it appears to meet some requirement to some degree." Some questions that should immediately occur to you are:

- What's the "it"? What part of the product are we talking about?
- What was the appearance? What specifically was observed?
- Which requirements were checked? Correctness? Performance?
- To what degree was the requirement fulfilled in order to pass the test? Did it work just okay, or supremely well?
- When does it work? What range of circumstances were covered by the test? How far can you safely generalize from them?

You don't have to ask these questions out loud if you don't want to. The point is that the phrase "it works" is ambiguous without further qualification. What you think "it works" means might not match someone else's definition.

In the end, all you have is an impression of the product.

Whatever you know about the quality of the product, it's conjecture. No matter how well supported, you can't be sure you're right. Therefore, any time you report the status of product quality, you should qualify that report with information about how you tested and the known limitations of your test process.

Don't confuse the test with the testing.

What does it mean to create tests? It might mean that the tester performed a session of exploratory testing, resulting in ephemeral tests without documentation or test product. It might mean that the tester produced a set of executable test programs or a set of explicit test procedures. It might refer to a high-level test matrix, test outline, or a set of test data.

The concept of a test that stands self-contained, tangible, and distinct from other tests is convenient (we'll use that convenient concept throughout this book because it's the standard jargon of the craft), but it's also limiting. It's the testing that matters, not how you parse the testing into packages you call tests. The testing is anything that involves at least these four activities:

- *Configure.* Prepare the product for the test. Put it into the right starting state. Otherwise, your test results may be tainted by rogue variables.

- *Operate.* Feed the product data. Give it commands. Interact with it in some way. Otherwise, it just sits there, and what you're doing is reviewing, not testing.

- *Observe.* Collect information about how the product behaves, output data, the state of the system as a whole, interactions with other products, and so on. You can't observe everything, but anything you don't observe may blind you to a bug.

- *Evaluate.* Apply rules, reasoning, or mechanisms that will detect bugs in the data you observed. Otherwise, you will either report no problems, or you will just pass the data through to your clients, who will have to perform the evaluation themselves.

Test creation may take many forms. Don't get too hung up on form, just make sure these four activities are happening. Focus on the thinker who is performing them and how well the tests fulfill the intended strategy and mission of testing.

When testing a complex product: plunge in and quit.

Sometimes complexity can be overwhelming. You might feel intellectually paralyzed. So, when you're testing a complex and daunting feature set, do it in bursts. Your mind has an amazing ability to cope with complexity, but don't expect to comprehend a complex product all at once. Try throwing yourself at it for 30 minutes or an hour. Then stop and do something else. This is the method of plunge in and quit. Don't worry about being unproductive for this short time; if you feel too confused, quit early.

The great thing about this method is that it requires absolutely no plan other than to select a part of the product and work with it. After a few cycles of plunge in and quit, you will begin to see the patterns and outlines of the product. Soon, more organized and specific testing and studying strategies will come to mind. It works like magic. Eventually, you'll know enough to design a comprehensive test plan, if that's what you think will serve your mission.

Use heuristics to quickly generate ideas for tests.

A *heuristic* is a rule of thumb; a way of making an educated guess. The word comes from Greek, meaning "serving to discover." Heuristics are not guaranteed to lead to the right answer or the best answer, but they are useful nonetheless. A seminal book on using heuristics is *How to Solve It* (Polya 1957).

Because the number of possible test cases is infinite, we are stuck making guesses about what small population of test cases will be effective under the time and budget constraints we face. Experienced testers collect and share testing heuristics that improve the quality of their guesses. A good set of heuristics helps us generate tests very quickly. Here are some examples of testing heuristics:

- *Test at the boundaries.* Boundaries are more likely to reveal ambiguities in the specification.

- *Test every error message.* Error-handling code tends to be weaker than mainstream functionality.

- *Test configurations that are different from the programmer's.* The programmer will already be biased toward making sure his own configuration works.

- *Run tests that are annoying to set up.* Easy-to-set-up tests are more likely to be performed, all other things being equal.

- *Avoid redundant tests.* If a test is truly duplicating another test, what new value is it giving you?

To use heuristics wisely, remember one thing: There is no wisdom in heuristics. The wisdom is with you. All the heuristic does is make a suggestion for your consideration. Blindly following heuristics that you don't understand is not good testing practice. As you collect heuristics, try to understand the reasoning behind each one and the conditions under which it's more or less likely to work.

You can't avoid bias, but you can manage it.

You are biased. That causes you to select some tests with greater likelihood than other tests. If there is a long edit field, you are probably more likely to enter something like 1111111111 than 3287504619, because it's easier to enter a string of repeated characters than the digits 0 to 9 in random order. This is a minor bias, perhaps, but it's still a bias. More ominous is the fact that most testers are biased in favor of testing the most visible functions, whether or not they are important functions. Also, most testers are biased toward users who think like them and toward very simple and very outrageous input as opposed to realistic input of moderate complexity.

Here are a few popular biases:

- *Assimilation bias.* I am more likely to interpret future test results as generally confirming my opinion of the product.
- *Confirmation bias.* I am more likely to pay attention to test results that really do confirm my opinion of the product.
- *Availability bias.* If I can readily bring to mind a scenario in which a user will behave in a certain way, I will also tend to think that behavior is more likely.
- *Primacy bias.* I will give more credence to the first observations I make.
- *Recency bias.* I will give more credence to the most recent observations I make.
- *Framing effect.* My reaction to a bug report is strongly related to how it's phrased, regardless of what it means.
- *Prominence bias.* I will give more weight to the opinions of users I happen to know.
- *Representativeness bias.* I expect that small problems probably have small causes, whereas large problems require large causes.

You can't avoid these biases. They are, to a large extent, hard-wired into our brains. What you can do is manage the biases. For instance, just by studying biases and practicing at becoming aware of them, you can become better equipped to compensate for them in your thinking. Diversity is also a protection against too much bias. If multiple testers brainstorm tests together, that can minimize the impact of any one tester's biases.

By definition, a heuristic is also a bias. We use heuristics because they bias us in ways that we hope will be helpful.

Lesson 40 You're harder to fool if you know you're a fool.

Con artists say that the person easiest to con is one who is absolutely convinced he cannot be fooled. You can put that principle to work for you as a tester. Convince yourself that you are *easy* to fool. It's not hard, just watch carefully for your own mistakes while testing. Notice whenever another tester finds a problem that you could have found, but didn't.

If you know in your bones that you're easy to fool, you become a little more alert. You work your mind harder over the details of your test strategy. This is one of the quickest ways for a novice tester to improve, because knowing you can be fooled is an attitude, not a matter of special skill or knowledge. The problem for novice testers is that for them this principle is just an article of faith ("I'm told that I'm supposed to think I can be fooled. Whatever . . . "); whereas the senses and reflexes of experienced testers have been awakened and sharpened through the pain of actually screwing up ("I remember the great recall of '94. We never imagined a virus could infect our golden master disk. I lost my innocence that day.").

When you miss a bug, check whether the miss is surprising or just the natural outcome of your strategy.

If you flip a coin and guess heads, but tails appears instead, does that mean you made a bad decision? Not by any rational standard. Unless it's a trick coin, there's a fifty-fifty chance of heads or tails. It wasn't surprising that tails appeared, just unlucky. Your strategy is sound.

It's the same issue when you don't find a bug in the test process, and it causes trouble for your clients. Don't beat yourself up over it until you examine what happened with the test strategy. Did you miss it because you were faithfully following a good test strategy and just happened not to find that particular problem? If so, then stay the course. These things happen. But, if you missed the bug because your test strategy is focused on the wrong kinds of problems, take this opportunity to improve it.

Confusion is a test tool.

When you feel confused, that could be telling you something important.

- *Is the spec confusing?* Ambiguities in specifications are often there in order to cover up important disagreements among influential stakeholders.
- *Is the product confusing?* It may be broken.
- *Is the user documentation confusing?* This part of the product may be too complex, too many special cases and inconsistencies, to describe.

- *Is the underlying problem just difficult to understand?* Some systems that we try to automate are inherently complex or involve difficult technical issues. The programmers will find them complex and difficult too, and that will lead them to mistakes of omission, misunderstanding, and oversimplification.

The more you learn about the product, the technology, and testing in general, the more powerful a compass your confusion becomes, showing you where important problems lie.

In testing, if you know nothing else about a product, you at least know that you're confused. In that situation, confusion can become your best deliverable, in the form of issues and questions that perhaps no one else has the courage to raise.

Fresh eyes find failure.

Making sense of something is a rich intellectual process of assimilating new information into what you already know, while modifying what you know to accommodate the new information. After you've made sense of a product or feature, you have a mental map of it, and your mind doesn't work so hard. This can be a problem for testers. When you know a product well, you make more assumptions about it, and you check those assumptions less often.

This situation has at least three implications for your testing:

- When you come to a product or feature for the first time, pay special attention to what confuses and annoys you. That may tell you something about how a user would react, too.

- When you work with new additions to the team, test alongside them. Watch how they react to the product as they're learning it.

- Beware of getting into a testing rut. Even if you're not following rigid test scripts, you may get so familiar with a particular feature that you test it in progressively narrower ways. Introduce variation wherever you can or switch testing duties with another tester.

Avoid following procedures unless they followed you first.

Beware of other people's procedures. It's common for test cases and procedures to be expressed in a way that says nothing about the underlying design goals of the test. That creates the strong likelihood that you will follow the tests without quite understanding how to set them up or what to look for. In other words, you won't really follow them. In general, test procedures are poorly written and poorly designed, because few good testers are good at what amounts to programming humans like computers. If you're going to follow test procedures, prefer to follow the ones that you designed, you own, or that you thoroughly comprehend.

For best results, *you* should be in control of your testing, not your documentation. Make it follow you.

If you are convinced that procedures are a good thing, at least study how they work. See *Things that Make Us Smart: Defending Human Attributes in the Age of the Machine* (Norman 1993) and *The Social Life of Information* (Brown and Duguid 2000).

When you do create test procedures, avoid "1287."

One of us, Bach, once witnessed a tester write a test procedure that included the line "Type 1287 characters into the field." Where did 1287 come from? The tester explained that her test idea was simply to enter a very large number of characters into the little input field. Because she had heard that test procedures should be specific, she went back and carefully counted the number of characters she had entered, 1287, and that's what she put in the procedure—an arbitrary number, now enshrined forever like cat tracks in a cement sidewalk.

Over-specification is not helpful. When you write down a test procedure, avoid any specificity that is not germane to the concept of the test. Include any information and specificity necessary to frame and explain the test, but let the future tester exercise creativity and judgment. Let the future tester introduce variation that will keep your test procedure fresh and productive.

One important outcome of a test process is a better, smarter tester.

We often hear arguments against any form of testing that results in minimal or no documentation, as though the only value of testing is what comes from writing down our tests. This ignores a profoundly important product of testing: the tester herself.

Good testers are always learning. As the project progresses, they gain insight into the product and gradually improve their reflexes and sensibilities in every way that matters in that project. An experienced tester who knows the product and has been through a release cycle or two is able to test with vastly improved effectiveness—even without any instructions—compared to an inexperienced tester who is handed a set of written instructions about how to test the product.

Some consultants and writers in the field seem to believe that an ineffective tester can be transformed into an effective tester merely by handing her a test procedure. In our opinion, this is a bad practice. It reflects a fundamental misunderstanding of testing and the people who do it well.

When evaluating a test process, look first at the quality of the testers on the project. Look at how they think and how that affects what they do. Only then can you be in a position to evaluate the work products they produce.

You can't master testing unless you reinvent it.

Don't reinvent the wheel. Wait a minute. *Isn't the wheel the single most reinvented thing in history?* Isn't that a *good* thing? After all, we drive on pneumatic tires, these days, not granite disks. There are thousands, if not millions of variations on the wheel theme. Maybe that's a lesson. It seems to us there are at least two reasons to reinvent something: to adapt it to a new context, and to learn how it works. Mastery requires both.

We have colleagues who advise students of testing to *avoid* reinventing tests or testing ideas. We disagree. That's like learning a science by avoiding experimentation. It's okay to learn from other thinkers. We think it's important to learn that way—check the title of this book if you doubt that. But if that's the *only* way you learn, then you can never become a master of the testing craft. You'll be a technician, nothing more. Following instructions won't get you to mastery any more than following an interstate highway will get you to Mars. We encourage that you learn testing the way great mechanics or great programmers learn: Take things apart, ponder how they work, and put them back together in new ways. Don't restrict yourself to being a steward of received wisdom; be the author of your own wisdom.

Early in your learning process, your reinvented tests, ideas, techniques, or documents aren't very good. That's normal. Just keep your brain turned on, watch other testers, study, and continually evaluate how your ideas pan out. If you want to be good at this, you have to practice.

We've been at this for years, and we are still reinventing, still reworking old ideas. Every colleague we respect is working toward mastery that way.

CHAPTER 3

Testing Techniques

W hat does a tester do? In the first two chapters, our answer has been sage and learned, we hope, but also rather abstract. It's time to get more specific. Where do tests come from? What do tests look like? This chapter is about *testing techniques*, but we won't define every technique in detail. For that, you'll have to go to the main textbooks on testing. We suggest Kaner, Falk, and Nguyen (1993), Jorgensen (1995), Beizer (1990), Marick (1995), Collard (forthcoming), and Hendrickson (forthcoming). Whittaker and Jorgensen's articles (1999 and 2000) and Whittaker (2002) also provide useful ideas.

This chapter reads differently from the other chapters in the book for two reasons.

- First, the essential insight in this chapter is a structural one, a classification system that organizes the rest of the material. We placed this in the first lesson. The next five lessons list several techniques, but the primary purpose of those lists is to support the classification system. We provide this detail to make it easier for you to imagine how to apply the classification system to your work.

  This classification system synthesizes approaches that we have individually used and taught. Use this structure to decide which techniques are available and appropriate for a given problem and for generating ideas about combining techniques to attack a given problem efficiently.

  The lists of techniques sometimes contain detail beyond a quick description, but we saw that as optional. The level of detail is intentionally uneven. We expect that you'll learn more about the details of most techniques in other books and classes.

- Second, even though this is not primarily a how-to chapter on techniques, we couldn't bring ourselves to write a chapter on testing techniques without describing at least a few techniques in enough detail that you could actually use them. Hence the *Addendum*, which describes five techniques that we find useful, in ways that have worked well for our students in professional-level seminars and university courses on software testing.

Testing combines techniques that focus on testers, coverage, potential problems, activities, and evaluation.

Lesson 48

Our primary goal in this chapter is to present a classification system for testing techniques. We call it the *Five-fold Testing System*. Any *testing* that you do can be described in terms of five dimensions:

- *Testers. Who* does the testing. For example, user testing is focused on testing by members of your target market, people who would normally use the product.

- *Coverage. What* gets tested. For example, in function testing, you test every function.

- *Potential problems. Why* you're testing (what risk you're testing for). For example, testing for extreme value errors.

- *Activities. How* you test. For example: exploratory testing.

- *Evaluation. How to tell whether the test passed or failed.* For example, comparison to a known good result.

We also describe a few techniques in detail in this chapter and present insights about the use of a few others, but our primary goal is to explain the classification system.

All testing involves all five dimensions. A testing technique focuses your attention on one or a few dimensions, leaving the others open to your judgment. You can combine a technique that is focused on one dimension with techniques focused on the other dimensions to achieve the result you want. You might call the result of such a combination a new technique (some people do), but we think the process of thinking is more useful than adding another name to the ever-expanding list of inconsistently defined techniques in use in our field. Our classification scheme can help you make those combinations consciously and thoughtfully.

Testing tasks are often assigned on one dimension, but you do the work in all five dimensions. For example,

- Someone might ask you to do *function testing* (thoroughly test every function). This tells you what to test. You still have to decide who does the testing, what types of bugs you're looking for, how to test each function, and how to decide whether the program passed or failed.

- Someone might ask you to do *extreme-value testing* (test for error handling when you enter extreme values into a variable). This tells you what types of problems to look for. You still have to decide who will do the testing, which variables to test, how to test them, and how you'll evaluate the results.

- Someone might ask you to do *beta testing* (have external representatives of your market test the software). This tells you who will test. You still have to decide what to tell them (and how much to tell them) about, what parts of the product to look at, and what problems they should look for (and what problems they should ignore). In some beta tests, you might also tell them specifically how to recognize certain types of problems, and you might ask them to perform specific tests in specific ways. In other beta tests, you might leave activities and evaluation up to them.

Techniques don't necessarily fit on only one dimension. Nor should they; all testing involves all five dimensions, and so we should expect the richer test techniques to span several. Here's an example of what can be a multidimensional technique: If someone tells you to do "requirements-based testing," she might be talking about any combination of three ideas:

- Coverage (Test everything listed in this requirements document.)
- Potential problems (Test for any way that this requirement might not be met.)
- Evaluation (Design your tests in a way that allows you to use the requirements specification to determine whether the program passed or failed the test.)

Different testers mean different combinations of these ideas when they say, "requirements-based testing." There is no one right interpretation of this phrase.[1]

---

[1]The multiple meanings of requirements-based testing provide an example of an important general problem in software engineering. Definitions in our field are fluid. Usage varies widely across subcommunities and individuals, even when documents exist that one might expect to see used as reference standards. We'll postpone a discussion of the factors that we think lead many people to ignore the standards documents. Our point here is to note that we're not claiming to offer authoritative definitions or descriptions of the field's techniques. Some other people will use the same words to mean different things. Others probably agree with the sense of our description but would write it differently. Either position might be reasonable and defensible.

Despite the ambiguities (and, to some degree, because of them), we find this classification system useful as an idea generator.

By keeping all five dimensions in mind as you test, you might make better choices of combinations. As in beta testing, you may choose not to specify one or more of the dimensions. You might choose to not decide how results will be evaluated or how the tester will do whatever she does. Our suggestion, though, is that you make choices like that consciously, rather than adopting a technique that focuses on only one of these dimensions without realizing that the other choices still have to be made.

People-based techniques focus on who does the testing.

Here are some examples of common techniques that are distinguished by who does them.

User testing. Testing with the types of people who typically would use your product. User testing might be done at any time during development, at your site or at theirs, in carefully directed exercises or at the user's discretion. Some types of user testing, such as task analyses, look more like joint exploration (involving at least one user and at least one member of your company's testing team) than like testing by one person.

Alpha testing. In-house testing performed by the test team (and possibly other interested, friendly insiders).

Beta testing. A type of user testing that uses testers who aren't part of your organization and who are members of your product's target market. The product under test is typically very close to completion. Many companies think of any release of prerelease code to customers as beta testing; they time all beta tests to the milestone they call "beta." This is a mistake. There are actually many different types of beta tests. A *design beta*, which asks the users (especially subject matter experts) to appraise the design, should go out as soon as possible, in order to allow time for changes based on the results. A *marketing beta*, intended to reassure large customers that they should buy this product when it becomes available and install it on their large networks, should go out fairly late when the product is quite stable. In a *compatibility test beta*, the customer runs your product on a hardware and software platform that you can't easily test yourself. That must be done before it's too late for you to troubleshoot and fix compatibility problems. For any type of beta test that you manage, you should determine its objectives before deciding how it will be scheduled and conducted.

Bug bashes. In-house testing using secretaries, programmers, marketers, and anyone who is available. A typical bug-bash lasts a half-day and is done when the software is close to being ready to release. (Note: we're listing this technique as an example, not endorsing it. Some companies have found it useful for various reasons; others have not.)

Subject-matter expert testing. Give the product to an expert on some issues addressed by the software and request feedback (bugs, criticisms, and compliments). The expert may or may not be someone you would expect to use the product—her value is her knowledge, not her representativeness of your market.

Paired testing. Two testers work together to find bugs. Typically, they share one computer and trade control of it while they test.

Eat your own dogfood. Your company uses and relies on prerelease versions of its own software, typically waiting until the software is reliable enough for real use before selling it.

Lesson 50 Coverage-based techniques focus on what gets tested.

You could class several of these techniques differently, as problem-focused, depending on what you have in mind when you use the technique. For example, feature integration testing is coverage-oriented if you use it to check that every function behaves well when used in combination with any other function. It's problem-oriented if you have a theory of error for functions interacting together and you want to track it down. (For example, it's problem oriented if your intent is to demonstrate errors in the ways that functions pass data to each other.)

We spend some extra space on domain testing in these definitions and at the end of the chapter because the domain-related techniques are so widely used and so important in the field. You should know them.

Function testing. Test every function, one by one. Test the function thoroughly, to the extent that you can say with confidence that the function works. White box function testing is usually called unit testing and concentrates on the functions as you see them in the code. Black box function testing focuses on commands and features, things the user can do or select. It's wise to do function testing before doing more complex tests that involve several functions. In a complex test, the first broken function will probably stop the test and block you from finding, with this test, that several other functions are also broken. If you rely on complex tests instead of testing the functions individually, you might not know until very late that one function is broken, and you might spend an enormous amount of work troubleshooting the complex test, only to discover the problem was in a simple function.

Feature or function integration testing. Test several functions together, to see how they work together.

Menu tour. Walk through all of the menus and dialogs in a GUI product, taking every available choice.

Domain testing. A domain is a (mathematical) set that includes all possible values of a variable of a function. In domain testing, you identify the functions and the variables. The variables might be input or output variables. (The mathematical distinction between input domains and output ranges is not relevant here, because the testing analysis is the same for both cases.) For each variable, you partition its set of possible values into equivalence classes and pick a small number of representatives (typically boundary cases) from each class. The assumption of the method is that if you test with a few excellent representatives of a class, you'll find most or all of the bugs that could be found by testing every member of the class. Note that in contrast to function testing, the primary element of interest is the variable rather than the function. Many variables are used by more than one function. The domain tester will analyze a variable and then, based on that analysis, run tests that involve this variable on each function with this variable as an input or an output.

Equivalence class analysis. An equivalence class is a set of values for a variable that you consider equivalent. Test cases are equivalent if you believe that (a) they all test the same thing; (b) if one of them catches a bug, the others probably will too; and (c) if one of them doesn't catch a bug, the others probably won't either. Once you've found an equivalence class, test only one or two of its members.

Boundary testing. An equivalence class is a set of values. If you can map them onto a number line, the boundary values are the smallest and largest members of the class. In boundary testing, you test these, and you also test the boundary values of nearby classes that are just smaller than the smallest member of the class you're testing and just larger than the largest member of the class you're testing. For example, consider an input field that accepts integer values between 10 and 50. The boundary values of interest are 10 (smallest), 9 (largest integer that is too small), 50 (largest), and 51 (smallest integer that is too large).

Best representative testing. A best representative of an equivalence class is a value that is at least as likely as any other value in the class to expose an error in the software. In boundary testing, the boundary cases are almost always best representatives. But suppose that you cannot map an equivalence class onto a number line. For example, the printers that are Hewlett-Packard PCL-5 compatible are (or should be) an equivalence class because they should all work the same way. Now suppose that for a specific task, one of the printers is slightly more likely to have trouble than the others. This printer would be a best representative for that class. If it doesn't fail, we have some confidence that the other printers also wouldn't.

Input field test catalogs or matrices. For each type of input field, you can develop a fairly standard set of test cases and reuse it for similar fields in this product and later products. We give an example of this technique later in the chapter. (See the How to Create a Test Matrix for an Input Field.)

Map and test all the ways to edit a field. You can often change the value of a field in several ways. For example, you might be able to import data into the field, enter data directly into the field, have the program copy a calculated result into the field, have the program copy a recalculated result into the field, and so on. The field has constraints (restrictions on what values the field can take). Some constraints will be constant, while others will depend on the values of other fields. For example, if J and K are unsigned integers, they're constrained to the values of 0 through MaxInt. These are constant constraints. They depend on the programming language's definition of unsigned integers. However, suppose that N is also an unsigned integer, that N = J + K, and that N = 5. In this case, J = 5 − K, and J cannot possibly be bigger than 5 (the value of N). This is a variable constraint, whose range of allowable values depends on the value of N. To check that J is kept within its allowable range (5 − K), you would try changing its value using each way that you can enter data into J.

Logic testing. Variables have relationships in the program. For example, the program might have a decision rule that says that if PERSON-AGE is greater than 50 and if SMOKER is YES, then OFFER-INSURANCE must be NO. The decision rule expresses a logical relationship. Logic testing attempts to check every logical relationship in the program. *Cause-effect graphing* is a technique for designing an extensive set of logic-based tests.

State-based testing. A program moves from state to state. In a given state, some inputs are valid, and others are ignored or rejected. In response to a valid input, the program under test does something that it can do and does not attempt something that it cannot do. In state-based testing, you walk the program through a large set of state transitions (state changes) and check the results carefully, every time.

Path testing. A path includes all of the steps that you took or all of the statements that the program passed through in order to get to your current state. Path testing involves testing many paths through the program. You cannot test all the paths through a nontrivial program. Therefore, some testers do *subpath testing*, testing many partial paths. *Basis-path testing*, for example, involves testing most or all subpaths of a certain type (the basis paths), under the assumption that if you get all of these, few tests of longer paths would be likely to find bugs that these tests missed.

Statement and branch coverage. You achieve 100 percent statement coverage if your tests execute every statement (or line of code) in the program. You achieve 100 percent statement and branch coverage if you execute every statement and every branch from one statement to another. Designing your tests to achieve a high percentage of line and branch coverage is sometimes called "Coverage-based testing." (And after you achieve that, you can quit testing or quit designing additional tests). We call this *statement-and-branch coverage* to differentiate it from all of the other types of testing that focus on some other type of coverage. Configuration coverage is an excellent example of a technique that hits the same statements many times but with potentially very different results. There are many, many other examples (Kaner 1995a). Testing that is focused on achieving high statement-and-branch coverage numbers will characteristically miss many types of bugs, such as (but not only) bugs involving missing code, incorrect handling of boundary values, timing problems, problems of compatibility with hardware and software configurations, delayed-fuse bugs like wild pointers, memory leaks or stack corruption that eventually leads to stack overflow, usability problems, and other failures to meet customer requirements. This technique is much more valuable to identify incomplete testing (what code has not yet been tested), than as a minimum standard for the amount of testing needed. Indeed, it's dangerous to allow testers to stop merely because they achieved X percent coverage (Marick 1999).

Configuration coverage. If you have to test compatibility with 100 printers, and you have tested with 10, you have achieved 10 percent printer coverage. More generally, configuration coverage measures the percentage of configuration tests that you have run (and the program has passed), compared to the total number of configuration tests that you plan to run. *Why do we call this a test technique?* Ordinarily, we would just consider this a measure of how much of a certain type of testing we had achieved. However, some testers craft a special series of tests that will make high-volume configuration testing faster and easier. In their hands, the optimization of the effort to achieve high coverage is the test technique.

Specification-based testing. Testing focused on verifying every factual claim that is made about the product in the specification. (A factual claim is any statement that can be shown to be true or false.) This often includes every claim made in the manual, in marketing documents or advertisements, and in technical support literature sent to customers.

Requirements-based testing. Testing focused on proving that the program satisfies every requirement in a requirements document (or focused, requirement by requirement, on proving that some of the requirements have not been met.)

Combination testing. Testing two or more variables in combination with each other. We discuss this in the *Addendum on Techniques* later in this chapter. Combination testing is important, but many testers don't study enough of it. Most benefits provided by the program are based on the interaction of many variables. If you don't vary them jointly in your tests, you'll miss errors that are triggered by difficult combinations, rather than difficult individual values.

Problems-based techniques focus on why you're testing (the risks you're testing for).

Lesson 51

Risk-based testing carries at least two major meanings.

Amland (1999) provides an excellent description of risk-based test *management*. Under this view, risk analysis is done to determine what things to test next. Testing is prioritized in terms of the probability that some feature of the program will fail and the probable cost of failure, if this feature does fail. The greater the probability of an expensive failure, the more important it is to test that feature as early and as carefully as possible.

The other meaning, which is where we're more focused, is on doing risk analyses for the purpose of finding errors. When we study a feature of a product, we ask how it can fail. That question breaks down into many additional questions, such as: What would a failure look like? Why should this feature fail—what drivers of risk are likely to have affected this feature? We describe our approach to risk-based testing in the *Addendum on Techniques*.

Both of these approaches to risk-based testing are also discussed in *James Bach on Risk-Based Testing* (1999c).

Whittaker and Jorgensen (1999 and 2000) provide excellent discussions and examples of broad classes of errors that involve constraint violations:

Input constraints. A constraint is a limit on what the program can handle. For example, if the program can only handle 32-digit numbers (or less), the programmer should provide protective routines that detect and reject an input that is outside of the 32-digit constraint. If there is no such protection, the program will fail when it attempts to process input data that it cannot process.

Output constraints. The inputs were legal, but they led to output values that the program could not handle. The program might fail when it attempts to display, print, or save an output value.

Computation constraints. The inputs and the outputs are fine, but in the course of calculating a value (that will lead to an output), the program fails. For example, multiplying two huge numbers together might yield something that is too huge for the program to cope with.

Storage (or data) constraints. Inputs, outputs, and calculations are legal, but the operations run the program out of memory or yield data files that are too enormous to process.

Whittaker (2002) provides detailed suggestions for testing against these constraints.

Here are a few additional tips for the design of risk-based tests:

- If you do risk-based testing, you must also do comparable nonrisk-based testing to test for the risk that you didn't know the risks well enough to make the right decisions.

- Test for timing issues. Surprisingly, many American-educated testers fail to consider timing issues. Some classic timing issues include race conditions and other unexpected orderings of events that happen in time.

- When you create a test, always create a test procedure that will force the program to use the test data that you have entered, allowing you to determine whether it's using that data incorrectly.

Activity-based techniques focus on how you test.

Regression testing. Regression testing involves reuse of the same tests, so you can retest (with these) after change. There are three kinds of regression testing. You do *bug fix regression* after reporting a bug and hearing later on that it's fixed. The goal is to prove that the fix is no good. The goal of *old bugs regression* is to prove that a change to the software has caused an old bug fix to become unfixed. *Side-effect regression*, also called *stability regression*, involves retesting of substantial parts of the product. The goal is to prove that the change has caused something that used to work to now be broken.

Scripted testing. Manual testing, typically done by a junior tester who follows a step-by-step procedure written by a more senior tester.

Smoke testing. This type of side-effect regression testing is done with the goal of proving that a new build is not worth testing. Smoke tests are often automated and standardized from one build to the next. They test things you expect to work, and if they don't, you'll suspect that the program was built with the wrong file or that something basic is broken.

Exploratory testing. We expect the tester to learn, throughout the project, about the product, its market, its risks, and the ways in which it has failed previous tests. New tests are constantly created and used. They're more powerful than older tests because they're based on the tester's continuously increasing knowledge.

Guerilla testing. A fast and vicious attack on the program. A form of exploratory testing that is usually time-boxed and done by an experienced exploratory tester. For example, a senior tester might spend a day testing an area that will otherwise be ignored. She tries out her most powerful attacks. If she finds significant problems, the area will be rebudgeted, and the overall test plan might be affected. If she finds no significant problems, the area will hereinafter be ignored or only lightly tested.

Scenario testing. A scenario test (as we use the term) normally involves four attributes. (1) The test must be realistic. It should reflect something that customers would actually do. (2) The test should be complex, involving several features, in a way that should be challenging to the program. (3) It should be easy and quick to tell whether the program passed or failed the test. (4) A stakeholder is likely to argue vigorously that the program should be fixed if it fails this test. A test with these four attributes will be persuasive and will probably yield bug fixes if it fails the program. However, you might have to spend days developing an excellent scenario test.

Scenario testing. Tests derived from use cases are also called scenario tests (Jacobson 1992, Collard 1999) or *use case flow tests*. (Many people would classify these as coverage-based tests, focusing on coverage of the important use cases.)

Installation testing. Install the software in the various ways and on the various types of systems that it can be installed. Check which files are added or changed on disk. Does the installed software work? What happens when you uninstall?

Load testing. The program or system under test is attacked, by being run on a system that is facing many demands for resources. Under a high enough load, the system will probably fail, but the pattern of events leading to the failure will point to vulnerabilities in the software or system under test that might be exploited under more normal use of the software under test. Asbock (2000) is an excellent introduction to load testing.

Long sequence testing. Testing is done overnight or for days or weeks. The goal is to discover errors that short sequence tests will miss. Examples of the errors that are often found this way are wild pointers, memory leaks, stack overflows, and bad interactions among more than two features. (This is sometimes called duration testing, reliability testing, or endurance testing.)

Performance testing. These tests are usually run to determine how quickly the program runs, in order to decide whether optimization is needed. But the tests can expose many other bugs. A significant change in performance from a previous release can indicate the effect of a coding error. For example, if you test how long a simple function test takes to run today and then run the same test on the same machine tomorrow, you'll probably check with the programmer or write a bug report if the test runs more than three times faster or slower. Either case is suspicious because something fundamental about the program has been changed.[2]

Evaluation-based techniques focus on how to tell whether the test passed or failed.

The evaluation techniques describe methods for determining whether the program passed or failed the test. They don't specify how the testing should be done or how the data should be collected. They tell you that, if you can collect certain data, you can evaluate it.

Self-verifying data. The data files you use in testing carry information that lets you determine whether the output data is corrupt.

Comparison with saved results. Regression testing (typically, but not always automated) in which pass or fail is determined by comparing the results you got today with the results from last week. If the result was correct last week, and it's different now, the difference might reflect a new defect.

---

[2]Sam Guckenheimer noted to us, "A performance difference might also reflect a change in a third-party component or configuration. For example, changes in the JVM with different Sun releases of the JDK have had remarkably different performance characteristics. Since this is a customer-updateable component, performance testing can yield surprising results even when your code hasn't changed at all!"

Comparison with a specification or other authoritative document. A mismatch with the specification is (probably) an error.

Heuristic consistency. Consistency is an important criterion for evaluating a program. Inconsistency may be a reason to report a bug, or it may reflect intentional design variation. We work with seven main consistencies:

1. *Consistent with history.* Present function behavior is consistent with past behavior.

2. *Consistent with our image.* Function behavior is consistent with an image the organization wants to project.

3. *Consistent with comparable products.* Function behavior is consistent with that of similar functions in comparable products.

4. *Consistent with claims.* Function behavior is consistent with what people say it's supposed to be.

5. *Consistent with user's expectations.* Function behavior is consistent with what we think users want.

6. *Consistent within product.* Function behavior is consistent with behavior of comparable functions or functional patterns within the product.

7. *Consistent with purpose.* Function behavior is consistent with apparent purpose.

Oracle-based testing. An oracle is an evaluation tool that will tell you whether the program has passed or failed a test. In high-volume automated testing, the oracle is probably another program that generates results or checks the software under test's results. The oracle is generally more trusted than the software under test, so a concern flagged by the oracle is worth spending time and effort to check.

The classification of a technique depends on how you think about it.

You might be puzzled about why we placed particular techniques where we did. If so, good for you: Your brain is turned on. Remember, all testing involves all five aspects of the Five-Fold System. We've listed techniques by category simply to give you a flavor of how different techniques emphasize some ways of thinking over others. Your taste may vary. For example, one reader argued with us that load testing should be classified as a problem-focused (or risk-focused test) rather than as an activity-focused test. Our answer is that you can think of it either way.

Let's look at this from a problem-oriented perspective:

- You can think of load testing in terms of the effect of denial-of-service attacks. An attacker could attempt to deny service by creating too many connections or users or by using too much memory (have every user issue a memory-intensive command at the same time) or by using tasks that eat too much processing capacity. You could do different load tests for each of these types of risk.

Now consider an activity perspective:

- Use a tool to track the patterns of activities of your customers. Which commands do customers use most often? What tasks are customers most likely to attempt? What percentage of customers do which activities? When you have a model of the usage patterns at your site, get a load test tool and program it with scenarios that look like each of the types of use. Have that tool randomly select among scenarios—in effect, create different sessions that represent different types of users. Keep adding sessions and watch how performance and reliability of the system degrades with increased load. Make changes to the software as appropriate.

When you think in terms of the risk, you think of a weakness that the program might have and ask how to design a test series that would expose that kind of weakness. When you know what type of test you want to run, think about the way that you'll run that test. If you were testing a telephone system, you might need a tool, or you might be as well off with 10 friends who make a bunch of phone calls. The criterion for the test design is that it must have power—the ability to detect the fault that you're looking for.

In contrast, when you think in terms of activities, you're asking how to do load testing. What tools? What will the tools do? And so on. The expectation is that if you use the tools competently, model customers accurately, and do the other activities associated with good load testing, then you'll probably find the types of bugs that load testing is likely to reveal.

Either classification is accurate, but the classification itself only helps you so much. However you classify a technique like load testing, when it comes time to test, you'll still have the same five dimensions of decision:

- *Who will do the testing?*
- *What aspects of the program are you testing?*
- *What types of problems are you looking for?*
- *What tasks, specifically, will you do?*
- *How will you tell whether a test passed or failed?*

Addendum to Techniques

Here are more detailed descriptions of a few of the key testing techniques that we've found particularly useful:

- How to create a test matrix for an input field.
- How to create a test matrix for repeating issues.
- How to create a traceability matrix for specification-based testing.
- How to do combination testing using the all-pairs technique.
- How to analyze the risks associated with some item or aspect of the program.

How to Create a Test Matrix for an Input Field

Start by asking, "What are the interesting input tests for a simple integer field?" Here are some of the tests we think of as routine for a field of this kind:

- Nothing
- Empty field (clear the default value)
- Outside of upper bound (UB) number of digits or characters
- 0
- Valid value
- At lower bound (LB) of value $- 1$
- At lower bound (LB) of value
- At upper bound (UB) of value
- At upper bound (UB) of value $+ 1$
- Far below the LB of value
- Far above the UB of value
- At LB number of digits or characters
- At LB $- 1$ number of digits or characters
- At UB number of digits or characters
- At UB $+ 1$ number of digits or characters
- Far more than UB number of digits or characters
- Negative
- Nondigits, especially / (ASCII character 47) and : (ASCII character 58)

- Wrong data type (*e. g.,* decimal into integer)
- Expressions
- Leading space
- Many leading spaces
- Leading zero
- Many leading zeros
- Leading + sign
- Many leading + signs
- Nonprinting character (*e. g.,* Ctrl+char)
- Operating system filename reserved characters (*e. g.,* "\ * . :")
- Language reserved characters
- Upper ASCII (128–254) (a.k.a. ANSI) characters
- ASCII 255 (often interpreted as end of file)
- Uppercase characters
- Lowercase characters
- Modifiers (*e. g.,* Ctrl, Alt, Shift-Ctrl, and so on)
- Function key (F2, F3, F4, and so on)
- Enter nothing but wait for a long time before pressing the Enter or Tab key, clicking OK, or doing something equivalent that takes you out of the field. Is there a time-out? What is the effect?
- Enter one digit but wait for a long time before entering another digit or digits and then press the Enter key. How long do you have to wait before the system times you out, if it does? What happens to the data you entered? What happens to other data you previously entered?
- Enter digits and edit them using the backspace key, and delete them, and use arrow keys (or the mouse) to move you into the digits you've already entered so that you can insert or overtype new digits.
- Enter digits while the system is reacting to interrupts of different kinds (such as printer activity, clock events, mouse movement and clicks, files going to disk, and so on).
- Enter a digit, shift focus to another application, return to this application. Where is the focus?

A list like this is often called a *catalog of tests*. (Marick 1995 defines the term and gives examples.) We find it useful to put the list into a matrix form, as in Table 3.1.

Table 3.1 Numeric Input Field Test Matrix

Numeric Input Field	Nothing	Empty (clear default)	0	LB-1	LB	UB	UB+1	Far below LB	Far above UB	UB number of chars	UB +1 chars	Far beyond UB chars	Negative	Non-digit (/ ASCII 47)	Non-digit (: ASCII 58)	wrong data type	expressions	Leading spaces	Non-printing char	O/S file name	Upper ASCII	Upper case	lower case	Modifiers (Ctrl, Alt, etc.)	Function keys

Across the top of the matrix are the tests that you'll use time and time again. Down the side are the fields that you would test. For example, in the typical Print dialog, one of the fields is Number of Copies. The range of valid values for Number of Copies is typically 1 to 99 or 1 to 255 (depends on the printer). On the form, you might write *Print: Number of Copies* on one row, then run some or all of the tests on that field, and then fill in the results accordingly. (We like to use green and pink highlighters to fill in cells that yielded passing and failing test results.)

The matrix provides a structure for easy delegation. When a new feature is added or a feature is changed late in the project, you can assign several of these standard matrices to a tester who is relatively new to the project (but experienced in testing). Her task is to check for basic functioning of the new feature or continued good functioning of older features that you expect to be impacted by the one that was changed.

The integer input field is just one example. You might find it valuable to create charts like this for rational numbers (of various precisions), character fields (of various widths), filenames, file locations, dates, and so on. If you run into one type of input field program after program or time after time in the program that you're testing, it's worth spending the time to create a reusable matrix.

How to Create a Test Matrix for Repeating Issues

The text matrix for an input field is just one example of a broad class of useful matrices you can create. Input fields aren't the only candidates for standardization. Whenever a situation recurs frequently, across and within programs, you have a basis for spending time and effort to create a testing catalog. Given a catalog, you can always format it as a matrix.

Here's an example that doesn't involve input variables.

In this case, the catalog lists the ways the program could be unsuccessful in an attempt to write a file to disk. In several situations the program would attempt to write a file, such as:

- Saving a new file.
- Overwriting a file with the same name.
- Appending to a file.
- Replacing a file that you're editing, with a new version, same name.
- Exporting to a new file format.

- Printing to disk.

- Logging messages or errors to disk.

- Saving a temporary file. (Many programs do this as part of their routine, so you might not think of it during user interface testing. However, if the disk is full, the program can still fail.)

Each of these situations will have its own row in the matrix. Similarly, if the software under test enables you to export to different formats, the test matrix will have one format per row.

The columns indicate the tests that you perform. For example, try saving a file to a full disk. Try saving a file to an almost full disk. Try saving a file to a drive that gets disconnected, and so on.

Here's a catalog of some of the interesting test cases for unsuccessful attempts to save a file:

- Save to a full local disk.

- Save to an almost full local disk.

- Save to a write-protected local disk.

- Save to a full disk on the local network.

- Save to an almost full disk on the local network.

- Save to a write-protected disk on the local network.

- Save to a full disk on a remote network.

- Save to an almost full disk on a remote network.

- Save to a write-protected disk on a remote network.

- Save to a file, directory, or disk that you don't have write privileges to.

- Save to a damaged (I/O error) local disk, local network disk, or remote disk.

- Save to an unformatted local disk, local network disk, or remote disk.

- Remove local disk, local network disk, or remote disk from drive after opening file.

- Timeout waiting for local disk, local network disk, or remote disk to come back online.

- Create a keyboard and mouse I/O during a save to a local disk, local network disk, or remote disk.

- Generate some other interrupt during a save to a local drive, local network disk, or remote disk.

- Power out (of local computer) during a save to a local drive, local network disk, or remote disk.

- Power out (of drive or computer connected to drive) during a save to a local drive, local network disk, or remote disk.

To create a catalog like this, we suggest you have two brainstorming sessions with colleagues. In the first session, try to think of anything that would be a test you would routinely run on the object (like input field) or task (like saving a file) under test. Budget an hour, fill lots of flip charts, and then send your colleagues away for a day while you organize the material from the brainstorms.

To organize the material, create a new set of flipchart pages. Write a theme heading on each, like "disk capacity" and "interrupted while writing." Under the heading, copy all of the items from the flipcharts that fit into that theme. Eventually, all items will be on one of the theme flipcharts or discarded. (Feel free to discard dumb ideas.)

Next day, brainstorm using the theme charts. People will add more items to "disk capacity" and to "interrupted while writing" and so on. Have a few spare charts ready for new themes. It's not uncommon to double the length of the list in the second meeting.

After the second meeting, sort tests into essential ones, which go onto the main test matrix; the infrequently used ones, which go to a secondary list that you might distribute with the main matrix; and the discards.

Nguyen (2000) provides additional examples of test matrices.

How to Create a Traceability Matrix for Specification-Based Testing

A traceability matrix enables you to trace every test case forward to an item (items) in the specification and to trace back from every specification item to all of the test cases that test it. Table 3.2 shows an example.

Each column contains a different specification item. A spec item might refer to a function, a variable, a value (*e. g.*, a boundary case) of a variable, a promised benefit, an allegedly compatible device, or any other promise or statement that can be proved true or false.

Each row is a test case.

Each cell shows which test case tests which items.

Table 3.2 Specification Traceability Matrix

	SPEC ITEM 1	SPEC ITEM 2	SPEC ITEM 3	SPEC ITEM 4	SPEC ITEM 5	SPEC ITEM 6
Test Case 1	X		X			X
Test Case 2	X	X		X		X
Test Case 3			X	X		X
Test Case 4			X	X		X
Test Case 5	X				X	X
Test Case 6		X				X
TOTALS	3	2	3	3	1	6

If a feature changes, you can see quickly which tests must be reanalyzed and probably rewritten. In general, you can trace back from a given item of interest to the tests that cover it.

This matrix isn't a perfect test document. It doesn't specify the tests; it merely maps the test cases to the specification items. You can't see from this matrix whether the test is a powerful one or a weak one, or whether it does something interesting with the feature (or other spec item) or something that no one would care about. You also can't see the testing that is being done of features that haven't been specified or of adjustments you've made in the testing to deal with specs that were incorrect. Despite these problems, charts like this can be useful for helping you understand:

- That one feature or item is almost never tested, while another is tested extremely often.

- That a change to one item (such as Spec Item 6 in Table 3.2) will cause revisions to a huge number of tests in the system. (This is a key issue in contract-driven development, because the client is going to pay a lot of testing money if they get the change they're apparently asking for, and they should be warned of that before the change is made.)

Traceability matrices are useful in more cases than just specification-driven testing. Any time you have a list of things you want tested (specification items, features, use cases, network cards, whatever), you can run that list across the top of the matrix, run the list of test cases down the rows, and then check which test cases test what. You'll almost certainly find holes in your testing this way. If your tests are automated, you may be able to generate a traceability matrix automatically.

How to Do Combination Testing Using the All-Pairs Technique

Combination testing involves testing several variables together. The first critical problem of combination testing is the number of test cases. Imagine testing three variables together, when each variable has 100 possible values. The number of possible tests of Variable 1 with Variable 2 with Variable 3 is $100 \times 100 \times 100 = 1,000,000$ test cases. Reducing the number of tests is a critical priority.

Start with Domain Partitioning

The first step is to reduce the number of values that will be tested in each variable. The most common approach involves domain testing. Partition the values of Variable 1 into subdomains and choose best representatives of the subdomains. Perhaps you can bring the number of tests of Variable 1 down to five this way. If you can do the same for Variable 2 and Variable 3, you now only have $5 \times 5 \times 5$ tests (125). This is still too many for practical purposes, but it's a lot less than a million.

The best discussions in print of partitioning are in Ostrand and Balcer (1988) and Jorgensen (1995). Jorgensen provides good examples of partitioning and of testing several partitioned variables in combination. We present a different approach to combinations from his, which we have found useful.

Achieving All Singles

The simplest set of combination tests would ensure that you cover every value of interest (every one of the five that we'll test) of every variable. This is called *all singles* (in contrast to all pairs and all triples) because you're making sure that you hit every single value of every variable. You can achieve this as follows:

1. Let V1, V2, and V3 stand for the three variables.
2. Let A, B, C, D, and E be the five values of interest in variable V1. In particular, suppose that V1 is the operating system; A is Windows 2000; B is Windows 95; C is Windows 98 original; D is Windows 98 with the first service pack; and E is Windows ME.
3. Let I, J, K, L, and M be the five values of interest in variable V2. In particular, suppose that V2 is the browser; I is Netscape 4.73; J is Netscape 6; K is Explorer 5.5; L is Explorer 5.0; and M is Opera 5.12 for Windows.

4. Let V, W, X, Y, and Z be the five values of interest in variable V3. These refer to five different disk drive options on the system.

To test all combinations of these variables' values, we would have $5 \times 5 \times 5$ = 125 tests.

Table 3.3 is a combination test table that achieves "complete testing," when the criterion of completeness is that every value of every variable must appear in at least one test.

This approach is often used in configuration testing to reduce the number of configurations under test to a manageable number.

A serious problem with the approach is that it misses predictably important configurations. For example, a lot of people might be using Explorer 5.5 with Windows ME, but that test isn't listed here. Instead, the table shows Opera 5.12 with Windows ME.

A common solution to this problem is to specify additional test cases that include key pairs of variables (such as Explorer 5.5 with Windows ME) or more key combinations of more than two variables (such as Explorer 5.5, Windows ME, HP 4050N printer, 256M RAM, and a 21-inch color monitor being driven at 1600×1200 resolution.) Marketing or technical support staff might specify these, naming perhaps 10 or 20 additional key configurations, for a total of 15 or 25 tests.

Achieving All Pairs

In the *all pairs* approach (Cohen *et al.*, 1996 and 1997), the set of test cases includes all of the pairs of values of every variable. So, E (Windows ME) isn't just paired with M (Opera). It's also paired with I, J, K, and L. Similarly, E is paired with every value of V3.

Table 3.3 All Singles—All Values are Represented at Least Once

	VARIABLE 1	VARIABLE 2	VARIABLE 3
Test Case 1	A *(Win 2K)*	I *(Netscape 4.73)*	V *(Disk option 1)*
Test Case 2	B *(Win 95)*	J *(Netscape 6)*	W *(Disk option 2)*
Test Case 3	C *(Win 98)*	K *(IE 5.5)*	X *(Disk option 3)*
Test Case 4	D *(Win 98 SP1)*	L *(IE 5.0)*	Y *(Disk option 4)*
Test Case 5	E *(Win ME)*	M *(Opera 5.12)*	Z *(Disk option 5)*

Table 3.4 All Pairs—All Pairs of Values are Represented at Least Once (25 Instead of 125 Tests)

	VARIABLE 1	VARIABLE 2	VARIABLE 3
Test Case 1	A	I	V
Test Case 2	A	J	W
Test Case 3	A	K	X
Test Case 4	A	L	Y
Test Case 5	A	M	Z
Test Case 6	B	I	W
Test Case 7	B	J	Z
Test Case 8	B	K	Y
Test Case 9	B	L	V
Test Case 10	B	M	X
Test Case 11	C	I	X
Test Case 12	C	J	Y
Test Case 13	C	K	Z
Test Case 14	C	L	W
Test Case 15	C	M	V
Test Case 16	D	I	Y
Test Case 17	D	J	X
Test Case 18	D	K	V
Test Case 19	D	L	Z
Test Case 20	D	M	W
Test Case 21	E	I	Z
Test Case 22	E	J	V
Test Case 23	E	K	W
Test Case 24	E	L	X
Test Case 25	E	M	Y

Table 3.4 illustrates a set of combinations that will meet the all-pairs criterion. Every value of every variable is paired with every value of every other variable in at least one test case. This is a much more thorough standard than all singles, but it still reduces the number of test cases from 125 (all combinations) to 25, a big savings.

To show how to create an all-pairs test set, we'll work through a simpler example, step by step.

A Step-By-Step Example

Imagine a program with three variables: V1 has three possible values; V2 has two possible values; and V3 has two possible values. If V1, V2, and V3 are independent, the number of possible combinations is 12 ($3 \times 2 \times 2$).

To build the all-pairs table, start this way:

1. Label the columns with the variable names, listing variables in descending order (of number of possible values).

2. If the variable in Column 1 has V1 possible values and the variable in Column 2 has V2 possible values, there will be at least V1 $\times$ V2 rows (draw the table this way but leave a blank row or two between repetition groups in Column 1).

3. Fill in the table, one column at a time. The first column repeats each of its elements V2 times, skips a line, and then starts the repetition of the next element. For example, if variable 1's possible values are A, B, and C and V2 is two, Column 1 would contain A, A, blank row, B, B, blank row, C, C, blank row. Skip the blank row because it is hard to know how many tests (how many rows) will be needed. Leave room for extras.

4. In the second column, list all the values of the variable, skip the line, list the values, and so forth. For example, if Variable 2's possible values are X and Y, the table looks like Table 3.5 so far.

5. Add the third column (the third variable).

   Each section of the third column (think of the two AA rows as defining a section, BB as defining another, and so on) will have to contain every value of Variable 3. Order the values so that the variables also make all pairs with Variable 2.

Table 3.5 First Step in Creating the All-Pairs Matrix

VARIABLE 1	VARIABLE 2	VARIABLE 3
A	X	
A	Y	
B	X	
B	Y	
C	X	
C	Y	

Suppose that Variable 3 can have values 0 or 1. The third section can be filled in either way, and you might highlight your choice on the matrix so that you can reverse it later if you have to. The decision (say 1,0) is arbitrary. See Table 3.6.

Now that we've solved the three-column exercise, try adding more variables. Each of them will have two values.

To add a variable with more than two values, you have to start over, because the order of variables in the table must be from the one with the largest number of values to the next largest number and on down so that the last column has the variable with the fewest values. (You *could* do it differently, but our experience is that you'll make so many mistakes that you would be unwise to try to do it differently.)

The fourth column will go in easily. Start by making sure you hit all pairs of values of Column 4 and Column 2 (this can be done in the AA and BB blocks), then make sure you get all pairs of Column 4 and Column 3. See Table 3.7.

Watch this first attempt on Column 5 (see Table 3.8). It achieves all pairs of GH with Columns 1, 2, and 3 but misses it for Column 4.

The most recent arbitrary choice was HG in the BB section. (After the order of H then G was determined for the BB section, HG is the necessary order for the third in order to pair H with a 1 in the third column.)

To recover from guessing incorrectly that HG was a good order for the second section, erase it and try again:

Table 3.6   Second Step in Creating the All-Pairs Matrix

VARIABLE 1	VARIABLE 2	VARIABLE 3
A	X	1
A	Y	0
B	X	0
B	Y	1
C	X	1
C	Y	0

Table 3.7 Adding a Fourth Variable to the All-Pairs Matrix

VARIABLE 1	VARIABLE 2	VARIABLE 3	VARIABLE 4
A	X	1	E
A	Y	0	F
B	X	0	F
B	Y	1	E
C	X	1	F
C	Y	0	E

Table 3.8 Adding a Fifth Variable to the All-Pairs Matrix. (This one doesn't work, but it illustrates how to make a guess and then recover if you guess incorrectly.)

VARIABLE 1	VARIABLE 2	VARIABLE 3	VARIABLE 4	VARIABLE 5
A	X	1	E	G
A	Y	0	F	H
B	X	0	F	H
B	Y	1	E	G
C	X	1	F	H
C	Y	0	E	G

1. Flip the most recent arbitrary choice (Column 5, Section BB, from HG to GH).

2. Erase section CC because the choice of HG there was based on the preceding section being HG, and we just erased that.

3. Refill section CC by checking for missing pairs. GH, GH would give us two XG, XG pairs, so flip to HG for the third section. This yields a Column 2X with a Column 5H and a Column 2Y with a Column 5G, as needed to obtain all pairs. (See Table 3.9.)

If you try to add yet another variable, it won't fit in the six pairs. Try it with the IJs (the values of Variable 6) in any order, and it just won't work. (See Table 3.10.)

Table 3.9 Successfully Adding a Fifth Variable to the All-Pairs Matrix

VARIABLE 1	VARIABLE 2	VARIABLE 3	VARIABLE 4	VARIABLE 5
A	X	1	E	G
A	Y	0	F	H
B	X	0	F	G
B	Y	1	E	H
C	X	1	F	H
C	Y	0	E	G

However, this is easy to fix. We just need two more test cases. See Table 3.11. If you consider the second table, what is needed is a test that pairs a G with a J and another test that pairs an H with an I. The values of any of the other variables are irrelevant (as far as achieving all pairs), so fill them with anything you want. If you're going to keep adding variables, you might leave them blank, and decide later (as you try to accommodate Variable 7 and Variable 8 into the same eight test cases) what values would be convenient in those rows.

If we tried to test all of the combinations of these variables, there would be 3 $\times$ 2 $\times$ 2 $\times$ 2 $\times$ 2 $\times$ 2 = 96 tests. We've reduced our set of tests, using all-pairs, from 96 to 8, a substantial savings.

There are risks if you *only* use the all-pairs cases. As with all-singles, you might know of a specific combination that is widely used or likely to be troublesome. The best thing to do is add this case to the table. You've cut back from 96 to 8 tests. It's sensible to expand the set out to 10 or 15 tests, to cover the important special cases. For another worked example, see (Cohen *et al.* 1997).

How to Analyze the Risks Associated with Some Item or Aspect of the Program

Suppose you're testing some feature of the product. (You could just as well be testing a variable. This is not restricted to features.)

The feature might have a problem. That is, it might fail to live up to an important measure of the quality of the product.

To determine whether the feature has a problem, consider the problem drivers, the things that make a feature more likely to go wrong.

Table 3.10   These Six Variables Do Not Fit into the Six Tests in the All-Pairs Matrix

VAR 1	VAR 2	VAR 3	VAR 4	VAR 5	VAR 6
A	X	1	E	G	I
A	Y	0	F	H	J
B	X	0	F	G	J
B	Y	1	E	H	I
C	X	1	F	H	J
C	Y	0	E	G	I

VAR 1	VAR 2	VAR 3	VAR 4	VAR 5	VAR 6
A	X	1	E	G	I
A	Y	0	F	H	J
B	X	0	F	G	I
B	Y	1	E	H	J
C	X	1	F	H	J
C	Y	0	E	G	I

Table 3.11   All Pairs with Six Variables in Eight Test Cases

VAR 1	VAR 2	VAR 3	VAR 4	VAR 5	VAR 6
A	X	1	E	G	I
A	Y	0	F	H	J
				G	J
B	X	0	F	G	I
B	Y	1	E	H	J
				H	I
C	X	1	F	H	J
C	Y	0	E	G	I

Quality Attributes

If a feature lacks or violates any of these attributes, it's probably due for a bug report:

- Accessibility
- Capability
- Compatibility
- Concurrency
- Conformance to standards
- Efficiency
- Installability and uninstallability
- Localizability
- Maintainability
- Performance
- Portability
- Recoverability
- Reliability
- Scalability
- Security
- Supportability
- Testability
- Usability

To determine whether a feature is defective, ask yourself how you would prove that it lacks or violates one of these attributes.

For example, consider *usability*. How could you prove that the feature under test is unusable? What would unusability look like? What traditional usability tests could you apply to study this feature? Ask questions like these (and run appropriate tests).

These tests are constrained by your imagination, but many of the ideas that could enter your imagination might come from the problem drivers list.

Problem Drivers

Here are some factors that suggest a likelihood of errors to us. You can treat each of these as a small or large (your judgment) warning flag and design tests to determine whether the program actually has the vulnerability that these factors suggest.

New things. Newer features may fail.

New technology. New concepts lead to new mistakes.

New market(s). A different customer base will see and use the product differently.

Learning curve. Mistakes are made because of ignorance.

Changed things. Changes may break old code.

Late change. Rushed decisions, rushed or demoralized staff lead to mistakes.

Rushed work. Some tasks or projects are chronically underfunded, and all aspects of work quality suffer.

Poor design or unmaintainable implementation. Some internal design decisions make the code so hard to maintain that fixes consistently cause new problems.

Tired programmers. Long overtime over several weeks or months yields inefficiencies and errors.

Other staff issues. Alcohol problems, health problems, a death in the family . . . . Two programmers who won't talk to each other (neither will their code) . . . .

Just slipping it in. A programmer's pet (but unscheduled) feature may interact badly with other code.

N.I.H. (Not Invented Here) External components can cause problems.

N.I.B. (Not In Budget) Unbudgeted tasks may be done shoddily.

Ambiguity. Ambiguous descriptions (in specs or other docs) can lead to incorrect or conflicting implementations.

Conflicting requirements. Ambiguity often hides a conflict; the result of which is the loss of value for some person.

Unknown requirements. Requirements surface throughout development. Failure to meet a legitimate requirement is a failure of quality for that stakeholder.

Evolving requirements. People realize what they want as the product develops. Adhering to a start-of-the-project requirements list may meet the contract but fail the product. (Check out www.agilealliance.org.)

Complexity. Complex code may be buggy.

Bugginess. Features with many known bugs may also have many unknown bugs.

Dependencies. Failures may trigger other failures.

Untestability. Risk of slow, inefficient testing.

Little unit testing. Programmers find and fix most of their own bugs. Shortcutting here is a risk.

Little system testing so far. Untested software may fail.

Previous reliance on narrow testing strategies. For example, regression and function tests, can yield a backlog of errors surviving across versions.

Weak testing tools. If tools don't exist to help identify and isolate a class of error (*e. g.,* wild pointers), the error is more likely to survive undetected.

Unfixability. Risk of not being able to fix a bug.

Language-typical errors. Such as wild pointers in C. See for example, *Pitfalls of Object-Oriented Development* (Webster 1995) and *Java Pitfalls: Time-Saving Solutions and Workarounds to Improve Programs* (Daconta *et al.* 2000).

Use Error Catalogs

Testing Computer Software (Kaner *et al.* 1993) lays out a list of 480 common defects. You can use this list or develop your own. Here's how to use one:

1. Find a defect in the list.

2. Ask whether the software under test could have this defect.

3. If it's theoretically possible that the program could have the defect, ask how you could find the bug if it was there.

4. Ask how plausible it is that this bug could be in the program and how serious the failure would be if it was there.

5. If appropriate, design a test or series of tests for bugs of this type.

Unfortunately, too many people start and end with the TCS bug list. It's outdated. It was outdated the day it was published. And, it doesn't cover the issues in *your* system. Building a bug list is an ongoing process that constantly pays for itself. Here's an example from Hung Nguyen (personal communication):

This problem came up in a client/server system. The system sends the client a list of names, to allow verification that a name the client enters is not new.

Clients 1 and 2 both want to enter a name, and Clients 1 and 2 both use the same new name. Both instances of the name are new relative to their local compare list and, therefore, they're accepted. We now have two instances of the same name.

As we see these, we develop a library of issues. The discovery method is exploratory and requires sophistication with the underlying technology. Capture winning themes for testing in charts or in scripts-on-their-way to being automated.

As you see new problems (within your time constraints), add them to your database to make them available to the testers on the next project.

Use Up-to-Date Sources to Add to Your Error Catalogs

There are plenty of sources to check for common failures in the common platforms. Here's a sample of the types of information available that we've found helpful:

www.bugnet.com

www.cnet.com

Nguyen (2001)

Telles and Hsieh (2001).

Bug Advocacy

A tester who can't report bugs well is like a refrigerator light that's only on when the door is *closed*. The situation may be illuminated very well—just not so that it matters. You are an information service, but to be effective you have to do more than fill out report templates and assume they are fully understood. Learn how to write and present your test results so that they *get* results. We call this "bug advocacy."

You are what you write.

Bug reports are the primary work product of most testers. These documents mold your readers' perception of you. The better your reports, the better your reputation.

Programmers rely on your reports for vital information. Good reporting of good bugs earns you a good reputation. Weak reporting generates extra (and in their opinion unnecessary) work for the programmers. If you waste enough of their time, they'll want to avoid you and your work.

Programmers aren't your only audience. Managers and executives sometimes read bug reports. Personnel-management issues catch their attention quickly and grate on their nerves. Reports that seem blaming, petty in tone, poorly explained, or inadequately researched or suggest that you're blowing small issues out of proportion will create a negative impression in the minds of the people who approve your raises and promotions.

Everyone benefits if you take the time to research and write your reports well.

Your advocacy drives the repair of the bugs you report.

Any bug report that you write is an advocacy document that calls for the repair of the bug.

Some bugs will never be fixed. Your responsibility is not to make sure that all bugs are fixed. Your responsibility is to report bugs accurately and in a way that allows the reader to understand the full impact of the problem.

How well you research and write the report will often have a substantial effect on the probability that the bug will be fixed.

Make your bug report an effective sales tool.

Whether you think of it this way or not, your bug report is a sales tool; it's designed to convince people to give up precious resources in order to obtain a benefit that you propose. In the case of bugs, the resources are time and money. The benefit is the improvement in quality that arises from fixing this particular bug.

Sales strategies generally involve two goals.

State the benefit so that your prospect will want it. Your bug report should make it clear to the reader why he should want to fix this bug. For example, you might explain how the bug interferes with normal use of the product, what data it corrupts, or how often people will run into it. You might point to a magazine review or other published complaint that savaged a competitor for a bug similar to this one. You might quote technical support statistics to show that bugs like this one in other products have cost a lot of money. You might show that the program passed this test in a previous release. (This is a key issue in some companies.) Or you might make sure that the report is drawn to the attention of someone whose pet feature is interfered with by this bug. In many cases (see the following), you can take a relatively minor-looking bug and discover more severe consequences by doing follow-up testing, rather than reporting the first version of the bug that you see.

Anticipate objections to the sale and counter them. Some bugs are dismissed as too minor, not reproducible, impossible to understand, unlikely to ever happen in the real world, as a problem that occurs only on a very specific equipment configuration that no one will have, too risky to fix, or not likely to bother the actual users of the product. You can routinely address these potential objections by following good reporting practices: Write clearly and simply and check (and report) that the bug replicates on multiple configurations. Other objections vary from bug to bug. You might anticipate one and include some relevant information in your bug report, or you might wait, see the initial reactions to the report, and add the information as the bug goes through review. We're *not* saying that you should argue for the bug in the report. Rarely or never say, "I know you're thinking of not fixing this, but if you think it's unimportant for *this* reason, then you should know about *that*." Instead, we're suggesting that if you think of a key objection, you might include some relevant facts, like "A similar bug was shipped in Release 2 of this product. Technical support's manager estimates that it resulted in over $100,000 in tech support costs."

Lesson 58 **Your bug report is your representative.**

You're not usually present when your bug report is received and read. When you write a bug report, you're asking a programmer (whom you don't manage) to do some more work. Programmers rarely have enough time to fix every bug. Much bug fixing is done on their time—after hours or on weekends. You're asking them to give this time up for the bug you found.

In some companies (especially as the project gets closer to an end), various managers decide what to fix. The group of decision-makers might be called the Change Control Board. (At different companies, this group is called the project team, the triage team, the war team, or just the bug review team.) These people recognize that every change costs money, takes time, and carries the risk of breaking something else.

To get a bug fixed, you have to convince the Change Control Board to approve the fix or convince the programmer to fix it on his own (perhaps late at night, when the Board isn't looking[1]). The bug report is your primary (often only) vehicle for persuading people to fix the bug. You may have an advocacy opportunity at the Change Control Board meeting, but in many companies, only one tester (perhaps your test lead or test manager) attends

---

[1]Getting people to improve the product behind the back of the Change Control Board is exactly the right strategy at some companies and exactly the wrong strategy at others. Pay attention to your corporate culture.

this meeting. How well that person will advocate for your bug will depend on your bug report.

Take the time to make your bug reports valuable.

Because so many people read and rely on bug reports, take the time to make each report informative and understandable. This provides value to your company.

Bug reports serve several purposes in most companies. For example:

- They alert people to defects, and help programmers troubleshoot the underlying problems.
- They alert people to problems in specifications and (depending on the company policies) possibly in test documentation, user documentation, or development tools.
- They provide background information for technical writers who are developing troubleshooting sections for the manual or for the company's Web site.
- They flag issues that might need work in customer training.
- They provide key information for post-sale support of customers who run into problems that weren't fixed or (oops!) weren't completely fixed.
- They provide information to management on the status and quality of the product under development.
- They provide starting-point suggestions for improvement at the start of the next release of the product.

Any stakeholder should be able to report a bug.

A stakeholder is a person who has a vested interest in the success of the product. This person might be an employee of the company making the product or might be a customer or user who relies heavily on it.

Your entire company has a stake in releasing a high-quality product, within budget, on time, and with the right features. Anyone in any part of the company who is convinced the quality is wrong or the feature set is wrong should be able to record that protest in a way that gets to the design and implementation team. The testing group should never stand in the way of this communication but should instead always facilitate it, even when—

especially when—the complaints come from outside Product Development (including the testing group).

You might not show the bug tracking records to everyone. The bug tracking data should be treated as confidential if you treat your source code and other development decisions as confidential. However, a wide range of people should be able to get information *into* your records.

Be careful about rewording other people's bug reports.

Add comments but don't edit people's material without their permission. You wouldn't want your name signed to something you didn't write and didn't approve. Neither do the other people in your company who report bugs, even the ones who write lousy bug reports.

Rewording a report without permission also risks losing important information.

Whenever you add anything to a bug report, especially someone else's report, initial and date your comment. For example, it's common to start additional information on a new line of the report and to start that line with something like "[CK 12/27/01]." This also makes it easy for people to ask the right person questions about these added details.

Report perceived quality gaps as bugs.

Quality is value to some person. (Weinberg, 1992)

Different people have different expectations of a product, but if a legitimate stakeholder is disappointed by the product and feels that it's less valuable because of something that it does or doesn't do, she should write that up as a bug report.

Your task as a tester is to help this person make a report that articulates her concern clearly and effectively.

Some stakeholders cannot report bugs—you're their proxy.

The customers of commercial off-the-shelf software (such as consumers) can't report bugs during development because they don't have the software yet. Other stakeholders on your project might be unavailable. As the tester, you're a stand-in for the absent stakeholders. To understand what to report on their behalf and to make your reports persuasive, you have to study the ways that they'll use the product and the things they'll value or hate about a product of this type.

Draw the affected stakeholder's attention to controversial bugs.

If you think it might be difficult to convince the programmers to fix a bug, but you want it fixed, consider who else in the company will benefit if this bug is fixed. For example, inconsistencies in the user interface might seem of minor consequence to the programmers. Attempting to reason with some project managers about issues like this is a waste of time.

Inconsistencies drive up the costs of documentation, training, and technical support. Additionally, if they're unavoidable in sales demonstrations, they can cost sales. If they affect accessibility, government agencies who require ADA compliance may not be able to purchase the product. If they would be evident to product reviewers, they might result in bad press (describing the product as sloppily designed or hard to use). None of these costs hit the programmers' budgets.

Write the bug report (or a memo attached to a copy of the report) so that it will catch the attention of the people whose budgets will be depleted by the bug. They will argue for you that the bug must be fixed. If they don't think the bug has sufficient impact, they won't advocate for the fix, and maybe you should drop it and advocate for the repair of some other bug.

Never use the bug-tracking system to monitor programmers' performance.

It is soooooo tempting to report that one programmer has a huge number of bugs open, that he takes forever to fix his bugs, or that he tries to defer everything. However, after you use the tracking system data to attack or embarrass one programmer, the rest of the programmers will respond defensively to the system. The most likely consequence is that programmers will argue that design bugs aren't bugs, that similar bugs are duplicates, that nonreproducible bugs shouldn't be reported, and that you're incompetent or unfair in your testing. That's not unreasonable. As soon as you (or anyone else) uses the bug-tracking system for political or human resources management purposes instead of technical purposes, people will treat it that way.

Never use the bug-tracking system to monitor testers' performance.

If you (the test manager) reward testers based on the number of bugs they report, you'll influence their behavior in ways that you might not prefer. For example, to bring up their bug counts, testers will probably report easier-to-find, more superficial bugs and will be more willing to report multiple instances of the same bug. They will be less likely to spend time coaching other testers or to work on the bug-tracking system or other group infrastructure. And programmers will be more likely to dismiss design bugs as nonbugs that testers put in the system to raise their bug counts.

Report defects promptly.

Don't wait until tomorrow or next week to report a bug. Don't wait until you've forgotten some key details. The longer you wait, the less likely the bug is to be fixed.

Another risk of late reporting: If managers know that you're testing an area of the product and they see no bug reports, they'll incorrectly conclude that you haven't found bugs and, therefore, that this area must be stable.

Never assume that an obvious bug has already been filed.

Other people make the same assumption, and the result is that some obvious bugs are never reported until beta testers complain about them. If you think a bug might have been reported, check the tracking system to see how it was described and what the response was. Maybe you can strengthen that report with your comments or added information. Maybe a new report is necessary if the old report was weakly written and was rejected.

We've seen this happen for some serious bugs. Lots of people knew about the bug, but everyone assumed that someone else had reported it. In one case, the bug wasn't actually fixed until after the product shipped. *Ouch!*

Report design errors.

Computer programs provide benefits to people. That's their job. The program is part of a system that involves equipment, other software, and humans. A software product has less value if it is hard to use, confusing to use, uncooperative to the software around it, or bound to a narrow range of hardware. You might be the only member of the development staff to see or appreciate the design errors and how they affect the running system. If you don't report these problems, who will?

Some people (including some testing consultants) claim that testers should not file reports of design errors, because the design of the program should have been settled earlier in the project, and the testers don't have the expertise to evaluate the design anyway. We think this is a mistaken viewpoint on both grounds.

Regarding late criticism of the design. Even if the product was fully designed in advance (as unlikely as that is in real projects in the real world), people don't fully understand the implications of a system until it is built. It's entirely reasonable for people to realize that a system is misdesigned only after they start working with it.[2] Problems must be reported when they're discovered, and many of them will not be discovered until the system is almost complete.

Regarding the problem of expertise. It's true that testers vary in their ability to understand and evaluate design decisions. On the other hand, testers are among the few people in the company who will put the full system through its paces before the software is sold or put into production. Exercise some caution if you don't have relevant expertise. For example, before criticizing the program's user interface, maybe you should check user interface design guidelines written for your system[3] and talk with other people who know more about design than you do. But if you're sure you're seeing an error, get it into the tracking system.

Test groups can make themselves more capable of evaluating design errors by hiring people into the group who have diverse backgrounds. A tester with domain expertise (deep knowledge of how and why this product will be used) can focus tests and explanations on issues that would bother a reasonable user. This is just one of the areas of subject matter expertise that will be useful to your group. If one tester knows database design, another knows network security, another knows user interfaces, and so forth, the

---

[2]This is why we're seeing such interest in modern development approaches like Extreme Programming and the Rational Unified Process (or more generally, the approaches that call themselves iterative, adaptive, evolutionary, or agile). These approaches take it as given that late requirements changes will happen and seek to minimize the risks associated with change. See, for example, Beck 1999, Kruchten 2000, and www.agilealliance.org.

[3]Apple, Microsoft, Sun, and several others have published user interface design guidelines for graphical user interfaces.

group as a whole is positioned to make knowledgeable and useful evaluations of many different aspects of the product's design.[4]

Extreme-looking bugs are potential security flaws.

Lesson 70

The majority of break-ins over the Internet take advantage of buffer-overrun bugs (Schneier 2000a and 2000b). These bugs might have been caught before release if only testers weren't so busy training themselves out of looking at extreme cases that they "know" the programmers won't fix. Anything that can interfere with the program's operation or result in corrupted data is an exploit-in-waiting.

A buffer overrun occurs when more data is entered than can fit into the memory assigned for it. The excess data overruns into other memory spaces. What happens then depends on what the data is and the intended use for the memory space. Sometimes nothing happens, sometimes you see garbage on the screen, sometimes the program becomes erratic, and sometimes it leads to a crash. A skilled cracker can use this flaw as a back door to gain control of the program or of the system running the program.

Suppose you can crash a program by pasting 65536 9s into a field that is supposed to accept a value between 1 and 99. Would anyone really do that? Yes, of course people will do this. Not your friends, maybe. And not the programmers who dismiss the bug, often saying "If anyone was ever stupid enough to do this, the crash would serve them right." But idiots aren't the only people who abuse software.

Any bug with severe consequences should be fixed regardless of how "unlikely" it would be to happen. After a skilled cracker has devised an exploit, he can write and distribute it so that it can be used by any script kiddie.

Uncorner your corner cases.

Lesson 71

Efficient testing often involves extreme values. The first errors you find will often be at the extremes. The idea behind testing at the extremes is that if the program can survive these, it can probably survive less extreme results. Thus, you can learn a lot from a few extreme tests. For example, to test an input

---

[4]It will not always be possible to collect the right set of people into the test group, in time for the project that needs them. You might have to retain outsiders—contractors or consultants—to train your staff or to perform some types of assessments.

field that is supposed to accept values between 0 and 999, you'd probably check −1, 0, 999, and 1000.

Some programmers cry "corner case" when they see a test result that involves an extreme value or a combination of extreme values. These programmers see these tests as unrealistic and unlikely to happen in the real world. In general, the concept of corner case is used as an excuse to not fix the bug.

Suppose the 0–999 program rejects 999. If you stop with this result, some programmers might ignore it ("Who would enter 999? That's the biggest possible value. No one would do that!").

Don't stop with this result. Instead, try smaller numbers until you learn what range of supposed-to-be-acceptable values are rejected. If the program rejects anything bigger than 99, you can report that it fails throughout the entire range of 100 to 999. *This* will capture attention. If the program fails *only* at 999, that is useful information, too. Report it explicitly.

As with all follow-up testing, there's a limit on the time that you can afford to spend on problems like this. If you feel that the research is taking too long to repay the investment, stop and look for new bugs. If the programmers in your company always take extreme-value bugs seriously, you can simply report them without further work.

Lesson 72 **Minor bugs are worth reporting and fixing.**

Minor errors confuse customers and reduce customer confidence in the rest of the product. Bugs considered minor might include spelling mistakes, minor screen formatting problems, mouse droppings (small blotches left on the screen behind the mouse pointer), minor calculation errors, graphs drawn not quite to scale, errors in the online help, menu choices that are inappropriately grayed out (or not grayed out when they should be), shortcut keys that don't work, incorrect error messages, mishandling of extreme values, mishandling of timeouts, and anything else that a programmer says will take more effort to fix than it's worth.

Several years ago, one of us, Kaner, in collaboration with David Pels examined the effect of minor bugs on technical support costs. Kaner was a software development manager; Pels managed technical support. Working with a strong-selling mass-market product, Kaner and Pels reviewed every letter and email ever received from customers, magazine reviews, customer call records, and the entries in the bug-tracking system. They classed an issue as a "cheap fix" if it would cost fewer than four hours (not counting testing time) to fix it. The fix might be a code change, a replacement of a driver or data file on the disk, a change to the user manual or to the text on the product's box. As long as it required less than four hours and would prevent subsequent customer complaints on that issue, it counted as a cheap fix. Under this criterion, they concluded that cheap fixes (of minor bugs) could have prevented over half of the technical support calls for this product. (They discuss this work briefly in Kaner and Pels 1997.) Over the next year, Kaner's group fixed many of these problems, and technical support cost per new customer dropped by half. There isn't a perfect cause-and-effect relationship here because Kaner's group also fixed some major bugs and added a few new features (and bugs), but it seemed clear to them (Kaner and Pels) that the general cleanup had a major impact on customer satisfaction. The market share of the product also increased substantially over the year.

Any product can get by with a few minor defects. But as the number increases, customer confidence declines. More disturbing is the corrupting effect of tolerating these bugs. At the point that you stop even reporting minor bugs (some companies pressure their staff to report only "worthwhile" errors), you'll find yourself and your company tolerating more and more serious ones. Down that road (unless you're in a monopoly position in your market), lies product failure. This progressive toleration of larger errors was an important factor in the Challenger disaster, as Richard Feynman vividly shows in his book *What Do You Care What Other People Think* (Feynman 89).

Keep clear the difference between severity and priority.

Severity refers to the impact or consequence of the bug. *Priority* indicates when your company wants it fixed. Severity doesn't change unless you learn more about hidden consequences. Priorities change as a project progresses. Generally, more severe problems are higher priority to fix, and minor and cosmetic problems are low priority. However, they're not the same. Severe problems may not be worth fixing—for example, suppose that you find a bug that will corrupt any new record that is created before December 1999. This would have been a high-priority bug a couple of years ago (when December 1999 was still a date in the future), it's still serious, but many companies would no longer fix it.

On the other hand, a start-up splash screen with your company logo backwards and the name misspelled is purely a cosmetic problem. However, most companies would treat it as a high-priority bug.

A failure is a symptom of an error, not the error itself.

When you see a failure, you're looking at a misbehavior of the program, not at the underlying error in the code. The failure might look minor (mouse droppings, for example), but the underlying problem might be much more serious (wild pointer, for example). If you hit the same bad code under slightly different conditions, the misbehavior that you see might be much worse.

Therefore, whenever you see an error that looks minor,

- Do follow-up testing to find more serious symptoms, which will make for a more compelling report.
- Do follow-up testing to show that the problem occurs under a wider range of circumstances and will be seen by lots of people.

If the problem appears hard to reproduce,

- Do follow-up testing to determine the critical conditions that will make it reproducible and then do follow-up testing to make the now-reproducible error look nasty.

Do follow-up testing on seemingly minor coding errors.

When you find a coding error, you have the program in a state that the programmer did not intend and probably did not expect. Data may also now have supposedly impossible values. If you keep using this program after the first failure, anything might happen.

When you see a minor failure, don't just make the bug reproducible and report it. The program is in a vulnerable state. Try to exploit this. Keep testing it, and you might find that the real impact of the underlying fault is a much worse failure, such as a system crash or corrupted data.

We recommend trying three types of follow-up testing:

Vary your behavior (change the conditions by changing what you do). For example, bring it to the failure case again and again. Is there a cumulative impact? Try things that are *related to the task* that failed. For example, if the program unexpectedly but slightly scrolls the display when you add two numbers, try tests that affect adding or that affect the numbers. Try things that are *related to the failure*. If the failure is unexpected scrolling after adding, try scrolling first and then adding. Try repainting the screen and then adding. Try resizing the display of the numbers and then adding. Or, try entering the numbers more quickly or *change the speed* of your activity in some other way. And of course, you can try a wide range of other exploratory testing techniques. It's sometimes useful to run many entirely unrelated subsequent tests, simply by continuing to use the program without restarting or resetting it.

Vary the options and settings of the program (change the conditions by changing something about the program under test). Typical changes are to use a different database, to change the values of persistent variables, to change how the program uses memory, or to change anything else the program allows you to change (any other option or preference or setting). In the scrolling example, maybe you would change the size of the program window, the precision of the digits being displayed, or the background activity setting for the spell checker.

Vary the software and hardware environment (change the conditions by changing the software that runs with this program or the hardware you're testing it on). This isn't configuration testing. You aren't checking out the bug on the standard configurations. Instead, you are asking what ways you could change the configuration that might make *this failure* more impressive. For example, if you think that timing might be a factor, use a different speed processor or video display or communications connection. If you think memory might be relevant, work on a machine that has less (or more) memory or change your virtual memory settings.

You can do follow-up testing forever. How much should you do? Do at least a few minutes of follow-up testing for every failure that you believe reflects a coding error (something unintended by the programmer).

For some failures, you'll do more testing, maybe even a day of testing. Trust your judgment. If you think a few more tests might yield valuable new information, try them. If you think you know as much about the bug now as you're going to know after more testing, stop this type of testing and report what you know. Trust your judgment.

Always report nonreproducible errors; they may be time bombs.

Nonreproducible errors can be the most expensive bugs your company might release. Sometimes the program misbehaves in a way that you can't replicate. You see the failure once, but don't know how to get it again. If that happens to a customer, it will erode confidence in the product. If the support staff has to go to great lengths to assess the customer's data or environment, the customer will get more annoyed.

Programmers have tools that you don't have. If you report the symptoms clearly, the programmer can often trace through the code, asking how you could have gotten a certain message or what could possibly have happened when you were looking at a given dialog or clicking on a given control. It is not unreasonable to believe that programmers can fix 20 percent of the "nonreproducible" bugs that are reported to them.[5]

Even if you are in a company whose programmers ignore nonreproducible bugs as a matter of policy, we suggest that you still report them. Don't report a bug that you haven't made a competent *effort* to reproduce. But if you still can't reproduce the bug, it's still worth reporting. Scan the database periodically looking for patterns in the nonreproducible bugs. The same problem might show up several times and (if you always report nonreproducible errors) be reported several times. Each of these reports will be slightly different. Together, they might give you strong hints about the underlying conditions.

When you report a nonreproducible bug, make it clear that you cannot replicate the bug. Some tracking systems have a field for this (Can you reproduce this: yes/no/intermittent/unknown). Some companies rely instead on conventions, such as flagging the bug as NR (not reproducible) in the summary line or on the first line of the description.

Using PrintScreen, a screen recorder like Spector, or even video recording can help you prove the existence of UFOs (Unidentified Funny Objects) that some programmers would otherwise say could never have appeared.

77 Nonreproducible bugs are reproducible.

Failures occur under specific conditions. If you know the conditions, you can recreate a failure. If you don't know the critical conditions, you probably cannot recreate the failure.

When you encounter a bug that you can't reproduce, there must be something important that you're not noticing. If you could find out what that condition is, you could recreate the bug. Here are a few examples of

---

[5]Obviously, the percentage will vary across products and across the toolsets available to the programmers. We have seen programmers work at this success rate in commercial software. Credible people have told us of programmers and projects that sustained rates as high as 80 percent.

conditions that we've found helpful to think about (things that people often don't pay enough attention to, except in retrospect):

- The bug might have a delayed fuse, such as a memory leak, wild pointer, or corrupted stack. If you suspect problems that develop over time, consider working with the programmers to use Bounds Checker (www.numega.com), Purify (www.rational.com/products/purify_unix/index.jsp), or similar tools, or use methods to monitor the software's behavior over time (videotape the output, use a utility that captures the screen every second, monitor memory usage, and so on).

- The bug might only show up the first time you install or use the product or a certain feature of the product. Use Drive Image (www.powerquest .com/driveimage/), Ghost (www.symantec.com/sabu/ghost), or a similar tool that helps you create an exact copy of a clean system (a system that has never yet seen your application). Restore the clean system, reload the application, and see if you can replicate the problem now.

- The bug might depend on specific data values or on a corrupted database.

- The bug might occur only at a specific time or date. Look for end-of-day, weekend, quarter-end, and year-end bugs.

- The bug might depend on your doing a series of related tasks in a specific order. What were you doing before you did the failing task?

- The bug might be a remnant of a previous failure. For example, did you restart the machine after the last GPF?

- The bug might be caused by an interaction of the application under test with other software running in the background or with software that is competing with your application for access to a device. Perhaps the failure reflects an unexpected problem in interacting with the device.

There are several other ideas—too many and too detailed for this book. We are reviewing this area thoroughly in Volume 1 *(Tester's Volume)* of the new edition of *Testing Computer Software* (Kaner et al. *forthcoming*), but in the meantime, you might consult Nguyen (2000), Kaner et al. (1993), and Telles and Hsieh (2001) for useful ideas.

Be conscious of the processing cost of your bug reports.

We've told you to report all minor problems and nonreproducible problems. Now we have to backtrack a bit and tell you to exercise some judgment in what you report and how you report it.

Bug reports carry processing costs. It takes time to write the report. Then the programmer and/or project manager reads it. In some companies, the full Change Control Board reviews the bug to decide what to do with it. In others, the bug goes to the Change Control Board only after the programmer or project manager decides not to fix the bug. That's a lot of readers. Add up everyone's time, and you might discover that it takes your company between two and eight person-hours to review and reject a minor bug. Late in the project, if you flood the company with minor bug reports, you might single-handedly kill the productivity of the programming and project management teams. You may elicit a surprising amount of resentment or anger by reporting very minor problems or by writing unclear (unnecessarily time-consuming) reports later in the project.

When you report a minor bug, take special care to make your report clear, and well analyzed (see the points on follow-up testing later in this chapter). If you're about to report a collection of minor bugs late in the schedule, talk with your test manager about group policy. Perhaps you should report the bugs into a secondary database that will be formally reviewed as input to the next release but that will be ignored in this release. This preserves your work but gets it out of the way.

When you're about to report an irreproducible bug, especially when you do this late in the schedule, take extra care to try to reproduce the bug. If you do solid follow-up testing and you still can't recreate the bug, say explicitly that the bug is nonreproducible and describe the troubleshooting that you did and the symptoms that you encountered.

Give special handling to bugs related to the tools or environment.

If the program fails because of a known weakness in the operating system or in another application or system that your program communicates with, and the failure is totally outside of the programmers' control, you might reasonably decide to not report it. On the other hand, you might have discovered a fault easily fixed with appropriate error handling code.

However, the program might fail because it interacts badly with a known weakness in the operating system (or in some other product or system). For example, perhaps the programmer can revise the program so that it doesn't make the critical system call and, therefore, won't cause the system crash. This is partially an O/S bug, but because the failure can be prevented at the application level, it is also an application bug. If you think this is the situation, report it this way. As always, report the steps to reproduce the problem first. But then add a note saying that you know this appears to involve an interaction between the application and the O/S, but you're hoping the application can work around the O/S-level bug. Before reporting a lot of bugs this way, consider talking with someone you trust who knows a lot about the underlying system.

Also consider using appropriate tools to make snapshots of the configuration on which the failure appears. For example, Rational distributes a free install analyzer to record the details of a Windows installation and compare to a reference (VeriTest-Rational Install Analyzer, available at www.rational .com/products/testfoundation). A similar tool is InCtrl5, available at zdnet.com.

Similarly, programmers often blame failures on third-party code that is integrated into the application. Report these bugs in every case, because they're failures caused by errors in the package of code your company is giving to customers. Advocate for the repair of these bugs if you reasonably believe the programmers could work around the problems in the third-party code they're using.

Ask before reporting bugs against prototypes or early private versions.

Sometimes a programmer will show you a private version and ask for private testing. If your company allows this, respect the implicit rules. Bugs discovered when you review early code probably aren't reported in the bug-tracking system. Instead, they're reported in conversation or in notes or emails to the programmer. If you make public the bugs that a programmer shows you in an early, private release of the code, you will break the programmer's trust. The most likely result will be that you won't get to see these early releases again.

At some point, the program will become public within the company, ready for regular testing. Use the notes that you took during your private preview of the program. Any bugs you found before, which haven't yet been fixed, should go into the tracking system.

We must note abuses of this arrangement. We have encountered programming groups who tried to hide their schedule problems by hiding their bugs. They wanted to call every release of the software to Testing a prototype or a private release until the final version. They didn't want any bug reports entered into the tracking system (where management might find them) until that final version.

If you run into this situation, work with your manager. If you're the test manager, you may have to consult the project manager's manager or other key stakeholders. The underlying question is whether your company considers the prerelease bug-tracking data to be a tool primarily for the programming group or a corporate resource that key stakeholders are entitled to see. Try to be cooperative and helpful. And never participate in conduct that your company will see as a cover-up.

Duplicate bug reports are a self-correcting problem.

Of course, it is usually better to add data to an existing, open bug report than to write a new report of what you believe is the same bug. If you know that you're reporting a bug that is similar to another one, cross-reference them.

In some companies, especially companies that pay too much attention to bug statistics and bug curves, project managers and programmers get upset about duplicate bug reports or argue to management that the bug counts are inflated by the duplicates. In these companies, do a cursory search for a previous report of the same bug. However,

- Don't let your search time get out of hand. If the database is big enough, you can spend a lot of unproductive time searching for duplicates. Manage your time.

- Every well-written report of the same bug carries new information that can help make the bug easier to fix.

- Whether two reports represent duplicates can be a matter of opinion. You may have two failures caused by the same fault. Or, multiple faults may be involved in a failure. Until the matter is settled and the bug fixed, retain all the information you've collected (Pettichord 2000a).

The project manager who protests that duplicates are driving up the bug numbers can easily fix this problem by getting these bugs fixed.

Every bug deserves its own report.

Don't merge different bugs onto the same report in an effort to appease a project manager or programmer who constantly complains about duplicates. If you write a report that has multiple bugs on it, some of them will probably never be fixed. When you compare the bug in the database to the bug you want to report, use this criterion: If you would run different tests to check whether your bug and the bug in the database have been fixed, report them as different bugs.

Pettichord recommends you manage similar bugs a bit differently:

> Sometimes in the interests of efficiency you may include a list of similar, minor bugs in a report, on the assumption that they can all be fixed at once. If any remain open after the report is marked fixed, open new reports on each of the open bugs, with a reference to the old one, which can now be marked fixed.

The summary line is the most important line in the bug report.

This field, sometimes called the headline or the title, is critically important because the project manager, other managers, and executives will read it when reviewing lists of bugs that haven't been or won't be fixed. Bugs with weak headlines might be dismissed during bug triage meetings. (At a bug triage meeting, the project team decides which bugs to fix, at what priorities.) Executives and other managers from outside the programming group are more likely to spend additional time on bugs with interesting summaries. The summary line is your best tool for selling the bug to these managers.

A good summary gives the reader enough information to help her decide whether to ask for more information. It should include the following:

- A brief description specific enough that the reader can visualize the failure

- A brief indication of the limits or dependencies of the bug (How narrow or broad are the circumstances involved in this bug?)

- A brief indication of the impact or consequences of the bug

You can't get all this information into your summary, because your summary can only be a line (maybe 65 characters) long. (You can enter a longer one, but the management reports that list multiple bugs typically show only one line of summary. The rest of your entry is invisible.) Pick what is most important for your report and leave the rest to the report's detailed description sections.

Never exaggerate your bugs.

Your credibility is fundamental to your influence. If you make the bugs you report seem more serious than they really are, you'll lose influence.

Your company has a severity ranking scheme for bugs, such as minor, serious, and critical. We are not defining a severity ranking here because the definitions vary widely across companies. Whatever your company norms are, work within them. Don't rank a bug as "serious" that would normally be classed as "minor" just to get it added attention. If you believe your company's severity ranking scheme would incorrectly apply to the bug you're reporting, use the rank that you believe is appropriate, but explain yourself at the end of your description of the problem. ("I know that normally a problem like this would be classed as minor, but I believe this particular bug should be classed as serious because . . .)

Report the problem clearly, but don't try to solve it.

Your job is to report problems, not to identify root causes and not to push for specific solutions.

Without studying the underlying code, you aren't in a position to know the root cause of a failure. Too often, we have seen reports that focused so much on the tester's (incorrect) theory of the cause, that they didn't report enough of the actual data for the programmer to readily understand what the tester actually saw.

Some programmers are likely to reject reports whose "solutions" they know to be invalid, without considering the underlying problem. Don't make it easy to reject your reports.

Deciding on the solution that fits the bug is the product designer's role. For example, suppose you discover an error message that disappears as soon as the user moves the mouse, rendering it difficult to read. You may be tempted to write a bug report that says "the error message should appear in a dialog box that is always on top until explicitly dismissed." If you do that, don't be surprised if the designer writes back a curt note telling you to mind your own business. The fact is, there are several solutions to the error message problem. The designer gets to pick the one that he thinks fits best.

Another problem with solution-oriented bug reporting is that many testers get so caught up in their proposed solution that they don't provide clean, accurate information about the failure itself. If the tester misunderstands the underlying cause of the failure, the proposed solution is worthless at best. It is often worse than worthless because the tester unintentionally omits key information or writes a report that draws the programmer's attention to the wrong details. Reports like these sometimes bring a lot of laughs to the programming group. You might not want to be the person at whose ignorant suggestions they're laughing.

A better way to report the disappearing message problem might be "an error message appeared, but I was not able to read it, because it disappeared as soon as I moved the mouse." If you have a good relationship with the designer, you might also add, "If it was a modal dialog, that might solve the problem." Note that this suggestion does not sound like an imperative.

If it's common knowledge on the project that some part of the program is supposed to work in one and only one way, then the difference between a problem and the lack of a solution may be the same thing. Otherwise, you're crossing the line.

Be careful of your tone. Every person you criticize will see the report.

No benefit is gained by adopting a blaming or patronizing tone in your bug report. It never pays to call the programmer unprofessional, closed-minded, or a fool. It might feel good in the moment, but you lose credibility, invite micromanagement of your work, and will be less likely to get many of your bugs fixed. Watch your formatting, too. For example, reports written in ALL CAPS read as though you were SCREAMING. If you're not sure how the report will be read, have someone else read it and LISTEN CAREFULLY to their comments.

If tone has been an issue for you or for some programmers in your company, try reading your report to yourself out loud. Use your voice to make the words sound threatening, sarcastic, or callous. Another approach to checking tone is to hand the draft report to someone you trust for their review.

Make your reports readable, even to people who are exhausted and cranky.

A remarkable number of bugs are fixed (and deferred) in the last weeks of the project, by programmers who are working heavy overtime to get the product finished. On tough projects, the programmers are often sleep-deprived, under stress, and over-caffeinated. Write reports that these programmers can understand.

Make your description of the reproduction steps simple:

- Walk through the bug one step at a time.
- Number each step.

- Don't skip any steps that are needed to reproduce the problem.
- List the shortest set of steps that take the reader to the failure.
- Use whitespace to make the reports easier to scan.
- Use short, simple sentences.
- Indicate what happened and what you expected to happen.
- If the consequences are serious, but you have any reason to suspect that the programmer won't understand why they're serious, explain why you think so.
- Include additional comments if they'll make it easier for the programmer to recognize the problem or easier for you to retest the bug after the fix.
- For complicated products or problems, consider using the first three lines of the description to make an executive summary of the problem. Then give details.
- Keep your tone of voice neutral.
- And don't make jokes; they'll be misunderstood.

Improve your reporting skills.

Study bug reports in the tracking system for ideas on how to improve your reporting. For example,

- Compare closed bugs that were fixed and not fixed. Look for differences in the way they were reported. If you want yours fixed, report them like the ones that historically do get fixed.
- Read programmers' (and others') answers to bug reports. What makes them confused? Angry? Unreceptive? Appreciative?

Use market or support data when appropriate.

When possible, compare your product's behavior to a leading competitor's. This helps you describe user expectations, and it helps marketing managers assess (from their point of view) the severity of the problem.

Ask salespeople and sales engineers what questions they face from customers, how they demonstrate the product, what they need to show, and how they want to show it. Use their stories when reporting bugs.

When possible, tie a bug you're reporting to technical support records about related or similar bugs. To gather this data, you'll probably have to work closely with your company's technical support staff. If possible, estimate the support cost of deferring the bug, or the aggravations people (customers or support staff) will face if the bug is left in the product.

Review each other's bug reports.

Some groups have a second tester review reported defects before they go to the programmer. The second tester:

- Checks that critical information is present and intelligible
- Checks whether she can reproduce the bug
- Asks whether the report might be simplified, generalized, or strengthened.

This tester might review:

- All defects
- All defects in her area
- All of her buddy's defects.

If she finds problems, she takes the bug back to the original reporter.

- If the reporter was a tester, she points out problems with the objective of furthering the tester's training.
- If the reporter was outside the test group, she simply checks basic facts with him.

This is a useful way to train staff and clarify reports, but beware of overburdening the reviewing testers. This process takes time. Additionally, decide when the reviewer should reproduce each bug and when she should just check for plausibility and understandability of each report.

Meet the programmers who will read your reports.

You're more likely to write a courteous and thoughtfully worded report and to research it in a way that makes it easier to understand when you know the person who will read the report. If the programmer is anonymous, you're more likely to see her as an idiot than as a fallible human trying to do a good job.

The best approach may be to demonstrate your bugs to the programmers.

As soon as they find a bug, some testers walk over to the programmer who covers that area and describe it or show it off. Based on the discussion, they might do further troubleshooting or just write up the report as is. Some companies encourage this practice, and others discourage it. We generally like this practice, but unless you've got a strong working relationship with the programmer already, we urge you to work with the bug a little bit (make it reproducible, perhaps do some follow-up testing) before approaching the programmer. The less well you know the programmer, the better prepared you should be before meeting with him.

This approach works particularly well when you're testing a complex product and there is data the programmer may need that the tester doesn't know to provide. The tester can learn from the programmer, and the programmer has access to the system at the time of failure.

If the programmer looks focused and busy when you drop by, don't interrupt him. Instead, send an email that says you found an interesting problem and you'd like to talk with him soon before putting it into the bug-tracking system. Let him talk with you when he's ready. If he's too rarely ready, just file your bugs without him.

When the programmer says it's fixed, make sure it isn't still broken.

Under time pressure, many programmers take the fastest route to fix the symptoms described in the bug report. The fix might or might not address the full generality of the bug. When you retest the allegedly fixed program, you might find that it fails under slightly different circumstances, such as with different data. Perhaps you'll find that the fix caused a new problem. Do follow-up testing to ensure that the symptom doesn't crop up somewhere else.

Verify bug fixes promptly.

When you're told that one of the bugs you reported has been fixed, test it as soon as you can. Giving prompt attention to verifying fixes shows respect to the programmer and makes it more likely that he'll respond quickly to your bug reports in the future.

If you find a problem with the fix quickly and report it quickly to the programmer, he'll probably still remember what he did to the code and be able to take care of the problem right away. The longer you wait, the less the programmer will remember. (See DeNardis 2000 for more useful suggestions like this one about basic operations of testing groups.)

When fixes fail, talk with the programmer.

If a bug fix fails repeatedly or fails very late in development, don't just enter this feedback on the bug report and file it in the tracking system. Take it directly to the programmer. If you work in the same building, walk it to the programmer's cube. If the programmer is farther away, call him. (Caution: If the programmer works for another company, you may need the project manager's permission to phone the programmer. In that case, start by walking the bug to the project manager.) Your tone and attitude should be friendly and helpful. You aren't taking this to the programmer to say "Bad! Bad programmer!" You are doing the programmer the favor of getting the information to him right away and making yourself available to clarify any ambiguities in your report and demonstrate the bug if he wants to see it.

Bug reports should be closed by testers.

When a bug has been marked as resolved, a tester should review it. If the bug was marked as fixed, the tester should try to show that the fix was incomplete. If the bug report was rejected as nonreproducible or not understandable, the tester should fix the report. If the bug was deferred or rejected as a nonbug, the tester should decide whether to gather additional data in order to challenge the deferral or rejection. If the bug was rejected as a duplicate, the tester should decide whether she agrees. Some project teams bury bugs by marking them as duplicates.

Normally, the tester who reported the bug will retest it, but if a nontester reported it, the bug should be evaluated by the tester most familiar with that part of the program. When feasible, that tester should also consult with the original reporter.

No bug should be marked as closed unless it has been reviewed and closed by a tester.

Don't insist that every bug be fixed. Pick your battles.

Sometimes there are good reasons for not fixing certain bugs. One of the most important reasons involves risk. Every bug fix (and every other change to the code) can create new bugs. When the programmer fixes a minor bug, he might create a more serious one. If he does this near the end of the schedule, you might not have enough testing time between his change and the release date to find the bigger problem. The fear of undiscovered side-effects makes experienced project managers cautious about making late changes to the code.

Another excellent reason is that the customer might not be willing to pay for the fix. This is particularly apparent in the cases of custom, contract software and of in-house development. The customer is actually paying for your time. Some bugs are less expensive to deal with than the cost of their repair. But even remote customers have value tradeoffs. Imagine working on an update release that will fix a critical error that erases some customers' data. The program with the bug is in use, in the field. Now imagine delaying that update release so that a spelling mistake can be fixed. The answer in the case of this update release seems obvious (don't fix the spelling mistake). For less obvious decisions, the project team is responsible for imagining and evaluating the tradeoffs, in order to reach the right balance of time, cost, feature availability, and reliability.

If you cannot build a case that a bug is important or find a stakeholder who cares enough to actively support your appeal of that particular deferral, we suggest that you leave that bug alone and challenge something else.

Don't let deferred bugs disappear.

Deferred means that the bug you reported is real, but it's not going to be fixed in this release. Therefore, bugs that were closed as deferred in this release are open issues at the start of the next release. Many groups set up their bug-tracking systems to automatically reopen the old deferred bugs or to transfer them (as open bugs) into the new file for the next version product. They often also reopen bugs that were rejected as "works as designed," if the relevant design decisions are under review in the new release.

Products that pass through many releases pick up a collection of annoying bug reports that will never result in code changes or documentation improvements. Some groups do a review with project managers and permanently close some bugs as INWTSTA ("I never want to see this again").

It's best to do this review at the start of the project, when schedule pressures are at their minimum and the project manager is at her calmest and most reasonable.

Testing inertia should never be the cause of bug deferral.

You know you have a fatally flawed process when the test manager asks the programmers *not* to fix a bug (coding error or design error) on the grounds that the change involved would affect too many checklists, scripts, or other testing artifacts and, therefore, would take too long to manage.

Appeal bug deferrals immediately.

If a bug of yours is deferred or rejected (the program works as designed), decide whether or not to appeal the decision. Some companies allow for appeals as a normal part of their process in project team meetings (bug scrubs, triage meetings, and so on). In other companies, appeals are made in private meetings between a tester or test manager and an executive.

If you decide to appeal a deferral or rejection, do it soon. Don't attack a decision months after it was made. Unless there are special circumstances, you won't get a sympathetic hearing.

When you decide to fight, decide to win!

If you do appeal, don't rely on the words and information in your original bug report. That report was unpersuasive. If you don't build your case more effectively, you'll not only waste your time, you'll damage your credibility.

To prepare your appeal, you might:

- Talk with other stakeholders, such as Technical Support, Documentation, Sales, and so on. Find out whose budget will be most affected if the bug is left in the product, how much it will cost them, or how bothered they are by it.

- Do additional follow-up testing, looking for more serious consequences of the bug or looking for ways to show that it happens under a wider range of circumstances than are described in the bug report.

- Develop some scenarios, stories that illustrate how a reasonable user could encounter the bug in reasonable use of the product.

■ Check the press for discussions of problems like the one you're reporting. One of your competitors might have shipped a product with a similar bug. If it showed up in *any* news report, that is strong evidence that the bug should be taken seriously.

The principle that we urge you to adopt is that every appeal you make must be persuasive. Even if you don't win every appeal (you won't, of course), you should develop a reputation that every appeal of yours *deserves* to win.

CHAPTER 5

Automating Testing

Robots that make you breakfast. Flying cars for commuters. That's science fiction. But software can do *anything*. So, why not make software test software? The reasoning goes, if one computer can do the work of three million mathematicians using sticks and sand, then surely one computer is worth an army of human testers. Indeed, test automation is an exciting idea that holds great promise. But beware. Automating some of your testing might or might not be helpful. Automation can save time, speed development, extend your reach, and make your testing more effective. Or it can distract you and waste resources.

Your investment in test automation is valuable to the extent that it helps you achieve your mission. The role of testing is to gain information. What information is your automation providing?

Automation efforts have been spectacularly successful for some groups but have left others unhappy and frustrated. Some of the failing groups have deluded themselves and their management into thinking that the work they put into automation yielded something that was helpful.

Use automation when it advances the mission of testing. Evaluate your success at automation in terms of the extent to which it has helped you achieve your mission.

Reviewers of early drafts of this chapter have separately urged us to emphasize some contradictory points:

Design your tests first, before deciding which to automate. This prevents you from falling into the trap of automating tests that are easy to automate but weak at finding defects.

Design automated tests differently from manual tests. Much of the power of automated testing comes from using a computer to do things a person cannot do. Look for opportunities, such as being able to repeat the same tests over thousands of different data files. This prevents you from falling into the trap of only automating tests from the existing (manual) test plans and missing the big opportunities for test automation. When designing manual tests, you aren't likely to consider tests that apply repetitive operations over thousands of files; it would simply be too much work.

These conflicting messages derive from two important lessons:

- Automating without good test design may result in a lot of activity, but little value.

- Designing tests without a good understanding of automation possibilities may overlook some of the most valuable opportunities for automation.

We think that to reliably succeed, you must have good test designers *and* good automators contributing to the selection and design of your automated tests. That's easy for us to say. It's harder to make it happen.

Speed the development process instead of trying to save a few dollars on testing.

Test automation efforts aimed at reducing testing costs rarely get the attention and cooperation they need to ensure success.

If you want support, focus your efforts on reducing the risk of development failure.

Test cases are powerful to the extent that they help you and your team gain useful information about the system being tested. Automated testing adds power by helping you gather and disseminate information quickly, to give programmers fast feedback. The most successful companies automate testing to enhance their development flexibility. Some of the goals of their efforts are to:

- Quickly detect destabilizing changes in new builds.

- Expose regression bugs as quickly as possible.

- Report problems quickly, because this makes fixing easier.

Quick fixes keep code stable. Keeping code stable saves time (multiple people don't waste time on the same bug) and facilitates refactoring and other efforts to improve code structure and straighten out spaghetti code. If the code base is largely stable, and a strong suite of automated tests is in place, the programmers can attempt bigger changes at lower risk. The project team can also adjust the product's scope and release dates on short notice to respond to market opportunities.

Here are two examples of techniques for supporting the pace of development.

Automated smoke tests. The phrase "smoke test" comes from hardware testing. You plug in a new board and turn on the power. If you see smoke coming from the board, turn off the power. You don't have to do any more testing. Smoke tests (a.k.a. *build verification tests*) broadly cover product features in a limited time—typically over lunch or overnight. If key features don't work or if key bugs haven't yet been fixed, your team won't waste further time installing or testing the build. Getting it fixed becomes the programmers' top priority.

Automated unit tests. These tests also streamline a development process, prevent backtracking, and maintain development momentum. These are larger sets of tests that focus on testing the low-level functions and classes of your product.

The greatest value of automated smoke and unit tests is that they can be run at any time and by any one. Run them automatically as part of the build process. Their availability helps individual programmers create minibuilds that incorporate just one or a few of their changes. If one of those builds is broken, the programmer knows what to investigate. If the minibuilds are OK, the broader build that comes to you, which collects everyone's changes, is more likely to work. This is an invaluable benefit that your project manager is sure to appreciate.

These kinds of automated tests take time, effort, skill, and money to create. The unit tests will probably be created by the programmers, although you might encourage and speed that effort by writing the code with them as half of a programming pair. With these kinds of benefits, you'll have a far easier time securing the cooperation you'll need than if you were to simply focus on saving manual testing time (Beck 1999, Chapter 20).

Expand your reach instead of trying to repeat the same tests over and over.

Use automation to expand your reach and extend your senses, allowing you to see more and do more.

You just can't run some tests without automation. You can run others on a much larger scale. Here are some examples:

Load tests. What happens when 200 people try to use your software at the same time? What about 2000? You'll need automation to simulate these scenarios.

Performance benchmarks. Is system performance getting better or worse? You can instrument automated tests to capture time measurements each time you run them. By collecting these measurements and reviewing them as a time series, you can detect performance degradations. Use the same approach to benchmark uses of resources, such as memory or storage.

Configuration testing. Software often must work on different platforms, in different configurations, attached to different peripherals. How do you cover them all? Automation helps you increase your coverage. To make this work, your must ensure that your tests are portable across platforms.

Endurance testing. What will happen when your product has been in use for weeks or months? Memory leaks, stack corruption, wild pointers, and similar errors may not be apparent when they occur but will eventually cause trouble. One strategy is to run a series of test cases over a long period—days or weeks—without resetting the system. This requires automation.

Race conditions. Some problems occur only in specific timing situations. The coincidental timing of two threads or processes contending for the same resource results in an error known as a *race condition*. These are often hard to find and hard to reproduce. Automation can be a big help because you can repeat tests with many slightly different timing characteristics.

Combination errors. Some errors involve the interaction of several features. Use automation to test huge numbers of complex tests, each of which uses several features in varying ways.

These approaches focus on using automation to create new tests or to repeat product usage in ways designed to uncover new bugs. None of these tests is simple to implement. You may have to work up to them by automating different parts of the testing and developing tools to assist you. Nonetheless, we think this is often a better goal for your automation efforts than simply repeating the same feature tests again and again.

Select your automation strategy based on your context.

Strategies for test automation vary based on the testing requirements, the software product architecture, and the staff skills available for testing:

Testing requirements. Software products may have many features but often, only a few are key. These must be reliable. They may require extensive testing that justifies the effort to automate. Alternatively, you might focus on how automated testing can help manage the product's major risks. Manual testing may be good enough for other aspects of your product.

Software product architecture. Analyze the product architecture to determine the possibilities for test automation. What are the major software components? How do they communicate? What technologies are being used? What are the available touch points? The architecture describes the software components and their relationships to different parts of the system. The languages, environments, and components affect which test tools are suitable. The interfaces used determine the opportunities for automation (Hoffman 1999b).

Testing staff skills. Some automation approaches are good at leveraging nonprogramming testers. Others make full use of the skills of tester-programmers. One of us (Pettichord) was once requested to recommend a single test automation approach for a company with multiple products developed in multiple locations. He couldn't do it. Some locations primarily had testers who could program. Others had testers who couldn't. No single approach would work for everybody. Even though the products had similarities, their staffs' orientations and capabilities were too different.

Lesson 105 — Don't mandate 100 percent automation.

Some software managers suffer from the misconception that automated testing *always* equals better testing, and they mandate that all testing must be automated. Such mandates have harmed many projects.

If you have a gullible manager or executive, perhaps you or another senior tester should try to be in the room with her when she gets a demo of the latest test tool or a lecture on the latest silver bullet testing methodologies.

Be skeptical when consultants or tool salespeople tell you that leading companies commonly achieve 100 percent automation. Ask for evidence. Many leading companies are successful when using a mix of testing methods, including nonrepeated minimally documented exploratory testing. And they should be. Automating tests usually means running fewer tests more often. Many tests are worth running only once.

Another myth to dispel is that of testing happening at the push of a button, automatically reporting any bugs that are found. Tool vendors who offer integration between their testing and tracking tools encourage this irresponsible fantasy. We've never seen this improve testing, reporting, or bug tracking. If you don't have people analyzing failures before they're reported, you'll waste your programmers' time and cause programmers to revolt. They'll resent having to wade through so many false alarms and duplicates.

That said, it might be a reasonable goal to create the most extensive and thorough automated test suite you can, in certain situations:

- For contractual or regulatory reasons, you must prove that the final version of your product passed a strong battery of tests.

- You will be delivering tests with your product that customers can run themselves. (This practice is common in the telecommunications industry.)

- Your product has stringent requirements for backwards compatibility, which will remain for many versions.

- The only way that you *can* test *some* products is by writing programs to exercise them.

However, even in these cases, we think testers should always have the option for running unofficial manual or single-use, undocumented tests. Don't put artificial limits on testing.

A test tool is not a strategy.

A test tool won't teach your testers how to test. If your testing is confused, test tools will reinforce the confusion. Fix your testing processes before automating them.

Some test tools come packaged with rudimentary advice on testing strategy. But their suggestions are rarely well informed, they're not tailored to your situation, and they tend to overemphasize the importance of their type of automation.

We've talked to managers who thought they could buy a test tool instead of hiring testers. (We've met tool vendors who push this idea.) We've never seen it work. If you buy such a tool, you might get rid of your testers only to end up with a bunch of busy tool users, a lot of activity, and little or no bug finding. Where's the value in that?

Don't automate a mess.

If you have bad tests, automation can help you do bad testing faster. If your testing is disorganized, your automation project will flounder in the confusion. If your testers don't know or won't say what they're testing, they'll create automation that no one else will understand how to use.

Here's a scenario that we've been in and that other consultants have faced: A company retains the consultant to automate its software tests. Initially, the problem is getting the GUI test tool to work with the software under test. That costs time and money but eventually gets solved. As the automation project makes little further progress, the consultant realizes that the root problem is that there is no testing process. So, they put the tool on the shelf and focus on fixing the underlying problem. Only then do they start to see positive results.

If your checkbook is disorganized, a computer won't organize it for you. If your testing is disorganized, automation will distract you from what you really need to be doing.

Don't equate manual testing to automated testing.

When you perform a test by hand, you bring to bear the entire range of human capabilities. You can improvise new tests or notice things that you did not or could not have anticipated. Test automation is a faint, tinny echo of that rich intellectual process. That's why it's nonsensical to talk about automated tests as if they were automated human testing.

Automation does not make the computer do the testing that you do. It performs the testing you explicitly specify, unable to benefit from your tacit knowledge and awareness. The automated test does the same thing each time it runs, at the same speed, in the same order, with exactly the same mouse moves and key clicks. The manual tester, however, can't help but vary a test every time he runs it. These variations can uncover unseen bugs.

Automated results verification also has limitations. Take any test procedure. Does it tell you to listen for strange noises coming from the speaker? Does it tell you to look for unusual flickers on the screen? Does it tell you to report progressive performance degradation? Probably not. Yet, even without instruction, a good tester will notice and report such problems. The prepared mind is a fantastic test tool, beyond any conceivable automation. Your mind can notice hundreds of problems you're not even aware you're looking for until that moment you say "Oh, what's that? That can't be right."

Automation has many advantages, but it puts a lot of distance between the human tester and the tests. That means problems may be triggered but not noticed. Unlike automated tests, the human tester can immediately investigate anomalies that occur, preserving the context in which they occur. The human tester can also recognize and pass over a wide range of false alarms that would confuse automation.

So, don't compare manual tests to automated tests. Instead, look at automated tests as making it possible for you to extend your reach, to do things that you wouldn't do with manual testing.

Don't estimate the value of a test in terms of how often you run it.

The value of a test comes from the information it provides. Estimating this is difficult. Skilled testing is often a matter of exercising such judgments well.

Some testers have been advised to try to estimate whether automating will provide a return on investment by comparing the costs of automated tests to the costs of running the same tests manually (see, for example, Linz and Daigl 1998a and 1998b; Dustin et al. 1999, 52 and Fewster and Graham 1999, 519).

We think this approach measures the wrong things in the wrong ways (Hoffman 1999a).

Here are the equations that we think are fundamentally flawed:

$$\text{Manual testing cost} = \text{Manual preparation cost} + \left(N \times \text{Manual execution cost} \right)$$

$$\text{Automated testing cost} = \text{Automated preparation cost} + \left(N \times \text{Automated execution cost} \right)$$

... where N is the number of times you run the test.

As a simple approximation of costs, these formulas are fair enough. They capture the common observation that automated testing typically has higher upfront costs while providing reduced execution costs.

We have two principal objections to using them to justify automation efforts.

1. The tests themselves are incomparable. *Don't equate manual testing to automated testing* (Lesson 108). They just don't provide the same type of information.

2. It makes no sense to compare the cost of running an automated test, say, 50 times to the cost of running the same test manually 50 times. *Who would run the same tests 50 times manually?* It wouldn't be worth the effort. The value of the test—the information it provides—doesn't justify it!

Yes, automation makes it easier to run tests more often, but you save money every time you run them, only if you actually would have run them manually.

Like all testing activities, behind the decision to automate some tests is a cost and benefit analysis. If you get the analysis wrong, you'll allocate your resources inappropriately.

Automated regression tests find a minority of the bugs

Informal surveys reveal that the percentage of bugs found by automated tests are surprisingly low. Projects with significant, well-designed automation efforts report that regression tests find about 15 percent of the total bugs reported (Marick, online).

Regression-test automators typically find more bugs during test development than when they execute tests later. However, if you take your regression tests and find opportunities to reuse them in different environments (e.g. a different hardware platform or with different software drivers), your tests are more likely to find problems. In effect, they are actually no longer regression tests, since they are testing configurations that haven't been tested before. Testers report that these kinds of automated tests can generate yields closer to 30 to 80 percent.

New tests of old features are as likely to find regression bugs as old tests. And they have the added benefit of having a chance to find bugs that have been there from the start.[1]

Consider what bugs you *aren't* finding while you automate tests.

When you calculate the cost of automation, we suggest that you focus on opportunity costs. What else would you be doing with the time you spend on

---

[1]There are two exceptions: (1) If your project suffers from poor configuration management, old code may be reintroduced, bringing with it old bugs. However, proper configuration management is usually a cheaper and more effective solution than regression testing. (2) Poorly designed code can result in a situation in which a local fix to one problem causes another. When the second problem is later found and fixed, the first resurfaces.

automation? What tests aren't you running? What bugs aren't you finding (Marick 1998)?

An immediate impact of many automation projects is to delay testing and delay bug finding. This concern is also an argument for using upfront automation techniques that let you prepare automated tests before the software is ready for testing. For example, a data-driven strategy might let you define test inputs early. In this case, test automation might help you accelerate testing and bug finding.

The problem with bad automation is that no one may notice.

Products that have been around for a while often have automated test suites. Created in the past, they're still used to test the product.

Testers often feel lucky to have such test suites. We'd like to offer some warnings.

Tests may not do what you thought. How do you know that the tests are doing what they're supposed to? Automators sometimes code different test procedures from the ones they specified. Long ago, they may have had good reasons for this, or they may have been confused. How would you know? How easy is it to review the tests and read the code?

Tests may no longer be interesting. Reviewer Douglas Hoffman reports, "I recently discovered an automated memory test in use at a computer manufacturer which they called a 'lonely bit test.' It was a test used to find certain wiring errors in pre-1970s core memory. The biggest core memories were 16 Kb, and the tests took minutes to run. They now can take hours to run on large memory configurations. The error it looks for isn't possible in current memory systems. Another automated test I recently reviewed was designed to test a state machine of an embedded processor system. I saw that the documentation on the test was written in 1986, seven product generations earlier. And, no, no one had thought to update the tests when the state machines were changed each generation."

Coverage may be poor. People often focus on the number of tests in a test suite. It's easy to inflate the size of a test suite by adding lots of minor variations of the same test. Check the actual coverage of the test suite. You may be surprised at what isn't tested.

False alarms may be common. With time, careless automation programming and deferred maintenance can lead to lots of tests that fail because of automation bugs. Of course, you won't know for sure which failures are product bugs and which are automation bugs, so you'll have to investigate them all. Many of these are broken tests—tests that haven't worked in ages but that no one has had time to repair. Remove broken tests from your test suites. What good are they? They are dead. Accept this and bury them or repair them, now. But, don't leave their stinking corpses in your active test suites.

Test results may be false. Some tests don't check any results. They pass unless the product crashes. Others have bugs that can cause parts of tests to be skipped or will prevent detected failures from being reported. Other tests have invalid "golden" output files: when the tests failed, the golden output file was updated instead of reporting the bug. We're not making this up. These kinds of problems, in our experience, can be expected with relatively complex test suites. To avoid them, automators must keep things simple or use defensive programming techniques. These kinds of problems are bad enough, but we have also seen and heard about many cases in which tests were simply hard-coded to pass. They just say "result=pass." The automator couldn't have even *thought* these might work. We have speculated as to why this happens but don't have any convincing explanations.[2] All we can say is that it has happened in lots of different places. We keep hearing new stories from people who've seen it happen. What would you think about tests that pass, even if the product they're supposed to test doesn't exist on the system being tested?

Good test suites are living things. New tests are being added. Old tests are being repaired or removed. If this isn't happening, your test suite will start to ossify. Soon the creators will move on and the test suite will start to attain the status of a mythical grand old oak tree, the kind that characters in cartoons go to for advice. Somehow, the tree gains in stature and reputation as it gets older. The idea that the wise old oak tree must be correct because it has been around for so long might work well for cartoon characters, but we think that testers should be more skeptical. We call the syndrome of believing in the wisdom and coding of ancestral testers who created grand (now old) test suites the *old oak tree syndrome.*

Lesson 113

Capture replay fails.

The most popular test tools include recorders. These appear to offer an easy way to create automated tests without any programming. Just turn on the recorder while you execute tests. The recorder captures every user event— every keystroke, mouse movement, and mouse click—and stores them in a

---

[2]Mary Sweeney reports cases in which this happened because automators started with a template that contained the results=pass line and then mistakenly forgot to remove it.

script for playback later. You also have to indicate checkpoints. These are steps in the test where you press a hot key so that screen information is saved with the script. During replay, the script compares the current screen (or some programmatic attributes associated with the current screen) to the saved information. If they're different, the test fails.

The key problem is that the scripts are too tightly tied to the minor details of the user interface and the system configuration. In practice, tests are often as likely to fail due to intended product design changes as from unintended product regression bugs. Testers find that they spend more time analyzing test failures and re-recording tests than they previously spent executing tests manually.

Suppose you have 100 test scripts that include creating an account. Suppose the product changes. Now it walks you through an extra dialog in the account creation workflow. All these tests will fail. You'll have to re-record them. Or suppose that a label on a screen is renamed from "Login Name" to "User Name." Any tests containing checkpoints for this screen will now fail.

When tests fail, they can be exasperatingly difficult to analyze. Is it a setup bug, an automation bug, or a product bug? It's hard to tell when looking at a script that was machine generated on the fly. If you can't read the script, how can you tell how it's supposed to work?

More structured test automation strategies use the same tools but take longer to code and require programming skills. The resulting tests are much easier to update when the user interface changes.

Our experience, and the experience of most automators, is that capture replay test automation is an ice-covered slope with a brick wall at the bottom. Too many teams spend a significant amount of time recording automated test scripts, find that they break after only a couple builds, and then record them all over again.

Invest in the skill and planning needed to build automated tests that will last or stick with manual testing. Either of these will usually be more efficient and effective than capture replay.

(We realize that capture replay tools are useful for learning the tools and as aids to manually authoring test scripts. We object to treating them as a solution in and of themselves.)

Test tools are buggy.

Testers get indignant when they realize that the quality tools purchased at a serious price are themselves full of bugs. Indeed, test tools are often buggier than comparable (but cheaper) development tools. Plan to test your tools and spend time finding workarounds for bugs.

Some tools are designed to support the testing of particular component technologies. The lack of testability in these component technologies leads to one source of test tool bugs.

- The tool programmers must first wait for the technology to become available.

- Then they must reverse engineer it to figure out how to add testing support.

- During this time, your product programmers start using the latest component technology. You're frustrated that the tool vendor hasn't released the required tool update yet. The vendor rushes it through testing to get it to you when you need it.

- Surprise! The rush job results in lots of bugs.

This cycle will perpetuate as long as testability has to be reverse engineered into component technology, rather than being designed in from the start. We're hopeful and hear promises of improvement, but it's hard to say when this might start to happen. It's an industry-wide problem.

Test tools sometimes suffer from bugs in other components. One of us, Pettichord, worked with an execution tool that was executing unreliably. Mouse events sometimes weren't being generated. Eventually we tracked the problem to a bug in an operating system driver. The unreliability was reproducible without the tool. Why didn't manual testers find it? Because they didn't notice that an occasional mouse movement or click didn't register. If they noticed it at all, they probably blamed themselves or the mouse hardware. We reported the fault to the O/S vendor, who seemed unconcerned. The severe impact on testability was apparently of little importance. We did eventually work around the problem by using different mouse drivers.[3]

Other tools may impact the product you're testing so much as to make it unusable. Coverage and memory monitors must instrument the software and take up significant space in memory. Such tools may slow down your product to the point where you can no longer test it.

Because test tools have such a bad reputation, your programmers are likely to require that you replicate every bug found with automation outside the test

---

[3]Bob Johnson reports a similar problem using different technology: "The mouse driver really played no part in the required testing of our application. However to automate we had to track down this problem and in our case it took several days of both testers' and developers' time. That's several thousand dollars of hidden expenses to automation."

tool before they'll take it seriously. This adds yet another complication to analyzing automated test failures.

User interfaces change.

Keeping up with design changes in the user interface is a major complication of GUI test automation. If you're automating the GUI, plan for this.

Telling programmers they should freeze the user interface doesn't work. Early versions of user interfaces often need revision. Don't put yourself in the position of recommending against improvement. The GUI will change anyway.

Abstract the interface in your test automation design. When the user interface changes, you'll update the abstraction layer, rather than every test that accesses the changed interface.

Here are some techniques for providing abstraction from the product GUI:

Window maps. GUI test tools support various techniques for identifying window controls, such as internal names, various properties, adjacent labels, and ordinal position. Rather than embedding the identification technique in every reference to a control, use window maps to associate a name to the identification technique for a control. If a user interface change forces you to change the technique particulars, you need only update the window map. Some test tools include support for creating and using window maps, which are also called *GUI maps* or *window declarations*. If your tool doesn't include built-in support, you can usually create one without too much trouble. Window maps provide support for minor GUI changes, such as renaming labels or relocating controls onscreen. They also can be used to provide support for reusing tests with user interfaces that have been translated into other languages.

Data-driven test automation. (Lesson 127: *Data-driven test automation makes it easy to run lots of test variants*.) This technique provides some abstraction in that you should be able to change a test procedure and still be able to use the test data you'd created for it.

Task libraries. (Lesson 126: *Don't build test libraries simply to avoid repeating code*.) Analyze the use cases into constituent tasks. Each task should be conceptually distinct. Pay particular attention to the start and end states of the task. Creating functions for these tasks can be used in your test scripts. If the user interface for a task changes, you should have to update the task only, not the tests that use it. This provides a significant degree of abstraction, but also can be a significant amount of work to design and create in the first place.

Keyword-driven test automation. (Lesson 128: *Keyword-driven test automation makes it easy for nonprogrammers to create tests.*)

API-based automation. (Lesson 132: *Automate tests using programming interfaces.*) Avoid the GUI altogether.

Select GUI test tools based on compatibility, familiarity, and service.

We're often asked to recommend test tools. The best choice depends on your specific situation. Some GUI test tools aren't compatible with particular development environments or support them poorly. Subtle factors can cause trouble. It's difficult to predict in advance what will work or won't work. It really is a matter of trial and error. So, where do you start?

Find out what tools your team already knows. Or whether they already know the language used by one of the tools. The cost of training and learning how to use the tool (whether in formal classes, self-study, or trial and error) are often quite significant. Familiarity can be a deciding factor in your success with a tool, assuming, of course, that it actually works out.

Another important factor is the vendor's ability to support the tool. Even if the tool works well with your product today, what is going to happen when you have to test it on a new platform next year? When you buy a tool, you're investing the vendor's ability to maintain the tool and keep it current with new technologies. Check their online support forums and talk to other users about the vendor's history.

You'll need some time to test the compatibility of the tool with your product and check the vendor's service record. Get the tool on a trial basis (30–90 days), or at least get a 30-day money back guarantee. During this time, you'll probably run into some problems. Test their support to see whether you get timely and informed responses. You should also ask to bundle training with the tool purchase. This may give you a better price. We've also found that important tips for using some tools are only available in their training. These tips are not in the tool manuals.

We do have strong opinions about what kinds of features are helpful in a tool, but for most teams, the preceding considerations winnow the options down to a single choice. For further suggestions, see Hendrickson (1999).

Lesson 117

Automated regression tests die.

The biggest problem facing automated regression tests is decay and premature death. You design regression tests to detect problems in features you've already tested—problems due to programmers' mistakes when fixing bugs or adding new features.

Regression tests decay for several reasons, such as the following:

Change of the user interface or output formats. These changes are the major cause of decay. Because of them, a large set of tests that used to pass will fail even though nothing obvious has been done to affect the features that the tests are aimed at. The changes may be so minor that manual regression testers would barely take notice. Automated tests, however, are sensitive and brittle, unable to differentiate between improvements and bugs.

Designed-in assumptions about the test environment. Test suites may break when moved to different machines or when necessary resources are relocated.

Errors in maintenance. Automators repairing tests make mistakes, introducing bugs into the test suites. Regression test suites thus develop regression bugs themselves.

Changing operators. Test suites may require special skills and knowledge to operate and maintain. When a test automator is reassigned, valuable knowledge can walk away. For instance, Sheila disables the disk I/O tests temporarily, due to a particular bug in the product, then leaves to take that programming job in Topeka. Sheila's replacement assumes that the tests are entirely obsolete and moves them to an archive, never to be seen again.

Testers invest in regression automation with the expectation that the investment will pay off in due time. Sadly, they often find that the tests stop working sooner than expected. The tests are out of sync with the product. They demand repair. They're no longer helping find bugs. Testers reasonably respond by updating the tests. But this can be harder than expected. Many automators have found themselves spending too much time diagnosing test failures and repairing decayed tests.

Exercise prudence when selecting tests to automate, because anything you automate, you'll have to maintain or abandon. Uncontrolled maintenance costs are probably the most common problem that automated regression test efforts face.

Maintenance costs alone should convince you to mistrust the tales that automation will turn your job into a vacation.

Test automation is a software development process.

Test automation projects often fail because of a lack of discipline and project management. Many testers don't realize that when they automate tests they're actually developing software.

Weinberg (1992) presents a scale for assessing organizational development. Like similar scales, level one is the chaotic organization; level two is repeating; and so on up to level five. However, he has an additional level at the bottom. Level zero is the *oblivious* organization. These organizations don't even realize they're developing software. Many test groups, unaware that test automation is software development, fall into this category.

Any successful software development project requires that some basic rules be followed. Testers are often the first to complain when programmers don't follow the rules. Testers shouldn't be surprised when test automation projects run into trouble after cutting corners.

What are the rules? Plan your project and establish milestones and deliverables. Define requirements. Use source code control for the tools, the automation code, and the tests. Design tests before coding them. Review the code and test it. Track automation bugs in a bug database. Document how to use the automation and plan for it to be used by people other than the ones who created it.

The failure to treat automation as software engineering has led to expensive automation fiascos, such as test teams finding themselves far behind in their testing with no useful automated tests.

We won't tell you which development process to follow, but follow a process.

Test automation is a significant investment.

It takes time and costs money to automate tests. Expect that a well-designed automated test will take 10 times as long to automate using a GUI test tool as executing it manually. This figure is affected by a host of factors, but many experienced automators use this as a reasonable first estimate (Kaner 1998a). We have reviewed a few claims suggesting that tests can be automated with only two or three times the effort. We find that these claims result from developing throw-away tests, failing to account for the full efforts involved in automation, or good luck. If you're prudent, you won't use a lower figure until you have particular evidence specific to your own circumstances.

Effective uses of test tools involve skilled programming and design. Like the automation of anything else, automation of testing is a software engineering problem.

Test automation can help you reduce costs when you have good reason to reuse the same test many times. It can help you create and run tests that are expensive or impossible to run by hand. It can help you measure aspects of program operation (timing and memory usage) that you can't do by hand. It can help you run a massive test series, looking for defects that wouldn't show up until after months of normal use and would take too long to run by hand. Any of these benefits might justify a substantial investment in test automation, but if you staff and budget your automation project on the assumption that it can be done part-time for almost no money, you'll be disappointed.

At the time of publication, many GUI test tools cost around $5,000 a seat. Load testing tools can cost $50,000 and up. As large as these costs are, we find that staff costs for training (whether formal or on-the-job) and implementation quickly dwarf these costs. Don't make the mistake of spending your entire test automation budget on test tools. It's just the tip of the iceberg.

Test automation projects require skills in programming, testing, and project management.

It's unusual to find people who are good at *both* test design and automation. It's usually important to assign different people to test design and automation. Each is a full-time job. Using specialists gives you the best results.

Testing. Articulate your testing goals for the automation. What purpose will the tests serve? How will they help you find bugs? Which bugs? Are the tests informed by an understanding of the product user domain? Well-intentioned programmers with little insight into testing can easily create test suites that are interesting but of little value. Provide guidance from people who understand testing and how the product will be used.

Programming. Test automation is programming. Tool strategies that promise to allow testers to create test suites without programming fail. Don't solely depend on junior programmers or programmer rejects either. Managing, installing, configuring, and maintaining the tools requires programming skill. Each automated test is a program or a feature in a larger automated test application. Test automation isn't easy and won't succeed without following software engineering principles.

Project management. Without sufficient management attention, automation projects may not actually address the initially conceived objectives. Don't make automation a side-project. Don't staff it with part-timers.

A good balance of skills is particularly important for projects expected to create tests that will be useful for a long time. You'll need people trained on the languages and tools that you're using. The automation approach you use will determine the exact mix of skills.

Lesson 121 Use pilot projects to prove feasibility.

Use a pilot test automation project to validate your approach, confirm that your tools work with your product, and determine what kind of payoff you can expect from automation. Plan to show results in a month or so. Then scale up to a larger effort.

A pilot project will help demonstrate your ability. This will make it easier to secure the resources and cooperation you'll need to be successful with the larger effort.

Automated tests will change your development and testing processes. The sooner you have some, the sooner you can start making changes. The longer your team uses manual testing processes, the harder it is to get the maximum advantage from automated suites.

Lesson 122 Have testers and programmers charter automation projects.

Automation projects benefit when they're jointly chartered by product testers and product programmers.

Product testers. Place product testers in a position to define requirements for test automation. Also, have them verify that the automation developed is useful, understandable, and trustworthy. It is not enough that the automation tests well. It must also earn the faith and confidence of the testers. If they don't trust it, they won't use it. The automation must serve the testers' interests.

Product programmers. Product programmers are experts in software development and should review the automation architecture. Involving them develops teamwork and provides increased opportunities for product testability hooks.

Set clear goals and define the requirements with regard to these key areas that are often overlooked (Pettichord 1999):

Reviewability. Who needs to be able to review tests? How hard will this be?

Maintainability. Who will maintain the tests? What will they have to know?

Integrity. How will you know the tests are to be trusted?

Design automated tests to facilitate review.

You test software because coding mistakes happen. Coding mistakes happen in test code, too. What should you do about that?

You could test your test code. Good idea. Should you automate that testing? Should you test the code that automates the tests of your automation? It hurts just to think about it.

Another approach is to focus on reviewing your test code. Design your test framework to make it easy for different people to review the tests. This will help them develop faith in the tests that your team writes, and help them develop faith in the tests you write. Keep code simple. Optimize test data formats to the needs of the testers. Use standard programming languages.

Test automation can go wrong in many ways. By making reviews possible, you make major blunders much less likely. You also help your team learn from each other. As they learn to review test code, they can learn how to start reviewing the product code as well.

A culture that encourages review leads to test automation that everyone can justifiably depend on.

We have limited experience with paired programming of automated tests. This is another form of review, and we expect (but cannot say from experience) that it will work well.

Don't skimp on automated test design.

You can assume that a reasonably intelligent and observant human being will run manual tests. You can assume no such thing about automated tests.

Here's a list of concerns that you may have to explicitly account for when you design your automated tests:

- Ensure that the test has been set up correctly.
- Specify expected results.
- Notice potential errors and side effects.
- Recover from potential test failure.
- Prevent tests from interfering with each other.

Document your test design so that people using your tests later will have some idea of what you were thinking.

Avoid complex logic in your test scripts.

Conditional logic in your test scripts makes tests harder to understand and more prone to error. Even more problematic is including code to throw and catch error-signals.

You may need logic to handle the setup for your test, to respond to checked output, or to handle custom controls. Place this logic in separate functions. You can test the functions in isolation (which is good), and your tests will be easier to review (which is also good).

Keeping your tests linear helps you focus on the purpose of the test (another good thing), rather than the automation support. When tests get too complicated, they tend to become buggy. Keep it simple. Keep your tests linear.

Don't build test libraries simply to avoid repeating code.

Standard programming wisdom recommends avoiding repeating code by placing the repeated code in a function that is called from each place where the repeating code resided. In test automation, this approach often leads to trouble. The opposite approach, which leaves the repeated code in place, is called *open coding*.

By their very nature, tests exhibit a lot of repetition. You test the same features in different scenarios, different orders, or in combinations with various other features. If you simply relocate the code you see repeated, you end up with a hodge-podge library. Functions contain sequences of tasks that frequently follow one another, even if they're part of different tasks. Naming conventions, results analysis, and testing strategy may also find themselves bundled into the hodge-podge library. The functions are hard to name meaningfully. In context, it's hard to infer what they do.

Tests using such libraries are hard to review, hard to debug, and hard to repair. We have reviewed test suites built with hodge-podge libraries on several occasions. The results are never pretty.

Test automation entails a lot of repetitive code. Useful libraries require stronger design principles than just avoiding the repetition of code. Useful task libraries focus on encapsulating user-perceived tasks, with particular attention on the start and end states of the functions. This effort isn't always justified. In such cases, stick with open coding.

Data-driven test automation makes it easy to run lots of test variants.

To test different inputs and input combinations with a common test procedure, use data-driven test automation.

Organize your test inputs and expected outputs into tables. Each row constitutes a test. Then create an automated test procedure that reads in a row from your table, executes each input step, and verifies the expected result. Spreadsheets are convenient for storing the test data. They make data entry easy. Most test tools and programming environments can access the spreadsheet data without much trouble. They can access the data in the native spreadsheet format or in delimited text files that can easily be exported (.CSV files).

After you've put together a data-driven test procedure, you can use it again and again to execute new tests. The technique is most powerful with product workflows that have lots of different data options. Use a more complex variant, *keyword-driven automation*, to support tests composed of varying sequences or several alternate paths.

Data-driven test automation supports nonprogramming testers. The automators create the data-driven test procedures, and the testers create the test data. In some cases, you might find it hard to automate the verification of the test results. Have your test procedure collect the results and present them in the context of the input data to simplify the manual results analysis.

Data-driven test automation is becoming commonplace. Many test tools include direct support for this technique (Dwyer and Freeburn 1999).

Keyword-driven test automation makes it easy for nonprogrammers to create tests.

Keyword-driven test automation builds on the data-driven technique. However, the tables contain directives (keywords), not just data.

First, the approach requires a general framework that includes support for running tests as well as libraries for setup, results analysis, and reporting. This will be used for all the keyword-driven tests.

Second, you'll have to create a task library that encapsulates the user tasks supported by your product. Identify each task function that can be used in testing and include an entry in the task library for each. Declare the start states that the task functions are valid in and the end states that they result in. This lets you tell which sequences of task functions are valid and so catch malformed tests.

Third, add support to read spreadsheet data, a row at a time. Using the declarations, interpret the first column as the name of a task function. The following columns are arguments to the function. Execute the function with its arguments. Then move to the next row.

The result is *keyword-driven* test automation. Using it *avoids complex logic in your test scripts* (Lesson 125). Because the tests are stored in spreadsheets, they're often easy for nonprogrammers to create and review. Because the tasks to be used and tested are all that the tester specifies, he can concentrate on the tests, not the control language.

In contexts that require many nonprogrammers to create automated tests, we believe this is one of the better solutions. One drawback of this approach is that you can't write a test unless supported keywords already exist for the tasks you require. Defining and implementing the task functions can become a major undertaking.

Reviewer Hans Buwalda reports, "Keyword driven approaches, like my own action words, can provide a good basis. However, over the years I have learned that testing and test automation remain very challenging areas and need the involvement of experienced specialists to do it right."

We have seen good results with this technique on projects that allowed significant advance time for automation development. We also have reports of teams that found that this approach required too much overhead and was unsustainable.

For more on this technique, see Pettichord (1996) and Buwalda and Kasdorp (1999).

Use automated techniques to generate test inputs.

Common programming methods can help in several situations:

Creating large files.

Creating lots of test inputs.

Setting up test beds. When load testing, start by preloading your database with a realistic amount of data. The amount of data available to be searched impacts database retrieval.

Creating random data. This is particularly useful with data-driven and keyword-driven tests.

Covering all combinations of inputs. Use algorithms to generate permutations and combinations.

However, using the previous methods usually leaves the expected results unspecified. This can entail a laborious effort to review or specify results manually. The following techniques are particularly valuable because they either reduce the number of test cases needed, provide a certain level of coverage, or specify the expected results.

Covering all pairs of representatives of equivalence classes. We've seen studies suggesting that most interaction bugs can be found if you test all pair-wise combinations of key equivalence class members. We discuss the all-pairs combinatorial technique in Chapter 3, *Testing Techniques*, in the section, "How to Do Combination Testing Using the All-Pairs Technique."

Covering interactions among logical conditions. When variables are not independent, techniques like all-pairs combination testing break down. *Cause-effect graphing* is a more robust approach (Elmendorf 1973 and Bender 1991). We have not used this technique. We've heard reports of failure and success in applying it.

Creating test scenarios with state models. The state-model test technique has seen serious academic study and significant results in industry. A state model, or state chart, identifies states of a system (document changed or unchanged; database connected or disconnected; transaction pending or completed) and the possible transitions between them. Skilled practitioners are able to build interesting and useful models without creating too many states. Others have sunk considerable efforts into this technique, generated massive state models, and received no benefit. This is called the *state-explosion* problem. The practitioners who see the most success are often able to see results shortly. If you use this technique, we suggest you create a state model for a feature or two, generate tests, and then reassess from there. If you can't see it paying off after a week's effort, it's probably not worth further investment (Robinson 1999 and Nyman 2000).

Separate test generation from test execution.

One strategy that supports separating test data from the execution code is data-driven test automation (Lesson 127). This separation facilitates test generation and has several advantages:

- Your tests will be easier to understand and review.

- You can use different test tools or programming environments for the generation and execution.

- A separate test case generator is easier to test. If you're using random methods, you should know that random number algorithms packaged with programming environments are often weak. Your data could be less random than you expected. Check and see (Park and Miller 1988). Kaner and Vokey (1984) provide a thoroughly tested set of parameters for a random number generator that you can program easily in Java or any other language that handles high-precision integer arithmetic.

- Tests are easier to repeat when the data is pregenerated. We've seen test scripts that changed the test every time they ran. If you can't pregenerate the data, you need to take other measures to ensure repeatability, such as logging the data or the seed used to generate it. Instrumenting your test scripts to use these logs adds complications.

- You'll have an easier time reporting any bugs found. The programmer's first instinct may be to question your tools.

- Different test specialists can each focus on different aspects of automated testing using whichever tools or languages they deem most suitable.

Use standard scripting languages.

If you're a tester who would like to learn more about programming, we suggest you learn Perl, Visual Basic, TCL, JavaScript, Python, or whichever scripting language is known and used by the programmers around you (Sweeney 2001). Some scripting languages, such as Unix shell scripts or DOS batch files have been around for a long time. Scripting languages are high-level languages optimized for ease of use rather than execution performance.

Many programmers are more productive and less error prone when they use scripting languages instead of system programming languages such as C/C++ or Java.

Scripting languages are very appropriate for most test automation. You can use them to generate test data, access programming interfaces, and validate results.

Many test tools have built-in scripting languages. Some wisely use standard scripting languages. Others have created their own proprietary languages, which we call *vendorscripts*. We see no compelling reasons for using them and note several problems.

They make coding difficult. Many of these are based on standard languages like C. If you can read C, you can probably read a C-based vendorscript. But you'll have a heck of a time writing much valid code. These vendorscripts won't support many of the standard language idioms, which makes writing much code about as easy as writing English without using the letter N.

They're hard to learn. The difficulty of finding training or books on vendorscripts makes them hard to learn. And if you do learn them, you can't use them for anything else. So, it's hard to motivate people to learn them. If you're hiring, it'll be hard to find people who already know them.

They interfere with collaboration between testers and programmers. We recommend that automation projects receive cooperation from both testers and product programmers. This becomes complicated when you're literally using different languages.

It's hard to build on the work of others. The libraries that are available for vendorscripts are pitiful compared to what is available for standard languages. This means that you're not going to be able to build on the work of others but will be spending your time rebuilding rudimentary libraries.

We suggest you avoid using tools with vendorscripts. More and more test tools are now using standard languages. If you must use a tool with a vendorscript, try to reduce the amount of code that must be written in the tool and do as much processing as possible in a separate language environment.[4]

---

[4] For further discussion, see Pettichord (2001a).

Automate tests using programming interfaces.

Nowadays, many software products have programming interfaces (public APIs) that can be used for testing. Those that don't may have hidden interfaces (private APIs) that can be exposed if you ask. Ask.

Public APIs are documented as part of the software product. They can't change much, and their stability makes them attractive for test automation. A private API can be extremely useful, but find out how likely it will be to change.

Unaware of these alternatives, many automators focus on what's most visible —the GUI. Sadly, this is usually the hardest interface to automate. Almost any programming interface is easier to work with—more stable and more reliable.[5] In earlier lessons, we discussed some of the problems with GUI automation and suggested strategies for dealing with them. But the best approach is to avoid them altogether. Programming interfaces tend to provide stability. They also facilitate error detection and isolation.

When we look at the many product testing efforts we've observed, we conclude that there is a strong correlation between the availability of programming interfaces for testing and the development of powerful automated test suites.[6] Programming interfaces include APIs, command-line interfaces, COM interfaces, HTTP, and more. You'll need to learn the lingo and the technology. Don't expect your programmers to give you a tutorial. Few have the patience, fewer the time. If you're serious about automation, you'll learn or get someone who knows this to help.

---

[5]Paul Szymkowiak disagrees, "My experience differs from this. I've found that many user interfaces are more stable than the available programming interfaces—certainly for the purposes of test automation. This seems to be because the user interface is visible to customers, used in training material and printed in user manuals. As such, there is more cost involved in accommodating ongoing change to it. I've worked with a number of project managers that have requested the user interface 'frozen' well before the equivalent programming interface is frozen. Many programming interfaces are poorly documented, and because programmers are the intended customers, the software vendor/developer assumes that they won't mind ongoing changes to the interface. I've also found many programming interfaces 'buggy', with an apparent lower 'usability threshold' than is normally expected of a user interface."

[6]Douglas Hoffman's experience is similar, "The most dramatic success I have had was with a prominent desktop publishing package. Its engine was invisible and the product was perceived in terms of its WYSIWYG GUI. Because the user interface was planned to be completely overhauled in release $n + 1$, we avoided automating GUI testing altogether. Instead, we used the public API for functional test automation and manually tested the GUI. We reported lots of defects (mostly found while automating the tests) and could much more easily identify GUI problems from functional problems."

Even GUI test automators find that they need to learn about details of GUI technology. On a technical level, it's actually more complicated than other interface technologies. One way or another you'll have to learn the details of the interface technology that your automated tests use. It's your choice. We think the GUI should be last on your list.

Here's a quick example. Lots of people have asked us for advice on automating installers using GUI test tools. The best approach is usually to chuck the tool. Most installers have scripting interfaces that provide a better approach. InstallShield, for example, is a popular install system that is used to create installers for many products. Many testers don't know they can run InstallShield installers with an option to record your selected install options. These are stored in a *response file*. The installer can later be run unattended, using the response file to specify the install options. It's easy; it's cheap; and the response file is simple to read and edit. It's a cost-effective way of automating installation (see Creating a Silent Installation http://support .installshield.com/kb/display.asp?documents_id=101901).

But you're not testing the GUI!—Focus your attention on where automation can help the most. Sometimes, you can effectively automate the GUI; other times you can't. Don't let people's preconceptions of what automation has to look like limit you.

Encourage the development of unit test suites.

Unit testing focuses on the smallest units that comprise a software system: the functions, classes, and methods that the programmers create. Most managers expect their programmers to unit test, and most programmers claim that they do. Actual practice, however, is extremely variable and often hard to confirm.

True unit testing tests units in isolation. Stubs are created to handle outgoing calls, and drivers are created to provide incoming calls. Building these stubs can be a major effort.

A more popular form of automated unit testing avoids stub development by testing units in context. We might call this *unit integration testing*. For systems that are built from the bottom up, this form of automation can be rather easy to automate.

You will need a scaffolding such as Junit or Xunit to manage test suite execution. This isn't too hard or too expensive. The code is tested through the normal calling interfaces that the languages support. Programmers write unit tests in the same language as the product software. Tests for Java are in Java; tests for C are in C. Use unit tests for regression testing, smoke testing, and configuration testing.

We caution against telling programmers what to do. But if managers are requesting more test automation, they should know the many ways that both programmers and testers can help. If programmers show an interest in unit testing, we suggest that you provide assistance. Unit testing is seen as a core practice of extreme programming and other agile methods (Beck 1999 and Beck et al. 2001).

Lesson 134 Beware of using automators who don't understand testing.

Automation requires programmers. What kind of programmers do you want?

Most programmers think they know a lot about testing. Unless they're terribly irresponsible, they test their own code a lot and often find they have to test other code that they're trying to use. They do know a lot about testing, except as compared to someone who focuses all his energy on testing: someone like you!

From the perspective of a tester, many programmers don't actually know much about software testing (just as many testers don't know much about programming). What they do know is often based on testing their own code. They overemphasize strategies appropriate to their own idiosyncrasies. People who understand testing requirements better should provide input and review.

Programmers' lack of knowledge about testing becomes a bigger problem when combined with the disdain that many programmers hold for testers. This disdain stems from a perception that testers are under-informed about software in general. Consequently, programmers may deliver automation that is quite clearly different from what was requested or expected. To guard against this, plan to review the test automation code. Programmers are accustomed to being given requirements they don't fully understand. A common strategy they use is to make a best guess, write a program, and then fix it later based on feedback. This strategy is understandable given the vagueness and confusion that often riddle requirements and other programming requests. The danger comes when this strategy is applied to test automation. Don't make the mistake of thinking that simply running the test suite will tell you if it works. Some test suite bugs will cause tests to fail; these you'll find and fix. Others will cause tests to pass when they have no right to, and you'll never know it. Use reviews, design strategies, and testing to guard against this.

Some responsible programmers may realize that they don't know enough about testing as they work on the automation project. They may try to slow down, giving themselves a chance to learn. Instead, urge them to move forward with pilot projects and reviews by testers. Or get them into testing so they can learn firsthand what testers need.

Avoid automators who don't respect testing.

Some programmers see testing as a low-status job beneath their abilities. We've seen such programmers assigned to work in testing. They naturally gravitate to test automation, which they're convinced they'll excel at, because they're such brilliant programmers.

Seeing testing as hardship labor, they have no incentive to learn how to test better. Instead, they demand some way to make the work interesting, fasten on automation tasks, and start developing tools that are of marginal value. Or, they'll redesign the bug-tracking system or create a fancy GUI for running tests—anything really to avoid testing.

We haven't seen this work out, we don't know how to make good use of such people, and we suggest that you avoid them if possible. If not, make sure they aren't in a position to cause problems for the rest of the test team. Maybe you can lend them to Technical Support. (Don't forget to claim your interdepartmental brownie points for doing Support such a big favor.)

Testability is often a better investment than automation.

In many circumstances, tests can be supported using either testability (test support code *inside* the product providing control or visibility) or automation (test support code *outside* the product). Testability often provides a better solution with less effort. Some examples:

■ After installing a product, users (and testers) had to search through a log to see if there were any installation errors. How do you automate this testing? The first idea was to write a script that would search through the install log for possible error messages. A better idea was to build this in as a feature of the product. It would probably be more reliable, would get better testing, and would actually benefit users directly.

■ Testers needed to simulate media errors on tape backup software, to test whether the software recovered gracefully. These are hard to simulate with automation. It would probably have required creating a tape drive simulator. Instead, testers worked with the programmers to allow the low-level tape writing code to (falsely) indicate that the media was bad.

■ Assertions are statements in the code that signal errors if assumptions are false. Assertions can be placed in the software under test to check that results are reasonable. This is often easier and more efficient than writing external code to verify results.

Lesson 137 Testability is visibility and control.

Any features that aid your ability to observe or control software operations improve testability. People often ask us for lists of potential features. Our list follows:

Access to the source code. Many companies will not allow testers to modify source code. However, you might still have access to view code. It is particularly important to be able to inspect change-records in the source control system.

Logging. Log error messages, sources of errors, usage profiles, resource utilization, system messages, and protocol communications. Allow different levels of logging to be specified. Logging mechanisms may already be present in the components used in your product. Programmers use logs to help with debugging. You can use them to catch bugs sooner, analyze bug patterns, provide detailed information in your reports, assess your test coverage, gather information on customer usage, and learn more about the software that you're testing (DiMaggio 2000, Johnson 2001, and Marick 2000).

Diagnostics. Diagnostics can alert you of potential problems. Assertions are one example. Data integrity checks verify that data is internally consistent. Code integrity checks verify that programs haven't been overwritten or modified. Memory integrity checks verify that memory is being used according to allocations. This can be a powerful tool when combined with logging, allowing you to enter debug mode or dump program information when an error is detected (Kaner 2000b).[7]

Error simulation. Your product has internal states, many of which are probably hard to induce, especially in a reproducible and systematic

---

[7]Noel Nyman reports, "Here's two diagnostic 'tools' Windows uses to help find memory errors. (1) Fill buffers with known patterns when they're initialized. That helps identify overruns, bad pointers, etc. (2) Put buffers at the end of allocated heap and work backwards into the heap. That forces buffer overruns and such to trigger Window's memory error notifications."

manner. Many error states are examples of this. Your software should be able to recover from media errors, lack of available memory or storage, network latency and disconnection, and similar problems. You may find these are difficult conditions to create, especially in a reproducible and systematic manner. Error state triggers can be placed at a low level of the product software to facilitate testing of error handling. (Tools also exist to simulate these errors from outside the product (Houlihan, 2001).)

Test points. Allow data to be inspected or modified at various points in the system (Cohen 2000).

Event triggers. Notifications of when internal tasks begin and end can help synchronize tests.

Reading obsolete data formats. Data formats may change several times while a product is in development. Provide means to convert data to the new formats so it doesn't have to be recreated.

Test interfaces. Programming interfaces are a major benefit for testability. A few products have actually added programming interfaces for this reason.

Custom control support. Allowing GUI test tools to work with custom user interface controls is probably one of the most requested testability features.

Permitting multiple instances. Allow multiple clients or agents to run on the same machine, even if this isn't supported in the field. This can allow testers to simulate a large network in a small lab.

Many software products have undocumented testability features that programmers have added to assist with their own testing and debugging. Ask about them.[8]

Lesson 138 | Start test automation early.

Automation is hard work, requiring planning, research, and design. If you're planning for lots of automated testing, start while the product is still being designed. You often have to address testability issues to automate effectively. Hard to specify in advance, testability solutions often result from trial and error.

Programmers are more open to testability suggestions early in the project. The features are easier to add when the design is still in flux. The programmer and project manager can put them on a schedule and budget

---

[8]On one embedded software project, Kaner and Hoffman discovered that the programming group had written more than 1100 diagnostic commands to check the state of the software and the device. All of them were available to the testers. The testers just had to build the appropriate commands into their test execution tool.

and plan for them. The uncertainties of the overall design motivate many programmers to help testing; less pressure is placed on the programmers if they know the code will be tested well.

Some test managers don't get this kind of head start but hope that they'll be able to catch up later. We've found that the later automation starts, the more difficult it is. We see several causes.

- After testing is in full swing, it's hard to divert resources to automation.
- After the test staff and processes are focused on manual testing, they resist change.
- After the design is set, programmers become less cooperative regarding testability requests.

If you want successful automation, don't delay. However, we urge you not to try and automate everything from the start. Build your infrastructure early but be judicious in your selection of which tests to automate.

Give centralized automation teams clear charters.

Some companies form a centralized automation team that supports multiple product test teams. This is often a wise arrangement.

If you're on such a team, make sure you have a clear charter describing the kind of assistance you give, how requests should be placed, and how you'll balance conflicting demands. This is important because the teams that are in the most trouble and clamoring for the most help are often the least able to benefit from automation. It's easier for them to say that they need help with automation, which is a technical skill, than that they need help getting their work organized, which presumably they should be able to do themselves. Not handling this well can lead you to being sucked into a vortex of ineffectiveness.

We suggest that you require teams receiving assistance to dedicate staff to work with you on automation projects. This can yield several benefits:

- You can assess their commitment and their actual problems.
- By training their staff, you can reduce continuing demands for maintenance and failure analysis.
- By pairing with the people who are requesting your services, you write their test requirements into your work from the start and throughout the project.

As a centralized automation group, you are a small in-house programming team with direct access to the people who are requesting your services. Read Beck (1999) and Jeffries et al. (2000).

Automate for immediate impact.

Too many people think test automation means automating manual testing. The result is an overemphasis on GUI regression tests.

Instead of thinking about test cases, pick some low-hanging fruit that will improve your efficiency. Focus on tasks that you can automate with high impact and little effort. Here are some good places to start:

System setup and preparation. New testers are often surprised by the amount of time they spend installing and configuring systems, getting them ready for testing. This work can be automated. Disk imagers allow the system to be reset to standard configurations. Install scripts can be used to automate setup. Sample data can be loaded automatically using common programming tools.

Diagnostic assistance. Some bugs are hard to surface. Defects that corrupt data or leak memory won't ordinarily be detected until the data is accessed or the memory runs out. Diagnostic tools can detect these faults when they happen. Tools for examining memory are available, and building tools for checking your product's data integrity or memory usage may not be difficult. Work with the project's programmers. They may already be using such tools themselves.

Session recording. Careful bug reporting requires the inclusion of complete configuration information. Programs can collect and report the necessary information automatically. This can also be used to help testers confirm that their system is configured as expected.

Test generation. *Use automated techniques to generate test inputs (Lesson 129).*

You don't have to automate a test from start to finish. Get some automated assistance in place first. It'll help build toward more comprehensive solutions.

You may have more test tools than you realize.

A stopwatch is one example of an excellent test tool. Measuring system response times is an important testing activity. Stopwatches are easy to use, flexible, and accurate. Some testers and programmers might think that an automated approach, using a call to the system clock, would necessarily be better, but stopwatches are often the best choice for black box time measurements. We recommend keeping one handy.

A test tool does not have to be labeled "Test tool." Testers have found dozens of other tools useful. Many are cheap and prosaic. Here are a few:

Disk imaging tools. Allow a system to be quickly restored to a known state.

Dependency walkers. Display the dynamic libraries used by a software application.

File scanners. Detect and catalog which files on a system have been changed.

Memory monitors. Track memory usage.

Macro tools. Make it easy to repeat certain tasks.

"Little languages" such as Sed, Awk, Grep, and Diff. These tools make it easy to automatically edit files, process output, search through data, and find differences. Initially developed for Unix, these are now available on most platforms.

Many system utilities and general programming tools also fit the bill. Moreover, they often come reasonably priced.

You can find a lot of useful freeware, shareware, and cheapware on the Net. Several useful programs are available at www.zdnet.com, www.pcmagazine .com, www.cnet.com, www.qadownloads.com, and www.softpanorama.org. Elisabeth Hendrickson is collecting a useful set of tool links at www.bughunting.com (see also Hendrickson 2001b).

CHAPTER 6

Documenting Testing

W e wrote this chapter to help you explore your requirements for test documentation. We don't provide sample documents. (See Chapter 3, *Testing Techniques*, for examples of tables and matrices.) Instead, we provide questions that might help you decide what you need.

This chapter starts out with a detailed evaluation of IEEE Standard 829 on Software Testing Documentation. We realize that you might never have read or even heard of this Standard—the IEEE sells the standard at a price high enough to probably dissuade most individuals from buying a copy.[1] We've met very few people who have their own copy of Standard 829. Not many of our client or employer companies have bought IEEE standards either. However, many of the test documentation templates that float around the field are derived from Standard 829. So, even though you may not know it by its name, if you've been in the field for a while, you've probably run into Standard 829.

If you haven't encountered Standard 829 and are not interested in test documentation templates, we suggest that you skip ahead to Lesson 147: *Analyze your requirements before deciding what products to build; this applies as much to your documentation as to your software.*

---

[1]We checked prices at www.ieee.org on July 30, 2001. Print copies of Standard 829 (64 pages, softbound) cost $65 to the public and $52 to IEEE members. Electronic access costs $98 to the public or $78 to members. Readers interested in a larger collection of standards can order the four-volume Software Engineering Standards 1999 set for $325 ($260 for members) or the Software Engineering Standards Subscription online for $850 per year.

The most recent document promoting Standard 829 is the *Software Engineering Body of Knowledge*, which we discuss here.

We quoted the *Software Engineering Body of Knowledge* (SWEBOK Version 0.95, 2001) in the preface. We'll have more to say about it in Chapter 10, *Your Career in Software Testing*. In this chapter, we note the SWEBOK position on test documentation:

Test documentation and workproducts

Documentation is an integral part of the formalization of the test process. The IEEE Standard for Software Test Documentation [829] provides a good description of test documents and of their relationship with one another and with the testing process. Test documents include, among others, Test Plan, Test Design Specification, Test Procedure Specification, Test Case Specification, Test Log and Test Incident or Problem Report. The program under test, with specified version and identified hw/sw requirements before testing can begin, is documented as the Test Item. Test documentation should be produced and continually updated, at the same standards as other documentation in development. *(IEEE Computer Society 2001, 92)*

We've attempted to develop IEEE Standard 829-style documentation, and we've seen the results of efforts by several other companies spanning several industries. We haven't been happy with the results. In fact, in our experience, Standard 829 has probably done more harm than good.

Part of our frustration with Standard 829 is the extent to which test groups have gotten themselves into trouble by attempting to follow it. Group after group has created test-planning templates based on Standard 829 and then created worthless documents that followed the template. Initially, we thought that the problem was in the people; they misapplied the standard. Later, we concluded that the problem must be deeper because it was widespread, and it snared people who we respected.

The pattern (or anti-pattern) that we saw was that a test group would create or borrow a template and invest a substantial initial burst of paperwork-filling energy that yielded an initial not-very-informative mass of material. They then ran into the costs and constraints of this type of documentation effort and gradually abandoned it. This left many groups to do purely *ad hoc* testing, because they had squandered all their planning time and budget on paperwork they would not use.

Abandoning the effort didn't mean that they publicly repudiated their work; usually, they silently stopped reading or updating it. If you asked them about test documentation, they were likely to produce the big binder full of paper (which no one was reading or updating). Several companies went through this cycle time after time, expecting to do a better job next time, blaming themselves for somehow not getting it right.

The problem is *not* that these companies were not doing Standard 829 in the right way.

The problem *is* that Standard 829 was not the right way to meet these companies' requirements.

To apply a solution effectively, you need to understand the problem clearly.

Lesson 142

Nowhere is this principle more apparent than in the use and misuse of test documentation. Accordingly, we have listed lessons from both sides of the debate regarding test documentation standards. We hope that you will think first about the problem that your test document needs to solve and then apply a form appropriate to the solution.

Don't use test documentation templates: A template won't help unless you don't need it.

Lesson 143

A test documentation template is no substitute for skill.

A template is a structure for creating test documentation. Fill in the sections or fill in the blanks, and you have your documentation.

The problem with templates is they make it easier to write a content-free document that looks good superficially. For some people that's a plus. But to use a template to write good test documentation, you have to own it. You must understand what each section of the template means, why it's there at all, and when it should be deleted. If you know all that, you don't need a template. If you don't know that, don't mess with templates. They'll steer you in counterproductive directions because you won't understand the requirements and tradeoffs that were balanced in the mind of the templates' author.

We've seen several organizations that created templates for themselves but used them ineffectively or counterproductively. The person using the template must be able to adapt it to the requirements at hand.

If you can writing effective test documentation without using a template, you may find that a template helps you write effective documentation more quickly.

Use test documentation templates: They foster consistent communication.

Suppose that you have to present your work to a third party. Perhaps you are writing test documentation that will be delivered to a customer as part of a custom-engineered product. The customer will take over maintenance and testing from here. Or perhaps you are writing test documentation that another company will use to test a product. Or perhaps you are writing test documentation that will be inspected by auditors or regulators or that might be used as courtroom evidence of good or bad testing after an accident involving your company's product kills someone. In each of these cases, your material will communicate more effectively and people will find your material easier to use if you use a standard, predictable format, present things in standard places, cover a standard set of issues, and use standard terminology.

Use the IEEE Standard 829 for test documentation.

The IEEE Standard 829 project was led by David Gelperin. He is a smart, thoughtful, considerate, open-minded person who has done a tremendous amount to foster diversity, creativity and the development and application of skill in the software testing field. His company, *Software Quality Engineering (SQE)*, organizes the *STAR Conference* (Software Testing Analysis & Review), which is one of the field's best and most successful conferences. SQE hosts several other conferences. We are regular speakers at SQE conferences. SQE also offers courses to the testing community, and we have taught courses for SQE. Our criticism of Standard 829 is not a criticism of David, who we consider a good friend, nor of the many public services that SQE has proudly provided, at its own expense, to the software testing community.

Many attributes of Standard 829 reflect David's strengths. None of the many categories of information in the standard is fluff. When we read the standard, we can understand why someone would want to know each and every piece of information that the standard calls for.

Nothing in the standard is mandatory. If you want to create procedurally scripted test cases, Standard 829 tells you what to call them and where in the document to put them. If you don't write test cases this way, you don't have to create this type of documentation just to satisfy the standard. The standard provides a framework, a structure, and a set of definitions, not a mandated set of sections.

The standard has been widely studied and discussed. People in the field know about it. This standard has been the basis for many (perhaps most) of the test documentation templates that circulate from company to company. It has become the basis of conversation about test planning and test documentation (for better or worse) in and across many companies.

Two of us, Bach and Kaner, have served as trial consultants (experts for use at trial) in cases involving defective products, and colleagues of ours have served in other cases and given us detailed debriefings. We've seen cases in which poor test documentation has been a part of an underlying problem that led to litigation. Even if the documentation was not a key problem, some of the companies whose products were allegedly defective or who were accused of fraud would have been better served if their test documents were clearer and better organized. Their mess weakened their defense. IEEE Standard 829 could have saved those companies a lot of money and might have helped them save their customers a lot of money.

Lesson 146

Don't use the IEEE Standard 829.

Each of us was enthusiastic about IEEE Standard 829 when we first read it. However, we have seen several problems in practice. When we would comment on these problems, we sometimes were told that the problems are due to misuse of the standard. After all, it is very flexible. Testers don't have to use the standard in an inappropriate way.

To us, this feels like a "Guns don't kill people, people kill people" type of argument. Sometimes this is a valid argument, but sometimes it's not.

Regarding the IEEE 829 case, we have seen problems enough times, in the hands of people we respect, in use by companies who have been working with 829-based templates for several projects, that we believe that the problems reflect weakness in the Standard, and they should not be dismissed as reflecting incompetence of the people using it.

The argument, "Guns don't kill people" reads differently if the gun in question has a hair trigger and no safety and is left loaded in a public place with an official-looking notice that says, "Use this gun for all projects."

Here are some of the issues that we have with the Standard, in practice:

- The assumption underlying the Standard appears to be a waterfall-like approach in which tests are developed early, documented carefully, and then not changed. The cost of change (the maintenance cost of the documents) has a chilling effect on change. In our view, you should create new tests that are more complex as the program gets more stable and more powerful as you gain more insight. To the extent that maintenance costs of test documentation encourage you to reuse old tests instead of developing more powerful new ones and to stick with your current testing strategy instead of improving it as you learn, the test documentation is part of the problem and not part of the process.

- Massive test documents create a compliance mentality. *Do what the plan says.* This is fundamentally different from the mentality of the alert, critical tester who pays attention to any hints available and follows up all promising leads.

- The standard provides no structure for analysis of the test documentation requirements. It provides no suggestions or guidelines regarding when to provide what type of information.

- There is no apparent awareness and no discussion of the (enormous) cost of providing all of these types of information. Time spent on that documentation may well be time not spent on testing.

- The standard appears to emphasize breadth of documentation. More seems to be better. It appears to be *a good thing* to generate a Test Plan, Test Design Specification, Test Procedure Specification, Test Case Specification, and so on.

- There are no criteria for deciding whether specific instances of test documentation are good or bad. In practice, volume seems to be the accepted substitute for clarity and coverage. We have reviewed or audited enormous test documents, that the authors considered adequate or complete, only to discover gaping holes—key testing strategies or areas of risk were completely missing. It is too easy to overlook the absence of even the most obvious tests when the test documents run hundreds or thousands of pages.

- The maintenance costs of these long documents are enormous. When the software changes, you don't just have to change the parts of the documentation that are tied to that aspect of the software. You have to search everything else to figure out what has to change. This is a parallel effort to searching through and changing your actual test files (code files if you automate). If the correspondence between documentation and code is not 1-to-1, there will be mismatches, and these will bring on their own mischief and time costs later.

- Documenting every test can seriously interfere with automated testing. If it takes an hour of documentation time per test case (we think this is an underestimate), and you want 10,000 automated tests on your project (this is definitely *not* an overestimate of the number of distinct tests used by many companies), then you have to spend 10,000 tester-hours on documentation. You also pay the cost of testing that the automated tests accurately implement the tests as documented. When the tests change, because of maintenance of the software under test, so will the test documentation, resulting in even more tester-hours. This is a huge tax on the automated testing effort. Companies that follow it will write fewer tests, and they may discard tests rather than face the cost of maintaining both them and their associated documentation. In our experience, companies have been much more likely to simply give up on the documentation, eventually rendering valueless whatever documentation-related labor they spent to that point (because it is incomplete, and it quickly goes out of date).

■ Automated testing paradigms that involve high volumes of tests (millions) generated or combined with random data or random sequences seem entirely foreign to the Standard. We can imagine shoe-horning the software documentation and the associated software models into the Standard's categories, but we don't see that done in practice. Instead, we see that these efforts (models, code, oracles, and so on) are documented elsewhere or not at all.

■ We previously mentioned our experience in lawsuits. We'll conclude this list of issues by mentioning a different experience. Several companies start with a carefully signed-off statement that the testing process will be documented to a certain degree, that a template (based on 829) will be followed, that the testing strategy will be thus and so. Then they get part way through the project and abandon the signed-off statement in favor of, as they see it at the time, getting real work done on a real schedule. They might have made the exactly correct decision, but think about how this plays in a lawsuit. They started with a thorough plan and an industry standard, then they quietly followed a lesser practice, and then they released a defective product. This looks bad, bad, bad. If you're not going to follow an over-ambitious plan, and your company has any risk of being sued, don't start your project by saying that you're going to follow that plan. An over-ambitious plan can do much more harm than good.

Having listed these costs, we come back to the question of benefits. If we spend all this money, add all this inertia to our projects, and encourage our staff to run their brains at a lower setting when they do (as opposed to write about) testing, what do we get back in return?

Many companies use substantially less paper. They track their status using a collection of brief lists and tables, status reports, and regular team meetings. They track their problems via well-written bug reports stored in a well-run, bug-tracking system. What added benefits would these companies gain from following Standard 829? How compelling are those benefits under *your* circumstances?

In many contexts, the added benefits are not compelling. In such cases, given the added costs and risks associated with developing and maintaining large test documentation sets, we submit that creating Standard 829-style documentation would be irresponsible.

Analyze your requirements before deciding what products to build; this applies as much to your documentation as to your software.

Your decision about what to include in a test documentation set and what to skip should be governed by your project's needs. IEEE Standard 829's format and categories might be useful, and they might not. Until you have completed your documentation requirements analysis, the choice of IEEE Standard 829 (or any other detailed specification) as your structure and user interface is, to say the least, premature.

We don't understand the mentality of someone who insists that code should never be written without a thorough requirements analysis but who is willing to write a large set of test documentation without a correspondingly thorough requirements analysis.

Please do not misunderstand this. We're not saying that IEEE Standard 829 is inappropriate for your product. It might be the perfect thing. Just like COBOL might be the perfect language for your project. All we're saying is, think about what you're going to build before you choose your programming language and your key tools.

To analyze your test documentation requirements, ask questions like the ones in this list.

We recommend Gause and Weinberg (1989) for a solid introduction to requirements analysis and for an excellent collection of context-free questions that are useful for any requirements analysis. Michalko (1991, 138) provides an additional set of interesting context-free questions (the CIA's Phoenix questions). In addition to those, we have collected a set of questions that are more specific to requirements for test documentation.

What is your group's mission, and what are your objectives in testing this product? The test documentation (like any other work product that you create) has no value if it doesn't support your mission and help you reach your objectives.

Is your test documentation a *product* or a *tool*? A product is something that you give to someone else to use. They pay for it. You will probably follow whatever standard they request, subject to their willingness to pay for it. In contrast, if the documentation is merely an in-house tool, it doesn't have to be any more complete, more organized, or more tidy than the minimum you need to help you meet your objectives.

Is software quality driven by legal issues or by market forces? If your software and testing are subject to inspection by regulators, you will probably follow a formal documentation format like Standard 829. Similarly, if your product might injure people or destroy property, your test documentation might play a role in a lawsuit. Standard 829's formal structure, the traditional bulk of 829-style documents and the "industry standard" status might make 829 a good choice. Impressive documentation might or might not help you improve the quality of your software, but it will help your company defend itself later. On the other hand, if the consequence of low quality in your market is lost sales rather than lawsuits, your customers won't ever see or care about your test documentation.

How quickly is the design changing? If the software's design changes quickly, don't build detail into the tests; the details will become obsolete too quickly. Don't spend many pages documenting the tests; the tests will be revised or discarded too quickly to justify the investment.

How quickly does the specification change to reflect design change? You cannot do specification-driven testing if the specification is chronically incomplete and out of date, nor would you want to tie your test documentation to the contents of such a specification. *NOTE: Beware of trying to wag the dog.* If the project isn't being run with up-to-date specifications, the project might or might not need better specifications. Inconvenience to the test group is not a particularly powerful argument for changing the project's specification policies. If you're not getting good specs, plan to adapt the test strategy rather than project policy. If you're going to fight for better specs, do so on the basis of the costs and risks created for other stakeholders, especially those who have a more visible role in the profit and loss of the company.

When you test, do you hope to prove conformance to specs or nonconformance with customer expectations? If you are doing custom software to a contractually agreed specification, your testing and documentation will probably focus on conformance to the specification. In contrast, if your product is intended for the mass market, then no one has signed off on the specification, no contract supports the product specification, and there is less assurance that the specification that you have on hand will produce a satisfactory product. In such a case, you might better serve the project by using your tests to prove that customers would hate the product than to verify the product against whatever specifications exist. Excellent test documentation for this purpose would include evidence of customer expectations, such as information about competitive products, common equipment that would be used with your software, critical magazine reviews of this product or predecessors, and other customer-focused and platform-focused material.

Does your testing style rely more on already-defined tests or on exploration? If you primarily reuse test cases, you might want operational and maintenance documentation for each. If you primarily explore, you might prefer strategic and tactical documentation (ideas about how to approach testing an area, but not test cases) and documentation of any tools that you've bought or developed that make exploration easier.

Should test documentation focus on *what to test* (objectives) or *on how to test for it* (procedures)? We prefer objectives-focused documentation, but step-by-step descriptions are certainly useful for describing the testing procedure to third parties.

Should the documentation ever control the testing project? Do you want testers to look in the documentation for operations information (such as scheduling info that lays out what to do next)?

If the documentation controls parts of the testing project, should that control come early or late in the project? Should testing be done primarily by reference to the testing documentation? If so, is that true throughout the project, or should early testing be more exploratory? Or should late testing (thorough shakedowns of the seemingly working product) be more exploratory?

Who are the primary readers of these test documents and how important are they? If you want testers and programmers to review the documentation (for example, to find holes in coverage), write it to emphasize design and to make it easy to see what the tests cover. Don't write it to emphasize the step-by-step description of the tests, or your reviewers will get lost.

How much traceability do you need? What documents (specifications or requirements) are you tracing back to and who controls them?

To what extent should test documentation support tracking and reporting of project status and testing progress? Should you create a processing system that lets you count the number of test cases documented and planned, the number attempted, the number passed, and the current number of bugs found? Should the test documentation play a role in that system? For example, should testers work with the documentation interactively as they test, marking it up as they run the documented tests? Should their checkmarks or status marks be collected and rolled into a status report?

How well should documentation support the delegation of work to new testers? To delegate effectively, you have to tell someone what to do, in enough detail that they will be able to do it. Effective delegation does not necessarily involve step-by-step instructions. We strongly prefer to teach new testers some skills, give them introductory tasks that familiarize them with product documentation (such as the user manual), and then give them instructions that assume they have the skills and the reference material. Rather than slow down (and bulk up the test docs) for testers who can't develop their own skills and look up their own answers, we replace people who can't cut it with people who can. If you think that detailed instruction is necessary, we caution that it takes a lot of skill to write effective, detailed instructions. For a light-hearted introduction to these issues, read Wurman (1991). Another critical aspect of delegation is your ability to determine what someone did and how well she did it. If you have someone mark up a very concise document (such as one of the matrices that we illustrated in the *Addendum* to Chapter 3, *Testing Techniques*) you might see patterns more readily than if you have to flip through dozens or hundreds of pages of marked-up test scripts.

What are your assumptions about the skills and knowledge of new testers? All writing is to an audience. The more your audience knows, the less you have to tell them.

Are you using the test documentation to document the project's process, to provide a collection of models or descriptors of the product that someone can test against, or to give the reader structure for finding bugs? These are very different objectives, for different readers with different skills and interests.

A test suite should provide *prevention*, *detection*, and *prediction*. Which is the most important for this project? If you create a test early enough and review it with programmers effectively enough, they might design the program in a way that ensures that it will pass the test. Because they were thinking about the test at the time of development, they simply didn't make the bug. Just going through the effort of developing the materials and, asking the programmers key questions can point out risks and weaknesses in their approach. These are examples of the prevention benefits of test planning. Later, you get code. If your plan steers you effectively, it helps you find those bugs that are present. This is the detection benefit of test planning. Finally, your test results might help you plan the rest of the project or future projects. They might highlight problem areas, common types of bugs, and effective versus ineffective strategies. They might also yield some statistics that you can use to set expectations about how long some tasks take and perhaps how much work is left in this project. *Your test planning effort will yield many benefits. Among these three (prevention, detection, or prediction), if you could only focus on one, which would it be?* Different groups have different answers to this.

How *maintainable* are the test documents (and their test cases)? How well do they ensure that test changes will follow code changes? Some product specifications are vision documents. They help the development team create its initial plan, but they are never updated. Later documents help the team address specific problems, as needed. Other companies create specifications that they update continually and that they tie, in detail, to every aspect of the product as it is built. *Which of these approaches is the right one for you?*

Will the test documents help you identify (and revise or restructure in face of) a permanent shift in the risk profile of the program? There's an old heuristic that an area of the program with some bugs will have more bugs. Therefore, test more heavily where you have found bugs before. At some point, however, this part of the product might finally be cleaned up. Some other part of the product that used to be in good shape might have become unstable. Do you intend to design your test documents in a way that would help you spot changes over time in the stability of different areas of the product.?

When we ask the preceding questions, we are not urging you to create a Requirements Document and write down all of the answers. We're suggesting that you think about the issues. Write down as much as you need, in as much detail as you need, to help you fulfill your test documentation objectives. You might need a multipage report that documents your choices and helps you get them approved by management. In some companies, test groups need this type of documentation to defend their work if the project falls seriously behind schedule or if the product shows unacceptable quality levels in the field. Alternatively, a one-sentence mission statement might be enough.

Summarize your core documentation requirements in one sentence with no more than three components.

Here are two very different summaries:

- The test documentation set will primarily support our efforts to find bugs in this version, to delegate work, and to track status.

- The test documentation set will support ongoing product and test maintenance over at least 10 years, will provide training material for new group members, and will create archives suitable for regulatory or litigation use.

These summaries will lead to vastly different documentation sets. Review your summary statement with every interested stakeholder on the project.

CHAPTER 7

Interacting with Programmers

Much of your interaction with programmers will come from the bugs you report. Chapter 4 is devoted to this important area. This chapter focuses on other aspects of your interaction with programmers.

Because programmers are experts at how machines think, they're often treated as machines themselves. Don't fall into this pattern of mistreatment. Programmers are not coding machines. They have feelings, and most care a lot about the work they do.

Many programmers mistreat testers. We think the best way to prevent or counteract bad relations is to build personal relationships based on mutual respect. Assume that the individuals you work with are worthy of respect and act on that assumption. Do your work in a way that should earn their respect. Refuse to accept mistreatment or abuse.

As an official critic of the programmer's work, you must demonstrate sensitivity, appreciation, and diplomacy. Don't go overboard as a cheerleader, but let people know when you see value in their work. If their work is poor, don't be nasty about it.

Be open and honest in your dealings with programmers. Start a conversation. You may want to discuss this chapter with them. Listen to what they say.

Understand how programmers think.

All three of us started out as working programmers before specializing in software testing. We still write code. Our experiences affect how we understand programmers and how, when we work as testers, we work with programmers.

Programmers and testers work under different conditions. We play different roles. In those roles, we think differently about our work. You can be more effective if you take into account some common differences in our perspectives and approach.

The best way for you to learn how to interact with programmers is to become one and to work with other programmers as your peers for a while. Come back to testing after you've written production code, had it criticized, condemned, and praised by testers, users, managers, and fellow programmers. Nothing we can say in this chapter can give you the insights you can gain from this experience.

The generalizations in this lesson will apply better to some people than to others. We urge you to get to know the person you are working with, rather than rely primarily on these observations. That said, you might find some of these notes useful:

Most programmers specialize. A programmer often focuses on a subsystem or module, depending on often-sketchy information about the other system elements that their code must interact with. In contrast, you are often a generalist regarding the systems you test. To test well, you have to understand how it all fits together. Indeed, you may be able to provide information about the complete system to the programmers you work with.

Programmers focus on their theory of the system. They have models for how the system components are related, which components are reliable, and how errors propagate. They must work from their mental model. When they tell you that a bug you reported can't happen, they're not saying they're infallible. They're saying that this type of error doesn't fit with their model and what they believe to be true. You focus on observation and evidence. This tests their model. Keep careful notes and logs, focus your reports on what you have actually seen, and let them find the flaws in their reasoning.

Programming is a complicated activity. Programmers use much of their energy just trying to understand the systems they're building. The concentration this requires often keeps programmers from attending to things you think are important. It also makes them impatient with interruptions.

Programmers often contend with difficult situations. They deal with ambiguous and changing requirements, buggy tools and component technologies, and work environments full of interruptions.

Many programmers dislike routine work, often building tools and scripts to automate the repetitive tasks they face. Many see testing as a repetitive task and, thus, one that naturally should be automated. They may suggest that there's something wrong with you if you are not automating your tests. Don't buy into this. Don't simply try to automate tests as a way of winning respect from programmers. There are better ways. *Your integrity and competence will demand respect* (Lesson 153).

For further discussion, see Pettichord's (2000b) article, "Testers and Developers Think Differently."

Develop programmers' trust.

Don't develop an unnecessarily adversarial relationship with the people who create the programs you test. You'll be more effective if the programmers you work with will share information with you, such as their plans, early drafts of their design documents, and early prototypes. Find out what kind of feedback they want and give it to them.

The earlier you can engage the programmers, the better off you'll be. Early engagement requires you to be sensitive and helpful. When you're dealing with early draft code, programmers know there are problems. They don't want to hear about the things they know about, such as the need for error handling that they haven't yet written. They want to know about serious problems. Find out what they define as serious and focus the information that you give them—for now. As the project develops, you'll have time to develop or influence more independent criteria.

If you disagree about whether something is going to lead to problems, state your opinion, but don't be a nag. It will become clear enough later whether you are right or not.

Provide service.

Offer to assist programmers directly. This builds trust and proves that you're someone they should cooperate with. Here are some services you can offer:

- Test third-party components. Share test results so that programmers can decide whether and how the components can be used in the product.

- Test private builds and prototypes.

- Set up test environments for programmers to use in their own testing.

- Review requirements documents for testability. Programmers have trouble with ambiguous requests. They may be very happy to get you involved.

Everything you do as a tester should be providing service. These are just examples of where the service is more direct and obvious. They give you chances to gain trust, but they also give you chances to display your competence.

Your integrity and competence will demand respect.

You are a customer advocate. Ultimately, your job is to report problems that users may experience. Programmers and managers may have trouble acknowledging these problems. If so, you are delivering an unpleasant message. You might not be loved for this. But if you find credible problems and report them accurately and directly, you will be respected. When reporting problems,

Report problems crisply. That is, lay a bug out step by step, with no (or few) unnecessary steps. Describe the failure symptoms accurately. Make your report easy to follow and easy to understand. Your work will be valued because you are showing respect for the programmer's time (as a bug report reader and as an investigator who relies on your report for clues).

Base your judgments on the actual observed behavior of the product. Often, you have used the software more than anyone else. This makes you an expert in the external behavior of the program. You are not an expert in the internals. Talk about what you can see, and don't spend a lot of time on your guesses about the nature of the underlying problem.

If a failure is irreproducible, show the work you did trying to reproduce it. When you submit an irreproducible bug report, the best impression to convey is that you did a thorough investigation, but better tools and information are needed than those you have. The worst impression to convey is that you gave up and tossed the job at the programmer at the first difficulty. Demonstrate respect for the programmer's time.

Deliver bad news directly. Don't go over people's heads until you've given them a chance to act on it. Tell them you're going to escalate a problem before you do.

Don't pretend to know things you don't. For example, if you don't know how serious a problem is, don't fake it. Either get evidence (*e. g.*, from technical support or marketing staff) or be quiet or be clear that you're stating a guess.

Don't exaggerate your bug reports. Don't minimize them either, and don't be bullied or cajoled into ignoring or hiding what you see. Stick to your guns—if you see a problem, report it and escalate it if you feel it's appropriate. Develop a reputation as a straight shooter, and you'll gain their respect.

If you have integrity, you can develop your competence. If you've lost your integrity, your competence won't matter.

Lesson 154 Focus on the work, not the person.

If you see bugs, report bugs. Don't report that Joe Programmer is a screw-up. He may be, but if you say this, you'll sabotage *your* effectiveness.

Many experienced testers use their observations of personal and organizational weaknesses to focus their bug hunting. They see a mess and predict bugs from it. Your successes at this may tempt you into thinking that it would be simpler and more effective to report the problems you see in the organization directly. *Wrong!*

As soon as you make it your job to report problem programmers, all of them will stop sharing information with you and stop inviting you to their meetings. This leaves you ineffective and makes you part of the problem.

Don't underestimate management's ability to notice these problems. People problems are much easier to notice than to fix. Remember that you are not the manager of the manager who is (seemingly and maybe actually) ignoring a problem employee. When you draw attention to possible programmer incompetence, you restrict management's options in how to handle it. Or you could be forcing managers to face a problem they've been trying not to notice. It's still a losing game.

Some testers go so far as to think it's their job to punish programmers for making mistakes, missing deadlines, and not following the process. Guess what happens to these testers? They become disposable. Some are dropped right away. Others are kept around as convenient bad cops until a Really Big Screw-up demands the sacrifice of a scapegoat.

If you see a pattern of problems that you fear isn't being addressed, discretely present the evidence to the right manager and let her handle it. You've done your job (Pettichord 2001c).

Programmers like to talk about their work. Ask them questions.

Lesson 155

Many testers report that they have trouble getting information from programmers. We find that programmers are often eager to talk about their work.

A good place to start is with whatever design documents they're working from. Start by doing your homework. Read the available documents. If you can, look at the code.

Programmers' documents will be confusing in places. Ask them about sections that seem important but that you don't understand. Sometimes you can use email for questions, but often face-to-face conversations work better, especially for follow-up questions. If they agree to a meeting, come prepared so that you don't waste their time.

If they don't have documents, ask for a picture of the system. Most programmers have an image of the system that they're working on in their minds and will be happy to share it.

You may get them to diagram the system on a whiteboard. One technique is to point to a random arrow or box and ask, "What happens if this fails?" This can uncover missing error handling or unquestioned assumptions. Questions like this to two or more programmers may reveal interesting differences in perspective between programmers.

Why are you asking these questions? To learn more about the system being built, the ways in which it can fail, and the attitudes and assumptions of the people building it. Don't audit or quiz them. If they feel this is happening, they won't cooperate.

When you get answers, write up your notes and share them with the programmer and other testers. Programmers don't like answering the same questions over and over to different testers.

It helps if you know their language. If they are programming in C++ or Java, you should have some idea what a class is. If the software runs on a multithreaded system, you should know what a thread is.

Active listening by itself may do a lot for you. In common conversations, each person contributes her own ideas, experiences, or wit. When you listen actively, you focus on trying to help the other person say what she has to say. This includes restating what she said in your own terms, asking questions that elicit additional information or context, and drawing inferences.

As a tester, it is your job to think about how the product could fail. But as a member of the team, you need to understand what is valuable about the product being built. Let the programmers know that you understand the value of what they are doing.

Don't tell the programmers they must provide certain documents before you can do your job. If they share draft documents that omit important information, ask. If you need information, ask for it. Explain why you need it and how it will help you in your job. They can't read your mind. (See Gause and Weinberg 1989, Chapter 6; Michalko 1991, Chapter 14).

Lesson 156

Programmers like to help with testability.

Most programmers want their programs to be tested well. They try to do good work, know that they can make mistakes, and expect you to find those mistakes.

For a tester, testability is anything that makes it easier to test software. When talking to programmers, a more practical definition is *testability is visibility and control* (Lesson 137). This definition states the nature of the features that will help you. Understanding that, they can suggest features that you haven't thought of (or didn't ask for) but that will be helpful. What kinds of features should you ask for? Lesson 137, *Testability is Visibility and Control,* provides a number of examples.

Many testers have been frustrated in their attempts to get testability features from programmers. We believe that there are three key points to being successful with such requests.

Speak their language. It is helpful if you can read design documents and code. You have to put your requests in terms they can understand. If you can specify exactly what interface you want in what part of the code, they'll give your request a fair hearing. Indeed, you may be surprised to find that they have already added features like those you've requested, to assist with debugging or for other reasons.

Ask early. See Lesson 138, *Start Test Automation Early.*

Be realistic. Some testability requests will be small enough that they can be scheduled with other implementation tasks. Others constitute new features and will have to be budgeted and scheduled just like any other feature. You'll have to champion these to management as well.

Most programmers like to program. If you make a specific, reasonable request, it gives them a chance to do their magic. What they don't like is trying to read people's minds. They will not welcome another ambiguous request.

Many testers have told us that programmers come back with excuses. "It will compromise the security of the software." "It will hurt performance." These are occasionally valid concerns for test code. But usually, we believe, these are code phrases for "we don't want to think about it." Making your case may require some salesmanship to help programmers realize that helping you is ultimately to their own benefit. You may have to seek out the right programmer, someone with the vision and influence to make it happen. Nonetheless, if you know what you're asking for, ask at the right time, and ask nicely, we think you can get constructive consideration of your requests.

We have seen many testability features that made significant benefits to product testing. Some were provided at the request of one of us. Others were suggested by testers or programmers on the teams. It can be a difficult case to make, but a worthwhile one. We encourage perseverance.

CHAPTER 8

Managing the Testing Project

Managing a testing project is like managing any other kind of project—in some respects. But there's at least one special feature of a testing project: It's driven by the programming project. What you do is a reaction to what they do. That's why using a tool like Microsoft Project to plot the tasks of testing can be so frustrating. You have to squint pretty hard to fit the work of your team into those little Gantt bars. In this chapter, we review the lessons we've learned about the dynamics of testing projects and how to control them.

Lesson 157 Create a service culture.

Project teams develop software in order to provide benefits to customers. The customers might be in-house or external, paying or nonpaying. The customers might be the same people as the developers (for example, when we build our own tools).

Testers provide services to the overall project. A typical service is finding and reporting bugs. Other services depend on your group's mission (see Chapter 1, "The Role of the Tester").

One of the fundamental issues running through the testing literature and the testing subcultures is whether your role is primarily service or control:

- A service provider controls the quality and relevance of the services he provides to the larger effort to develop the end result. *We provide excellent services to people who need them.*

■ A service provider does not control the quality of the end product, does not control the processes used by other service providers (programmers, writers, marketers), and does not approve or deny approval of the release of the product. The service provider is not the project manager; he provides services to the project manager.

Lesson 158 Don't try to create a control culture.

Testers often receive, and give, detailed advice about how projects should be managed. We think that much of that advice is naïve. The worst and most dogmatic of it comes from testers and consultants whose product development experience is limited to testing (or otherwise measuring or evaluating) the work of others.

Testers often see projects at their worst. Testers face the consequences of poor and incomplete decisions and half-done tasks, without noticing the planning and work that allowed the product to get as good as it is. What appear to be poor and incomplete decisions are often thoughtful business decisions with which you disagree. It is easy to believe that you know better and would do it better.

Some processes make it easier or harder for testers. However, a competent test group can provide solid services to a wide range of project managers, who work under very different project management styles, including the inconvenient ones and the ones that make the testing part of the project less efficient.

Some processes seem destined to produce bad products. This is a serious problem; someone should manage this. Unfortunately, the *worst* group to manage this is the testing group. Testing groups don't have the resources, the experience, or the political power to fix the broader development processes or to manage the fixed processes.

We are not saying that you (the human being who is doing testing today) should learn your place and stay in it. Far from that. We encourage you to expand your role and influence in the company. If you want to and have the competence to manage the project manager, do so. But, do that job from an appropriate role—as the project manager's manager. It is not the role of the test manager.

Lesson 159 Develop the power of the king's ear.

Your power in your company rests on your investigative skill and your freedom to communicate. Your power does not rest in a chain of command, because you aren't very high up in the project's chain of command.

In the ideal case, you can point out a problem to any group in the company that is affected by it. A significant problem that goes unfixed will cost some group(s) a lot of money. If they think a problem is serious enough, they'll argue to get it fixed. If they don't think that the problem is serious enough, the problem might not be fixed. Not all problems will be fixed.

Some companies (several, in our experience) accept it as a given that testers will show off their bugs and their status reports to anyone who will listen to them. Project managers get annoyed, complain, and are told by their peers and managers to stop whining: Testers will be testers.

Other companies have a more hierarchical attitude. In their cultures, it would be inappropriate for a tester to visit a marketer or a technical support manager to discuss a problem with a product under development.

If your task is to help the company make the right business decisions about the defects that you find, your effectiveness is limited if you cannot communicate your findings to the people in the business who are most affected by those defects. If you can't communicate those findings directly, in one-on-one meetings, you can communicate them indirectly. For example, you can give people access rights to the bug-tracking database and teach them how to use it to find problems that might interest them. Or, you can publish status reports that highlight key problems. As people in other groups come to value and rely on the information you provide, they will (often) be willing to advocate for and defend your right to provide it to them.

You have to evaluate your company's culture and work within bounds that won't get you fired or ostracized. Within those bounds, we suggest that you exercise and develop your influence by being a credible, high-integrity reporter of information that people value. In our experience, you can gain much more actual influence this way than you can from procedural authority, such as the authority to refuse to sign-off (approve) a release.

You manage the subproject that provides testing services, not the development project.

Lesson 160

The testing effort is a sub-project of the overall project. You apply resources and deliver services. You have a lot of control over how the testing project is run, and you should choose your style as carefully as you might wish the project manager had chosen his.

Sometimes project managers make mistakes, and sometimes they can benefit from your advice. By all means, offer it. Speak your mind. But the final decision on how to run the project is the project manager's. If he doesn't take your advice, so be it.

We don't write much in this chapter about the human issues involved in managing people under stress. We consider more of those in Chapter 9, "Managing the Testing Group." For now, we'll note that when project managers and executives make bad decisions, they sometimes subject testers to verbal abuse, demands for excessive overtime, and demands to compromise their integrity. This is not within the project manager's reasonable scope of authority. As a test manager, an important part of your job is to protect your staff from abuse.

All projects evolve. Well-run projects evolve well.

Throughout every project, you should expect (as the normal state of affairs) large and small refinements or corrections to the overall plan.

A project is a collection of tasks. Over time, the project team will discover that some tasks are harder or more time consuming than expected, that others can't be done yet because the key person for the task is busy with something else, and that others still seem more or less urgent to the marketing manager or the customer than they did last week. Additionally, every time you file a bug report, you add a new task to the pile.

The project provides a structure for integrating the new information and determining what (probable) tasks to do next and in following iterations until the product is complete. Think of a project as an ongoing structured conversation about what makes sense to do next.

There are always late changes.

Many traditional project management approaches are designed to limit and control change, but others embrace it (for example, see Weinberg 1992, Beck 1999, Beck et al. 2001, and Krutchen 2000). All project management approaches must nonetheless deal with change.

Imagine building a new chair to replace one that wore out. It is clear what is needed, who needs it, what they'll do with it, and what kinds of stresses they'll put on it. You can find people who have made chairs very similar to the one you're about to make.

Software isn't like that. In most software projects, no one has created exactly this product before, and even if others have, the people on *this* project haven't. Additionally, the people who will use this software haven't used it before. Even though they might have a good idea of what they want, they don't know how to specify their requirements because:

■ They don't know all of their requirements.

■ Their requirements will change as they try early versions of the software or competitors' products. They will discover new ways to use the software and imagine other uses they wish they could make, but can't (yet).

■ Different stakeholders have different needs, which are often in conflict. No one document can articulate all of the conflicting and potentially conflicting requirements and balance them.

Moreover, as components and tools are built and skills are learned, the expected costs to provide a given benefit will change, making it more or less easy to satisfy someone who wants that benefit.

Requirements are the result of ongoing struggles between what we want and what we can have (Bach 1999a). As the project progresses, the requirements change.

Projects involve a tradeoff among features, reliability, time, and money.

The project manager's job is to deliver the right set of features, at an appropriate level of reliability, on time, and within budget. This is a challenging tradeoff.

Features. Choose the right set of features, given that it would be too expensive to deliver everything that every stakeholder could want.

Reliability. Make the product work, but beware of spending infinite time and money making sure that it works perfectly under all conceivable circumstances.

Time. Put the product into production or up for sale as soon as possible.

Cost. Build the product at the lowest reasonable cost. Cost includes money and opportunity cost. While you use a critical resource (a specially skilled person or a unique machine) on your project, that resource is not available to some other project.

We characterize this as a tradeoff because the project manager can gain more on one dimension by spending or sacrificing more on another. For example, you can have more features if you spend more time (and/or money) building the product.

If you want to understand a project manager's odd-seeming decision, try to understand how it affects each variable (features, reliability, calendar time until the product is released or put into production, and cost).

Let the project manager choose the project lifecycle.

A lifecycle model is a description of the product design and development process from the time someone first thinks about creating this product until it is released to the public and put into use.

We reject the idea of a single best choice for a software development lifecycle. Each model nails down some aspects of the project and leaves others open to revision. The lifecycle models differ in what they leave open.

Some companies follow a standard lifecycle model, but in our experience, there is always some room for customization by the project manager. The wise project manager picks the approach that controls the things he finds difficult to manage fluidly and leaves open the issues he has particular strength in. Every choice carries risks and consequences. The choice is not always convenient for the testing group, and it is not always the choice that you would make. To the extent that there is a choice, it belongs to the project manager.

In the next two lessons, we look at the waterfall and evolutionary lifecycles. The waterfall, so often advocated by testing consultants, doesn't always support our interests. The evolutionary model is often better for testers but can be harder on other members of the project team.

We are not suggesting that you should advocate for an evolutionary approach over the waterfall. We're not suggesting that you advocate for any lifecycle. We're pointing out that common lifecycle choices are very different from each other and that the choice of one over the other is not simple.

Waterfall lifecycles pit reliability against time.

The *waterfall model* describes a specific lifecycle approach to project management that proceeds through phases. The phases include

- Problem definition (what are we trying to build and why)
- Requirements definition
- Internal and external design
- Coding
- Testing
- Installation
- Post-installation support
- Lawsuits by disappointed customers
- Problem definition (for the next version of the product)

The model gets its name from its phase diagram, which looks like a waterfall to some people. The term *waterfall* describes the linear character of this approach. You move from one phase to the next, and it is hard to move back to the previous phase, just like water that won't move up a fall.

In practice, a certain amount of backtracking happens (we discover some errors or impossibilities in the stated requirements when we try to design a product that will satisfy them), but it is discouraged with change control.

A variation of the waterfall describes a broader role for testing. This is called the V-Model. At the end of each phase, testers formally evaluate the work product of that phase. For example, testers review (and, presumably, approve) the requirements documents at the end of the requirements definition phase. They also write a series of tests, which are to be performed when later phases are complete and the relevant parts of the system become operational.[1]

The waterfall (with or without the V) looks like a tidy process, but what happens on projects that don't deliver everything in their appropriate phase? What if the project falls significantly behind schedule?

---

[1]We have several other concerns with the V-model. The process of writing detailed tests before code delivery is risky. As the product's design changes, your tests become outdated. By the time the code is complete, many of the tests you wrote will describe aspects of the product that were never written or that were written in substantially different ways than originally envisioned. On many projects, all of this paperwork—even worse if there is test code and extensive test data—have contributed nothing. They were made obsolete before they provided any value. Advocates of V-like processes have told us that these work products from the testing group can be used by the programmers, to help them discover ambiguities and weaknesses in a proposed feature before coding it. We certainly agree that reviews of designs can improve the designs and prevent problems. But if that's the goal, we suggest that design inspections and code reviews might contribute a great deal more to the quality of the product, in a lot less time, than pre-writing tests that will never be run. And rather than waiting until the end of a phase, we suggest reviewing designs and code as they become available for review.

Most software projects *do* fall significantly behind their original schedule. We've seen advice from experienced people that boils down to "Well-managed projects won't have this problem." But software projects carry a substantial amount of risk. *There are always late changes.* Saying "this won't happen" is wishful thinking.

So what *does* happen if the project falls significantly behind schedule?

Under the waterfall, by the time you get the code, all the features have been designed, and most or all of them have been coded. Most of the software development money has been spent. The key tradeoff is between time and reliability. Fix the bugs and ship the product late, or ship it sooner with more bugs.

This is the classic fight between project managers and testers: Ship it buggy or ship it (or put it into production) late. In response, many testers ask for stricter adherence to the waterfall project management model. This is not a solution. The late-stage tradeoff between reliability and time is inherent in the waterfall. You won't break out of that box by strengthening the box's walls.

Think carefully before you advocate for a waterfall or a modified waterfall (V-model).

Evolutionary lifecycles pit features against time.

In the evolutionary approach to software development, the project team adds one feature at a time. They design the feature, code it, test it, and fix it. When the product, with this feature integrated into it, meets the group's quality standards, they add the next feature (Gilb 1997 and Beck 1999).

The development team can release this product at any time. (Release the latest version that passed testing.) The difference between today's version and next month's is that next month's will have more features. Both of them work. There is no end-of-project tradeoff between time and reliability.

This approach poses its own challenges. Imagine being the marketing manager or the technical writer. Go to the project manager and ask, "What features are in this product?" The answer, of course, is "That depends. When are we shipping it?" Anyone who must know what will be in the product at the time the product is released, will find the evolutionary approach challenging. Some people feel that the problem of an indeterminate set of features and the risks of feature creep are more easily managed under the waterfall than under an evolutionary approach.

Be willing to allocate resources to the project early in development.

It's getting to be accepted wisdom that testers should be involved earlier in the development cycle. However, test groups are typically understaffed and overworked. What is so compelling about the results that can be achieved early in development that it is worth pulling a tester off of the crisis du jour?

■ If all you do is send the tester to early project team meetings, you are probably wasting his time.

■ If the tester is not fluent in the programming language, sending him to code reviews is often a waste of time, or worse, an opportunity for him to demonstrate ignorance and lose the respect of the programmers.

There *can be* valuable activities for testers early in development. Here are a few examples:

■ They can review any requirements documents for understandability, testability, and ambiguity.

■ As other project artifacts (documents, code, and so on) develop, test them. Don't wait for the whole thing. Start working with an artifact when the author says (and you believe) that it is far enough along for a useful test or review.

■ Facilitate code reviews. Code reviews are a big payback quality improvement effort. Your staff can make it easier for the company to have these meetings (thus, make them more likely) by taking care of the logistics (book the room, bring the cookies) and administration (run the meeting, circulate the agreements lists). Your staff member learns a lot during the meeting but isn't expected to (and should not) comment on the document under review. To facilitate code reviews well, your staff will require training.

■ Prepare a preliminary list of hardware configurations and start arranging to buy or borrow the equipment.

■ Ask for testability features. These take design and programming time. If you don't get them into the budget and schedule, they won't get into the code.

■ Discuss the possibility of code coverage measurement and use of other development support tools (such as Purify or Bounds Checker). To use these tools well, you will need support (the time and attention of at least one member of the programming team). If the project doesn't budget for that time (probably a 1/2 time commitment for much of the time that the software is under test), you won't get it.

- Prepare for test automation. This preparation involves reaching agreements on the breadth of automation and automation support staffing level.

- Research your test tools. Order automation support software and equipment. Learn how to use them.

- Order externally developed test suites, if any exist for your type of software. More generally, look for software that can serve as an oracle, in order to facilitate high-volume testing.

- Learn about the product's market and competition. Become an experienced user of at least two applications (other than yours) in this market.

Contract-driven development is different from market-seeking development.

When a company does software development under contract, the contract specifies the responsibilities of the parties. The contract might specify a set of features, how the program is to be coded, tested, documented, and supported. Your company's primary responsibility is to fulfill its obligations under the contract. If you build what is specified in the contract, your customer has to pay for it. (By customer, we mean the person or company paying for the software.) As the product evolves, the customer will probably change her mind about some aspects of the product. Many projects put controls on those changes because they affect the cost of the project. (Additionally, the change control process can be used to weaken the negotiating position of the customer.)

Much of the advice in software engineering texts applies well to large custom software development projects done under contract.

Market-seeking development is different. Customers don't buy your product until after your company has built it. Throughout development, your key concern is whether the product you release will sell to your target market. If a competitor releases a more appealing product, releases it faster, or does a better job in marketing, the fact that yours conforms perfectly to its specifications is irrelevant. Marketers and salespeople will ask for design changes throughout development, based on the ongoing flow of information they get about customers, competitors, and the expectations of the press.

In a contract-driven project, your primary activity might be to test the software against a set of specifications. In a market-seeking project, you are more likely to be concerned with discovering and testing the product against the expectations of different customers.

Lesson 169 Ask for testability features.

If you are the person who will lead the testing effort for a product, you are probably the first tester involved in the project. The sooner you request testability features, the more likely it is that the programmers and project managers will agree to budget and schedule for them. If they aren't budgeted and scheduled into the project plan, you probably won't get them.

In general, it's up to you to educate the project team about your team's needs and about the types of information and support that will make your team more efficient and more effective.

We discuss ideas for testability in more detail in Lesson 137, "Testability is visibility and control."

Lesson 170 Negotiate the schedules for builds.

Your processes should be compatible with the pace of software revisions. Does your company make new builds once a month? Once a week? Once a day? Three times per day?

You might not be able to manage builds that come to you too quickly. It takes time to qualify the build (verify that it passes basic tests) and then update everyone's computers. If builds come every day, you might test one build for a few days before updating.

Some programmers demand that you only report bugs against today's build. Anything reported against yesterday, they say, is of little value because they might have found and fixed that bug already. This is certainly convenient for them, but it can be a nightmare for you because you have to stop everything, every day to update your computer, and then replicate with the new build anything that you're half-way through before you can move forward on the work you were doing yesterday. A task that should take a full day might split across two or three days when all of the administrative time and distractions are added.

The only solution we know is to negotiate the schedule for builds. This includes agreements on how often you'll accept new software, how a new build will be qualified as fit for testing, and how bugs found in recent builds will be recreated in the current build.

Understand what programmers do (and don't do) before delivering builds.

Some programming groups do extensive unit testing before releasing a new build to testers. Others don't. Some programming groups do a smoke test as part of their build process. Others don't.

The programming group that you work with does what it does. Don't assume that they have or have not done certain types of tests or taken a certain level of care in preparing a build for you. Find out their process and base what you do on your knowledge of what they do.

Be prepared for the build.

It's important to have your test environments ready when the builds are ready. This is especially true in the Web space. In a fast-paced project, a test group without a well-managed test environment is useless.

Sometimes you should refuse to test a build.

Occasionally, you will reject a build and refuse to test it. There can be sound technical reasons for doing this:

- If the importance of this build is that it adds a critical feature, and you discover that the feature isn't present in the build or fails immediately, further testing is a waste of time.

- If key features that used to work are now badly broken, the build was probably made with the wrong files, or with files that will be swapped out quickly. Bugs that you report in this build will probably be ignored. ("Oh yeah, that was the bug with the bad blahblah file. Anything could have been polluted by that crazy file. Can you get that bug again now?") Your smoke test should catch this level of failure. Rejection of the build is typically automatic when a smoke test fails.

■ If you just received a build, but you know that another build is coming in a few hours, which won't be affected in any way by what you find in this build, depending on the cost to qualify and install a build, you might be better off ignoring this build and continuing to test on the old one while waiting for the next one.

The general principle is that you should refuse to test a build if it will make your work substantially less efficient without discernible benefit or if your work on this build will be ignored.

Use smoke tests to qualify a build.

A smoke test (a.k.a. sanity check or acceptance into testing) is a test suite whose goal is to check the basic functionality of the build. If the build fails the test, the build is declared so unstable that it is not worth testing.

Typically, when a new build is submitted to testing, one tester runs the smoke test (which might be an automated test, a manual test, or a combination of the two). The other testers ignore the new build until it passes smoke testing. It is common to have a standard, core series of tests in a smoke test and a few transitory tests (tests that will be retired in a few builds) that focus on bugs or features that are of special interest in this build.

The smoke test process is a public one. In companies that do this well, the programmers are welcome to copies of all documents that describe the tests and of all automated test code that runs the smoke tests. In some of these companies, the programmers run the smoke test as an automatic part of the build process. Everyone understands that if the program fails the test, it's rejected from testing. The process is without surprises. Under these circumstances, smoke testing is seen as a technical task rather than a political task, and most people on the project (including most or all managers) see it as reasonable.

Sometimes, the right decision is to stop the test and fix cycle and redesign the software.

If you keep finding bugs in the same area no matter how many bug fixes seem to be applied or keep finding the same user task confusing no matter how many little changes to the UI are made, it is probably time to stop testing and debugging in this area. The area probably needs a redesign and a rewrite.

As test manager, you can suggest this action to the project manager. You are in a good position to use the bug-tracking system to show the statistics (many reports, many repairs, many new failures) to back up your suggestion.

We suggest that you make this presentation or recommendation to the project manager privately and that you accept the real possibility that you might not convince the project manager to take the action you recommend. The project manager manages the project. You provide services to him, including good advice, but he gets to make his mistakes. His good decisions might initially look to you like mistakes.

As everywhere else in this book, corporate culture plays a role here. Some companies expect you to present these recommendations and their associated data publicly. Our primary suggestion applies to the tone of your suggestion at these companies: You are identifying a concern and making a suggestion, which the project manager can accept or reject.

Adapt your processes to the development practices that are actually in use.

A consultant, speaking at a recent software testing conference, advised the audience that testers should refuse to test a product unless the programmers provide them with thorough specifications. This is terrible advice.

Advice like this is dismayingly common and has been common for at least 20 years. We think it is more likely to blow the test manager's credibility, or get her fired, than to achieve any improvement in the company's processes.

Let's note and then set aside the religious question: Are documentation-heavy approaches that resist late changes (like the waterfall) *really* the only ones that qualify as "good engineering?" That's the assumption (often stated explicitly) behind this type of advice.

In our view, the key questions raised by this type of refusal are

- Should your test group design your practices in a way that requires your company's programmers to do things that they don't, won't, and currently don't have to do?
- Is this realistic?

- Since when have you become the project manager or the vice president of development? If you want to run the project, become the person who is chartered to run the project.

We suggest that you work with programmers as they are. Salespeople and drive-by consultants, who have no stake in your success and face no consequences from your failures, are poor authorities on the proper responsibilities of programmers in your company.

"Project documents are interesting fictions: Useful, but never sufficient."

— Brian Marick

Even in a project that attempts to fully specify the product, the development documents (such as specifications and requirements documents) will leave a great deal to the imagination. Don't fight this truth; it's fundamental.

Consider error handling. We've seen estimates that more than 80 percent of the code of a modern software project deals with error handling and less than 20 percent deals with primary flows. Yet even supposedly thorough specifications dedicate less than 20 percent of their space to error handling. That means that 80 percent of the code is designed by programmers as they write it.

Do ask for specific additional information to fill in the gaps when you work with a specification. *Don't* design your tests or plan your project on the assumption that what is on paper is complete, comprehensive, or accurate.

Don't ask for items unless you will use them.

Testers love to say, "There isn't a specification; how can I test without a specification?" If you demand a specification, use it. Make sure the project manager and the specification writers know you are using it and know how you are using it. Otherwise, in the future, they will refuse to give you anything that is inconvenient for them to give you. They'll say, "Why should I give you this? You made me waste all that time writing a spec for you, and you never used it."

Take advantage of other sources of information.

You aren't helpless if no one gives you a specification. Plenty of other sources of information can help you steer your thinking.

For example, ask marketing or development staff for use cases. These can be used to direct session-based testing, and they may reveal serious design errors faster than systematically tromping through the feature list.

Here are some other sources of useful information that you can use for points not covered by specifications:

- User manual draft (and previous version's manual)
- Product marketing literature
- Marketing presentations, selling the concept of the product to management
- Software change memos that come with each new internal version of the program
- Internal memos (*e. g.* project manager to engineers, describing the feature definitions)
- Published style guide and user interface standards (such as guides published by Apple computer and Microsoft)
- Published standards (such as C-language)
- Third-party product compatibility test suites
- Published regulations
- Bug reports (responses to them)
- Results of reverse engineering of the program
- Interviews of people, such as the development lead, tech writer, customer service and technical support, subject matter experts, and the project manager
- Header files, source code, database table definitions
- Specs and bug lists for all third-party tools that you use
- Prototypes and lab notes on the prototypes
- Interviews with the development staff from the last version
- Customer call records from the previous version (What bugs were found in the field?)

- Usability test results

- Beta test results

- Ziff-Davis SOS CD and other tech support CDs, for bugs in your product and common bugs in your niche or on your platform

- BugNet and other Web sites that describe common bugs, www.bugnet.com, www.cnet.com, and links from www.winfiles.com, mailing lists, new groups, Web discussion sites, and so forth, that discuss bugs and irritants in your product localization guide (probably one that is published, for localizing products on your platform)

- Compatible products (understand their features, bugs, and design, then see how your product compares). See listserv's, NEWS, BugNet, and so on.

- Exact comparisons with products you emulate

- Content reference materials (such as an atlas to check your online geography program)

Flag configuration management problems to the project manager.

What is the probability that a bug fix will break something else in the product or that a bug that was fixed will come back? The probabilities of side effects vary widely across companies and projects. We've seen projects in which there were almost no side effects, and we've seen projects that were plagued with them.

Side effects are likely if the code is old, heavily patched, heavily interdependent (high data coupling and/or code coupling), and poorly documented. But even relatively clean code suffers side effect problems sometimes. One of the common root causes is weak configuration management.

If bugs that were fixed come back, get fixed, come back, and get fixed time after time, you are probably looking at a source control problem. Either the programming group can fix this, or you will constantly have to retest code that was working in the last build.

Sometimes, the problem is not in configuration management. To illustrate this point, Rex Black told us about a "test subproject with hundreds of bugs across a four month period where the average bug was re-opened two-and-a-half times." He said "This wasn't a CM problem, it was a sloppy fix problem brought on by impossible scheduling."

In either case, talk with the project manager about this problem and ask for advice.

If the problem won't go away, flag the need for high levels of regression testing (and the work you are spending to achieve this) in your status reports. To the extent that this appears likely to be a recurring problem in your company, budget future projects to allow for extensive automated regression testing.

Programmers are like tornadoes.

A test tool salesman tried to convince a company to create user interface level test scripts by using a capture and replay approach. They told the salesman this wouldn't work, because the programmers could be expected to make late changes to the software's user interface and feature set. He responded that the testers should push the programmers to do *real engineering*. Real engineering, he said, means freezing the user interface and feature set relatively early in the project. Then the testers could do their jobs.

The primary value of a pitch like this is that it helps you recognize that this salesman (and his company) is someone you don't want to do business with. Like the bad advice mentioned before (refuse to test unless they give you a specification, Lesson 173), it is unreasonable to predicate your methods on things that the programming group in your company won't do.

In the Midwestern United States, houses have basements. Historically, the basement was, among other things, a place where you took shelter if there was a tornado. Of course, you don't *have to* go to the expense of building a basement. Maybe you should skip the basement and declare that the weather shall not include any tornadoes. *However, that declaration might not do much good, especially when the next tornado comes through.*

Programmers are like tornadoes. Think of them as forces of nature. They will do what they do. What programmers will do will vary from company to company, as it should. Design your practices accordingly.

Great test planning makes late changes easy.

If late changes are inevitable, then our task is to design testing processes that work well with late changes. Here are a few suggestions:

- Rather than developing a large suite of tests in advance of testing, develop tests as you need them. If later changes to the product obsolete these tests, at least they will have been useful for a while.

- Don't create enormous test documents that have high maintenance costs, such as detailed manual test scripts. Keep your paperwork as lean as possible.

- Don't tie manual or automated tests to specifics of the user interface, other than tests specifically intended for the user interface (UI). Even if you do end-to-end testing, which is necessarily through the user interface, don't tie your test to the fine details of the UI, because they will change.

- Design automated tests in ways that maximize their maintainability and their portability across platforms. (See Chapter 5, "Automating Testing.")

- Build a set of generic tests that handle situations that recur in program after program. This saves you planning time and eases delegation when a new feature is added or a feature is changed late in the project.

- Build a strong set of smoke tests, to detect basic failures in the software under test quickly. If the programmers are making significant changes, they are probably rebuilding software frequently and would probably be glad to send you new builds quickly, integrating the changes a few at a time and getting the changes into your hands as soon as possible. The smoke tests disqualify bad builds at a low cost, making it easier for you to cope with frequent (such as daily) builds.

- Seriously consider using Extreme Programming methods to develop automated tests (Beck 1999 and Jeffries et al. 2000). In particular, we recommend building an overall architecture and design for the automated test series and then designing and delivering code iteratively, delivering solutions in an order that minimizes project risk (the project here is the testing subproject), programming in pairs, and working closely with your stakeholders (other testers, programmers, and the project manager) to determine what needs to be done next.

- Develop a model of the users of the product and the benefits they will want to achieve from it. Derive complex tests from this model. Most of these tests will not change rapidly as the project progresses, because they are focused on benefits rather than implementation details.

- Help the programmers develop a large suite of unit tests and other tests of relatively simple functionality. These can be run every time the code is rebuilt, before it is sent to testing.

The suggestions are not as important as the general principle. Analyze your testing practices and your situation. Determine what costs and inefficiencies you face when late changes are made to the software. Then find ways to change your processes to reduce those costs or spread them throughout the development period, rather than having them appear at the end.

Test opportunities arise whenever one person hands off an artifact to another.

Programs aren't written all at once, they are written function by function and feature by feature. Similarly for specifications, requirements documents, and manuals: They are written section by section, chapter by chapter. An opportunity for testing arises any time that any part of the product is ready for review. This is the way to involve testing throughout the development of the product. Test what is ready to test, as soon as it is ready to test.

There is no universal formula for knowing how much testing is enough.

We wish there was a way to know for sure that we have done enough testing. In fact, many such formulas have been proposed. We think there are important problems with all of them. Furthermore, we think it's better to live with uncertainty about testing than to embrace false certainty. A good decision about how much testing is enough is necessarily based on your skill and judgment, as you consider the factors that bear upon that issue.

So don't worry about finding a formula. Worry about using your head.

"Enough testing" means "enough information for my clients to make good decisions."

Because testing is an information-gathering process, you can stop when you've gathered enough information. You could stop after you've found every bug, but it would take infinite testing to know that you've found every bug, so that won't work. Instead, you should stop when you reasonably believe that the probability is low that the product still has important undiscovered problems.

Several factors are involved in deciding that testing is good enough (low enough chance of undiscovered significant bugs):

- You are aware of the kinds of problems that would be important to find, if they existed.

- You are aware of how different parts of the product could exhibit important problems.

- You have examined the product to a degree and in a manner commensurate with these risks.

- Your test strategy was reasonably diversified, to guard against tunnel vision.

- You used every resource available for testing.

- You met every testing process standard that your clients would expect you to meet.

- You expressed your test strategy, test results, and quality assessments as clearly as you could.

If you do this skillfully and faithfully, any bad bug that arises after release will probably be for one of three reasons:

- You didn't understand the risk dynamics as well as you thought. Now you know better.

- You made a mistake in the testing. You'll do better next time.

- Your risk assessment was correct. But management elected to take the risk. Stuff happens.

Your ability to know what information is enough will improve as you gain experience with a product line. It's not a sin in testing to miss a bug. It's only a sin to be careless, thoughtless, or not to learn from your experience.

Lesson 186

Never budget for just two testing cycles.

Some test labs budget for two testing cycles. The first cycle, they say, will expose all the bugs. The second cycle will check all the bug fixes. As long as they don't add new tests, the product doesn't change in any way other than those bug fixes, and those fixes are all perfect, everything will work out just fine. Back in the real world, you will probably have to test the product much more than twice:

- As you learn more about the product (you know more the second time through than the first), you will think of new and better tests and find new bugs. If you work from a two-cycle model, you have strong disincentives to creating new tests in the second cycle of testing.

- Even if all the programmers attempted to fix all of the bugs found in the first cycle of testing, the probability that they will fix all of them and not create any new ones is tiny (unless only one or two bugs were found).

- Commonly, you'll find that some tests can't even be run the first time through because of defects that prevent you from even attempting to run them. These are blocking defects. The blocked tests won't get their first valid run until later. What if they find bugs then?

Time after time, we have seen projects budget for two cycles of testing and then fall behind. Because the initial expectation was unrealistic, the schedule changes were inevitable, but every change was treated as a failure and a delay by the test group.

To create a schedule for a set of tasks, estimate the amount of time needed for each task.

Your work will consist of a large number of tasks. Make a list. (See Kaner 1996b and any project management book that covers work breakdown structure estimation.) Some tasks you can only know in general terms; others you can break down fairly finely. To the extent that you can, create separate items for anything that takes longer than a day. Estimate (guess) how long each task will take; add them up; add 25 percent (or more or less, depending on your company) for meetings, training, and other nonproject work; and use this as your estimate for the total time required.

This method sounds easier than it is. Making a list of the tasks is nontrivial because it is so easy to omit tasks or to underestimate their scope.

Try some other estimation methods to develop converging estimates:

- If you've done other projects like this, estimate how long this one will take based on how long they took.

- If you have a sense of the length and complexity of the program and a model based on data in your current company that relates length and complexity to duration of testing, apply the model to derive an estimate.

- If you have a sense of the key risks associated with the project, estimate what it would take (time and tasks) to test for those particular risks and to lightly test the product as a whole.

- Some other factors will affect your estimates. For example, if you know that the programmers are particularly skilled in this type of application, their code will probably require less testing. If these individual programmers make more bugs than usual, the project probably will require more testing. If user documentation has already been written or if clear and detailed input from users is available, the testing will probably be quicker and easier.

You can make guesses about testing staff size at any point in the project, using methods like these. The later in the project (the more information available to you), the better your estimates should be.

The person who will do the work should tell you how long a task will take.

Managers routinely underestimate the tasks they delegate to others. If you want an estimate that makes sense, get it from the person who has to live with it and hold him accountable to it. If that tester's estimate is much longer than your estimate, don't start by trying to get him to change his estimate. Instead, try to understand what he sees as the scope of the task, what else he is doing, and what other factors lead him to the seemingly high number. This might be a great opportunity to help your tester work smarter. Maybe you can redefine the task for him, or maybe you have to revise your estimate. Bullying him to change his estimate will achieve a smaller estimate, but the task will still take just as long. Your schedule will catch up to reality later.

Having said that, we thought you might want to read a thoughtful response by Pat McGee.

> "The person who will do the work should tell you how long . . ." I don't like this practice much. I think that many people don't pay enough attention to how they do things that they can give reasonable estimates. I've seen situations where a programmer estimated it would take 2 weeks to do something, and the manager said it shouldn't take more than 2 days, and it really took only 1.5 days. It passed review on the first attempt, too. But, I've also seen cases where something like that happened, and it really took much longer. I think that the right person to make an estimate is the person who has paid the most attention to how long things take. Sometimes that's the manager. Sometimes it's the worker. Sometimes it's neither. Regardless, I think your original statement is oversimplified to the point of being useless.

The distinction between our approaches is that Pat takes the estimate from the person with the best knowledge. We take it from the person who will face consequences if the estimate is wrong (and who thus has an incentive to get the best estimate). Both approaches seem reasonable to us, and much better than the more common method of *estimation by wishful thinking*.

There is no right ratio of testers to other developers.

People often ask us what is the right ratio of testers to other developers. We think this is the wrong question (Kaner et al. 2000 and Hendrickson 2001a).

First of all, two people can mean very different things when they say they have a one-to-one ratio. Therefore, companies differ in who they count, when they start counting, and what tasks count when they start making tester-to-others comparison. This makes ratios incomparable across companies.

Second, the ratio focuses attention on itself, rather than on the work being done. Suppose that on the last project, the programmers spent 16 person-months designing and writing code, and the testers spent 24 person-months finding bugs. The ratio (24-to-16 or 3-to-2) is accurate but uninformative. Change the proportion of new code to third-party code, the amount of code that can be reused from previous projects, the balance of troubleshooting responsibilities in bug reports so that testers do more (or less) troubleshooting this time than last time, or many other variables, and the ratio from the last project is wrong for this one. Rather than talk about ratios at all, talk about what work you have to do and how many people it will take to do it.

Trade tasks or transfer people from tasks that they are failing at.

A tester who is brilliant at testing for data quality might be overwhelmed when he tries to plan for efficient testing of the product across a wide range of configurations. Different testers have different strengths. Encourage a tester to take risks and stretch, and provide her with a mentor for this type of work if you can, but watch the tester's progress. If a tester is exceptionally slow at the task or continues to write ineffective bug reports, the job is inappropriate (too hard, too technical in an area in which he is not knowledgeable, too boring, or involving a personal conflict with the developer). Don't keep testers on tasks that are inappropriate. In the ideal case, you can find another tester who would like to take on this task in return for giving up a different task of hers. Opportunities for task trading are often there, if you look for them.

Lesson 191

Rotate testers across features.

Don't keep a tester working on the same cluster of features from the start of testing a project to the end. First, this is boring to most testers. Second, over time, you specialize that tester so much that he becomes less valuable to you than a less experienced generalist. Third, if your specialist leaves, you'll have a huge knowledge hole in your group. Fourth, and most important, two testers will analyze the same feature in different ways. They will start out with different theories of error, create different tests, and find different defects. When one tester starts feeling confident about the quality of an important area of the program, move that tester out of that area. The new tester that you assign to the area will find defects that the previous tester never thought to check for.

Fran McKain suggests evaluation of your context:

> Some caution here. Some feature clusters are large enough that it takes a long time to know the area well enough to be effective in testing it. Rotating too soon just keeps the testers operating at a consistent low level of contribution.

We agree with the importance of specialization, but we wonder how to manage the risks created by it. Perhaps one way to mitigate the risks is to test in pairs, pairing the specialist with other testers in your group.

Lesson 192

Try testing in pairs.

A pair of testers, working together, can often do as well as (or better than) a skilled bug hunter. Pairs might be stable (two people regularly work together) or pairing might be much more fluid, as in *extreme programming*. In that case, the tester who is responsible for a given area will seek out short-term partners who have useful skills or knowledge for attacking some part of that area.

Pair testing is different from many other kinds of pair work because testing is an *idea generation activity*, rather than a plan implementation activity. Testing is a heuristic search of an open-ended and multidimensional space. Pairing has the effect of encouraging each tester to explain and react to ideas. When one tester must phrase his thoughts to another tester, that simple process of phrasing seems to bring the ideas into better focus and naturally triggers more ideas. If faithfully performed, we believe this process will result in more and better ideas that inform the tests.

We strongly encourage testing pairs to agree on a charter before they start a testing session. To create a charter, they might spend 5–10 minutes away from the computer (perhaps at a flipchart) thinking of the direction that they want to follow for the next hour or two. They might focus, for example, on risks to investigate, predicted bugs to find, features to test, or tools to use. This is an overall guide, not a detailed list of test cases. Testers are free to break away from the charter, to explore a new opportunity (for example, to track down suspicious behavior that they just noticed but that involves a different feature). However, when they pause after following that lead, they should look to their charter to help them decide what to do next. Without a charter, we expect that pairs will sometimes lose focus.

We also believe that pair testing helps both testers stay focused on the task, makes it easier for them to replicate and analyze bugs, and makes it easier for one tester to stay on a roll while the other fields interruptions or runs off to grab some needed thing. We also suspect that others will be less likely to interrupt them with minor issues. It's also more fun.

We suspect that it is at least as efficient to have testers working in pairs as having them work alone. They get more done in less time. This is a new area. *Try testing in pairs.* See how it works in your company. You might do it for some classes of tasks, or with some people, but not others.

Assign a bug hunter to the project.

A bug hunter is an experienced, enthusiastic exploratory tester. Here are some of the ways we use bug hunters:

- Do initial exploratory testing of a suspect area, to develop ideas for more detailed attacks that can be performed by less experienced testers.

- Explore an area that is allegedly low risk—can he quickly find bugs that would lead to reassessment of the risk?

- Troubleshoot key areas that seem prone to irreproducible bugs.

- Find critical bugs that will convince the project manager to slip a (premature) release date.

Charter testing sessions, especially exploratory testing sessions.

Before sitting at a computer, a tester (or a pair of testers) should have a clear idea of what he's up to, what he intends to do for the next 60–90 minutes. We call this the *session charter*. We're still experimenting with this approach, but it seems to work well.

The advantage of the charter is that it helps the tester focus and to avoid getting lost in an unproductive distraction. The tester isn't chained to the charter. If he sees something suspicious or has a brilliant idea, he is free to follow it up. But when he takes a breather, he checks in with his session charter and returns to it if nothing is much more attractive or more pressing.

We think it is particularly valuable to come up with an explicit charter when two testers are working together as a pair.

To come up with the charter, the tester might operate from a detailed project outline and pick a task that will take a day or less, or he might (instead or also) create a flipchart page that outlines this session's work or the work for the next few sessions.

A charter for a session might include what to test, what tools to use, what testing tactics to use, what risks are involved, what bugs to look for, what documents to examine, what outputs are desired, and so on.

Test in sessions.

A session is a protected block of time, between 60 and 90 minutes. During a session, the tester is doing focused testing. If you're the test manager, you protect the integrity of the session—in effect hanging a big "Do Not Disturb" sign on the tester's cube that everyone (including you) should respect unless a serious problem must be addressed urgently.

Testers who don't find ways to protect their time often have to work in short bursts because they are so frequently interrupted for questions and meetings.

Use activity logs to reveal the interruptions that plague testers' work.

If you don't think you need to defend your testing time from constant interruptions, keep an activity log for a week or two. In the log, list every phone call (and the time you took it), every burst of reading email and responding to email, every meeting, and every time someone poked their head into your cube with a question, a joke, or a hand grenade. What was the longest uninterrupted block of time that you were actually able to devote to planning or doing testing? Did you get *any* reasonable blocks of time during normal working hours, or do you have to come to work very early or stay late to find uninterrupted time? (For more discussion of time fragmentation, see Weinberg 1992, 284.)

If you're a test manager, working with a tester who appears to have a productivity problem, or who seems to be putting in excessive overtime in order to keep up with his task load, an activity log is a useful way to help the tester (and help you understand what you have to do to help the tester) focus and prioritize his work. We do not suggest that you use this as a disciplinary tool or as a formal performance evaluation tool. For that stuff, go to your Human Resources department for company-specific advice. What we are suggesting is that sometimes people get overwhelmed. If you are the manager of someone who seems overwhelmed, we hope that you will look for some coaching tools, things you can do to help the person focus on the tasks at hand, use time effectively, and clear off tasks that cannot be done. The activity log is one of those tools.

Lesson 197 Regular status reports are powerful tools.

The true power of a testing group is communicative, not administrative. You *persuade* people to give you the resources you need, to do the work you want them to do, and to reconsider releasing unsatisfactory products to customers.

Status reports are useful tools for getting across your message. Here are some tips for maximizing their power:

- Always write in a neutral, factual tone. Refrain from exclamation marks, all caps, and humor.

- Avoid singling out individuals. Talk about deliverables, bugs, and deadlines but focus on the thing, not on the person associated with the thing.

- Adopt a standard format, common to all projects. Don't set yourself up for complaints by a project manager (whose project is in trouble) that you are treating his project in a special way because you don't like him.

- Circulate the report on a standard schedule. Through some early parts of the project, that schedule might be once every two weeks. Later, the schedule may be once per week. Near the end, the schedule may be daily. Put all projects on equivalent schedules.

- Pick your content carefully. Keep the reports concise—pack them with lots of information in few pages.

- Circulate the report beyond the project team. Send it to the project manager's boss and perhaps to the boss's boss. Send it to all of the stakeholder groups in the company. The project manager might protest that you are circulating the report too widely. We suggest two responses: "We always circulate reports like this to these people," and "If this report is inappropriate for Ms. X, just get her to tell us that she doesn't want it. We'll be glad to stop sending it to her, on her request."[2]

There's nothing more dangerous than a vice president with statistics.

Lesson 198

When reporting status (or making other measurements), beware of what you count and with whom you share the data. Top managers, in particular, are prone to making decisions using data that they don't understand. By definition, a measurement is a thin slice of the whole picture. Any measurement that reduces the picture to a small set of numbers is a gross simplification. If you understand the context of a measurement, you have hope of using measurements productively. Top management often isn't presented with that context.

We encourage you to experiment with measurement. We use measurement to aid us in learning about how the project is going and how the quality of the product is coming together. Executives worry us because, in our experience, they use metrics not for learning but primarily to assert control over something they don't understand.

Does that mean you should never give numbers to executives? That's not a realistic option in many companies. But you can be cautious about what you provide, you can anticipate misunderstandings and flag problems upfront, and you can refuse to provide certain numbers. For example,

- Don't storm into some executive's office complaining that the average programmer takes 1.4 weeks to fix a bug, and Joe takes 5.3 weeks. After

---

[2]Several reviewers commented that in their company, this last tip could be dangerous and counterproductive. We understand that in some companies, information flow is more limited and that managers assert more right to control the flow of information. On the other hand, your effectiveness is limited if you cannot make the project stakeholders aware of the problems that you are discovering. Perhaps these suggestions will help:

- If you are just introducing the idea of testing status reporting to your project team, circulate the reports as widely as you reasonably dare, within the cultural context of your company. Use informal channels to let a broader group of people know of the existence of these reports and let them ask the project manager to include them on the distribution list. Eventually, if your reports are useful, you will build a broad list that you will reuse across many projects. At some point, the broad distribution becomes corporate practice. It is at this point that you can afford to say to the project manager, "We always circulate these reports to these people."

- If you provide services only to the project manager and have no broader responsibilities to the company, you don't have any reason to circulate your reports beyond the project manager. On the other hand, if you can be held accountable for not reporting key problems to other people in the company, you need an open channel for providing status reports to those people.

you volunteer individual performance data from the bug-tracking system, you'll be asked for a lot of it.

- When you send a memo that says the project is at least five weeks from shipping because of 200 open bugs, and the programmers only fix an average of 40 bugs per week, put a cautionary note near the number. You might point out that this number makes a useful point with large numbers of bugs, but when the number of open bugs is small, many other project factors have a bigger effect on the amount of time needed before release than the bug count.

- When asked for statistics about individuals (such as bugs per tester), say no. Explain, if asked, that as soon as you use the bug-tracking system for collecting human resources data, the character of the database changes. The bug reporting process will become more politicized, more adversarial, and less accurate.

Be cautious about measuring the project's progress in terms of bug counts.

Bug counts are a favorite scorecard for measuring project progress. Unfortunately, they are inadequate and often misleading.

Bug counts are useful for demonstrating that the project is far from its release date. If the project team can fix an average of 40 bugs a week, and 400 open bugs are supposed to be fixed before release, you can make a persuasive case that the product won't be ready to ship in the next month.

Bug counts are not useful for demonstrating that the project is close to release quality. If the open bug count is low near the desired end of the project, does this mean that the product is more stable, or that the test team is spending too much time writing reports, running regression tests (tests that rarely find new bugs), demonstrating the product at tradeshows, and doing other activities that aren't geared toward finding new bugs? We can't tell this from the bug counts.

We are particularly unimpressed with statistical models of bug arrival rates (how many bugs will be found per unit time) as vehicles for managing projects because we see no reason to believe that the assumptions underlying the probability models have any correspondence to the realities of the project. Simmonds (2000) provides a clear, explicit statement of the assumptions of one such model.

Hoffman (2000) gives some excellent examples of measurement fiascos involving such measures. See also Austin (1996) and Kaner (2000a).

The more independent coverage measures you use, the more you know.

You can measure how much of the product has been tested in many dimensions: bugs, requirements, code, configurations, change history, developer, tester, data, and so forth. No single measurement dimension is sufficient.

For example, one commonly recommended measure is the percentage of lines of code (lines plus branches or others of the several variations of this) that have been executed during testing.

As with bug counts, the lines-of-code measure is useful for showing how far away you are from adequacy or completeness. If you have only tested 10 percent of the lines of code, you should not have much confidence in the software's reliability. As you get near 100 percent line coverage, that doesn't tell you the product is near release. It just tells you that the product is no longer obviously far from release according to this measure. (See Marick 1999 for additional commentary on this measure.)

Suppose that you are developing a product for the mass market. You decide to test it on a dozen different variations of Windows, running under another dozen browser versions, using 10 different connections (modems at different speeds, Ethernet, etc.), and so on for several other configuration variables. You might boil this down to 100 standard configurations that the program must be compatible with, testing against all 100.

- After you've tested the product on the first few configurations, running your config tests against the others might not execute a single additional line of code or take the program down a single additional branch. If we think that lines of code is a measure of how close we are to being done, this should tell us to stop doing configuration testing. That decision would probably be disastrous for a mass-market product.

- If 100 standard configurations exist and you have tested 30 of them, you have a coverage measure that is independent of lines of code but still very important. You are at 30 percent complete for configuration testing.

A coverage measure involves a population of possible tests of a given type, a subset of that population that you intend to run, and another subset that you have actually run. You can measure coverage as the number of tests executed compared to how many you planned to execute or as the number of tests executed compared to the total population of interest. Either percentage might be useful. Neither of them measure anything more than your progress along one dimension, whether that is lines executed, configurations tried, data flows checked, classic risks checked (think of division by zero—the bug lies in the absence of code to prevent this division; such absences are invisible to line counters), or some other dimension. You could conceive of hundreds of possible dimensions, one for each class of possible failure (Kaner 1995a and 2000a).[3]

Lesson 201 — Use a balanced scorecard to report status on multiple dimensions.

Balanced scorecards are often used to measure the health of a business (Kaplan and Norton 1996, but see Austin 1996). Simpler metrics are inadequate.

- For example, if you focus on quarterly profits, you are likely to encourage behavior to maximize quarterly profits. Over the short term, you could boost quarterly profit by firing your research and development (R & D) staff. The company would make big profits for two years and then go bankrupt because it has nothing new to sell.

- Instead, maybe you should count the number of new patents issued, but down that road lies excessive investment in research and not enough investment in making salable products.

Several different numbers seem informative about the business's status, but any of them, considered in isolation, is prone to damaging side effects. A key point of measurement is to encourage people to do better on the measured scores, and so people who want to do a good job will try to find ways to bring up the score. Their methods might not be the ones that the metric designer had in mind. For example, laying off research staff to boost short-term profits might not be within the expectation of the person pushing to improve quarterly profits. But it might be a good faith response to the demand to increase this number.

A possible solution to the problem of measurement side effects is to use several numbers that have counterbalancing side effects. For example, a

---

[3]Even this is an oversimplification. As one of our reviewers, Noel Nyman, explained, "This implies that all tests have a single unit value, which is probably not true. Just as bugs have different severities, tests have different value and different run times. We could have run 80% of our tests and have completed only 20% of the test hours we need. We may have run 80% of our tests and still have 50% of our most important tests remaining to be done. Any metric that ignores this to give some value of 'coverage complete' gives false information, usually false hope."

scorecard that reports short-term profits, patents issued, and staff turnover would quickly highlight R & D failures beside high short-term profits.

A scorecard that is well balanced might be a valid measure of the health of the business, even though none of its components, considered alone, would be valid or safe.

We think that the same reasoning applies to project progress and testing progress. You can think of progress (or lack of progress) reporting along several different dimensions, such as

- How much of the product has been tested?

- How much of the planned testing has been done?

- How many problems have been found, and how many of those are still outstanding?

- How much confidence do we have in the quality of the testing (for example, we should have low confidence if beta testers are finding glaring errors missed by the testers)?

- How much testing work is being blocked because of unfixed defects or missing equipment or unmade decisions?

The best status reports we have seen use indicators of each of these types. The information they provide to management doesn't fit into a single, trivial number. But the pattern of information can be represented simply enough to guide decision-making.

Here's a suggested structure for a weekly status report.

Imagine the status report as a four-page document. The front page lists key issues, such as

- *Decisions needed.* (For example, how should we prioritize these features; what equipment are we testing; are we getting a new staff member or not?)

- *Bug fixes needed.* (Anything that interferes with your work has to be fixed on a high priority basis.)

- *Expected deliveries* (such as promised documents, equipment, functions, and tools) and the promised delivery dates. These go on the list a bit before they are due and stay on the list after they are overdue. Remove all delivered items. This is a list of what is missing, not a cumulative work list. Highlight anything that is holding up your work, such as access to a promised machine or the completion and delivery of a feature list.

- *Unexpected problems.* (For example, report loss of testing efficiency in an area because of staff turnover; a key tool doesn't work as expected; people need training; and so on.)

The second page describes your group's progress in completing your planned tasks. For example, you might list the areas of testing work on your schedule, how much you budgeted for each one (such as two weeks), how much you've accomplished on each one (such as 10 percent complete), and how much time you've spent on this work. In this example, if you've spent more than 10 percent of your budgeted two weeks, you are behind schedule for that area. Looking across the list, you convey an overall impression of progress (or lack of it) against a plan and schedule.

The third page provides the bug report statistics. We put bug numbers on an inside page for the same reason that newspapers put sports sections on the inside pages of a newspaper. The sports section is the most widely read part of the newspaper. If you put the bug numbers inside, you keep the front page for the news you think is important to report, and you can cram in advertising (other stuff you want to say) on the other pages.

The back page lists the bugs that have been deferred this week. The list probably includes only the bug number, the summary (or title) line, and the tester's rating of severity of the bug. The reader who wants more information can look it up.

A project dashboard is another useful way for showing status.

Lesson 203

The dashboard is a chart, drawn on a large whiteboard in a conference room open to anyone on the project team and anyone else with a stake in the project. It shows the status of the project at a glance. (See Bach 1999b for further discussion and illustration.)

The typical dashboard lists several areas of work, one area per row. Even a big whiteboard can't fit very many areas, if you want your words big enough to be readable. For each area, the whiteboard shows the current level of effort, the level of coverage planned for this area, the level of coverage achieved so far, and the tester's assessment of quality (on a scale of high, medium, and low). The board also allows room for the tester to make a few key comments to support the assessment.

The typical dashboard is updated weekly (early in the project) and then daily or even twice per day as the project draws near its end date. It has to be up-to-date enough for drive-by managers to want to look at it.

The details of project dashboards vary across companies. For example, some companies want other specific information (other columns) for each area or want a row or two to be variable, reserved for the status of the issue or feature of the week.

The exact layouts don't matter. The key point is to show the project's status at a glance.

Testing Dashboard				Updated: 2/21 Build: 38
Area	**Effort**	**C.**	**Q.**	**Comments**
file/edit	high	1	😊	
view	low	1+	😊	1345, 1363, 1401
insert	low	2	😊	
format	low	2+	😊	automation broken
tools	blocked	1	☹	crashes: 1406, 1407
slideshow	low	2	☹	animation memory leak
online help	blocked	0		new files not delivered
clipart	none	1	😊	need help to test…
converters	none	1	😊	need help to test…
install	start 3/17	0		
compatibility	start 3/17	0		lab time is scheduled
general GUI	low	3	😊	

Milestone reports are useful when milestones are well defined.

Some companies drive their projects by milestones and do a thorough status assessment at each milestone. Others don't.

If your company wants an assessment of the product at each milestone, you need to understand what you are assessing the product against. How does the company define the milestone? Which aspects of the milestone definition are you supposed to compare the product to? For example, if a milestone definition says that 50 percent of the functions have been coded, are you supposed to state whether this is true or not? How will you know this?

If your company does not have a standard definition of a milestone, you cannot defensibly say whether, for example, the product is ready for beta testing. Your judgment, in the absence of a company standard, is likely to create more political squabbling than insight.

If you are asked to assess progress relative to a milestone and there is no usable definition of the milestone, we suggest that you get the relevant managers to agree to a definition first and then provide the assessment against this definition. If they seek your advice on how to define a milestone, suggest that they think of the milestone as the completion of a project iteration. What are the exit criteria for this iteration? (Or, what are the entry criteria for the next one?) Lawrence and Johnson's (1998) work is very helpful for this, very detailed, and available at no charge.[4]

Don't sign-off to approve the release of a product.

Let the project manager or the project team decide when to release the product. Your job is to make sure that they have the best data available (the best data of the kinds that a tester can provide) for making that decision. Report your findings honestly, directly, with precision, and to every stakeholder. If they make a release decision that you wouldn't have made, that's their choice.

Do sign-off that you have tested a product to your satisfaction.

If someone insists that you sign a product release form (the form that authorizes the project manager to release the product to manufacturing or to put the software into production), make it clear that your signature means that you have tested adequately (in your opinion), that you have completed the agreed upon level of testing, or that your group did a fine job in the time available. You can make that clarification by memo (to the project manager or the project team) or by writing a short clarifying statement underneath your signature on the release forms.

---

[4]See www.coyotevalley.com/plc/builder.htm for a useful example of detailed definitions of several project milestones. We are not endorsing these as the "right" definitions, and we don't believe that Lawrence or Johnson think they are the "right" definitions. Instead, they illustrate the type of criteria that can be applied to define a milestone, and they are good starting points for a company that is in the process of creating its own definitions.

If you write a release report, describe your testing work and results, not your opinion of the product.

It is very difficult for a testing group to assess the overall quality of a product or its fitness for the market it will be sold into. You don't have the relevant data. You do have bug reports and your attempts to find bugs (tests that the product passed). Describe what you know.

List unfixed bugs in the final release report.

If you prepare (or help prepare) the final release report, you should include a list of the product's unfixed bugs. Also include the rejected design issues that you consider important in your list. Circulate this list in advance, so the final report contains no surprises.

A useful release report lists the 10 worst things critics might say.

If you're releasing software for resale, imagine writing a release report that lists the top 10 issues that might be raised by an unsympathetic magazine reviewer. If the problems are serious enough, your company's marketing communications (or other marketing staff) will hold the release. This might be the most useful quality assessment you can provide. (Note that this approach lets you maintain your position as a critic of the software, rather than attempting to provide a fair assessment of the software.)

CHAPTER 9

Managing the Testing Group

This chapter focuses on the challenges of managing the testing group. The difference between this chapter and Chapter 8, "Managing the Testing Project" is that Chapter 8 focuses on one project's issues. How do you work with the other members of the development team and the other stakeholders, to help get the right product out on time and within budget? In this chapter, we consider the group of people who work together on project after project, year after year.

Choosing among our personal favorite lessons was difficult because the three of us have plenty of management experience. We have run our own businesses, and we were tempted to write a very long, general-purpose discussion of the management of technical staff. Rather than do that, we suggest some references: Weinberg (1992, 1997a, 1997b, 1997c, 1998, and 2001), Humphrey (1997), Deming (1986), DeMarco (1997), DeMarco and Lister (1999), Brooks (1995), Constantine (1995), Black (1999), Drucker (1985), and Wiegers (1996). You can find some generic lessons here, especially involving recruiting. We included these because we get so many questions about hiring and job-seeking that we decided that no discussion of test group management would be complete without considering them.

Lesson 210

Mediocrity is a self-fulfilling prophecy.

- If you eliminate creativity by dehumanizing your processes;
- If your goal is to make your staff interchangeable cogs;

- If you standardize your staff's work, so that anyone can do exactly what they can do, in the same way that they do it;

- If you evaluate your staff using numbers that don't reflect their creativity, persuasiveness, judgment, or interpersonal sensitivity;

- If you alienate your staff from the results of their work, tell them that their job is to report bugs and someone else will decide what to fix without their further input, and prevent them from speaking up for their bugs at the bug triage meetings;

- Then don't expect them to show you their heart when the project most needs them;

- Don't expect them to speak up on matters of principle;

- Don't expect them to gladly work through the night when the project needs that extra push;

- Don't expect them to design brilliant tests for difficult but critical bugs;

- Don't expect them to lose sleep, searching for the words to explain a critical problem to a manager who just doesn't understand . . .

- *And* don't expect them to show you or your company loyalty when you need it the most.

If you declare there shall be no heroes in your company, you won't get any.[1]

Lesson 211 Treat your staff as executives.

Peter Drucker is often credited as the founder of modern management theory. In one of his excellent books, *The Effective Executive*, he teaches that an executive is anyone who manages the value of her own time and affects the ability of the organization to perform. Most knowledge workers are executives. Drucker points out that executives are always given more to do than they can possibly achieve. Effective ones pick a subset of tasks that they will do well and skip many other tasks entirely. Ineffective executives try to do everything, don't succeed, and don't do particularly well at much of what they did attempt. Different executives have different strengths and interests. Give two executives identical jobs (not tasks, but ongoing jobs), and they'll give very different performances.

Most testers are executives, within Drucker's meaning. Manage them on that basis. Don't supervise them as though they were factory workers, and don't

---

[1] For more on what we mean by heroes, read Sims and Manz (1996) and Lebow (1990).

spend your time trying to redesign their jobs into the equivalent of factory work. Instead, accept and manage around the fact that they have different strengths and interests.

In writing this, we're *not* just writing about senior testers. When we form or manage test groups, we hire a mix of experience levels and backgrounds. New testers require more supervisory attention. We expect to invest in training junior staff. But our intent is to create executives, and we show them respect as learning, thinking individuals from Day 1. We expect them to take on responsibilities quickly, to show enthusiasm, to establish their credibility, and to build their skills. If they want less demanding work, they can find it elsewhere.

Lesson 212 Read your staff's bug reports.

Some test managers or test supervisors read every bug report filed by their staff (easy for a test group of 7, much harder for a test group of 70). This helps you understand the situation of the product, the strengths and morale of your staff, and the communications and interpersonal issues affecting your staff.

For the purpose of evaluating the quality of the work of your staff, here are some of the questions you might ask about a tester's bug reports:

- Are the reports well written?
- Do they lay the problem out simply?
- Do they leave holes that cry out for follow-up testing?
- Do the tests that found the bugs seem routine or insightful?
- Was the bug difficult to find? Is the bug in a normally stable part of the application, and if so, does this reflect on the tenacity of the tester who reported the bug or on that tester's good luck?
- How is the tone of the report?
- Did the programmer understand it? What comments has the programmer made back on the report? Does it appear that the programmer and tester are cooperating or speaking past each other?

Lesson 213 Evaluate your staff as executives.

Bug counts are, at best, worthless measures of the effectiveness of your staff. They're misleading and demotivating, and they allow you to think you know a lot more than you know. At worst, they make the wrong people look good, and the best people look incompetent.

Bug counts survive as a measure because managers and executives protest that they need some way to evaluate the effectiveness of their staff, and they don't know what else to use besides bug counts. We don't have simple metrics to suggest, but we can suggest things you can do to appraise the work of a member of your staff:

- Read his bug reports.
- Read his code.
- Read his test documentation.
- Collect comments from the programmers and other stakeholders who work with him.

Consider the following:

- What fights does he get into and why?
- How well does he meet deadlines?
- How well does he keep his own promises?
- What kinds of problems does he miss?
- What types of assistance has he provided to other testers and programmers to make them more effective or more productive?
- Is he gaining new skills? How well is he transferring his skills to other testers?
- What issues has he taken stands on in your company? How do these reflect on his business judgment and personal ethics?

The information you get from this work will give you a rich picture of the work of your staff member and the situation of the projects he's working on. The information doesn't condense into a simple number, but you might be able to use it to build a report card. Imagine giving the tester a score from 0–5 on each area (bug reports, code, and so on). The resulting score card would show a pattern of strengths and weaknesses (as you perceive them). Multidimensional information, like this, will also help you develop a training and coaching plan with each member of your staff.

Many companies use self-evaluations as part of the formal performance evaluation and pay evaluation process. (In a self-evaluation, the employee fills out a form to evaluate his own performance.) These can be very useful, but some managers rely on them too much and don't take enough time to learn more about the actual work of the employee. Another concern we have is that formal evaluations are rare—every six months or every year. We encourage you to actively follow the work of your staff on an ongoing basis. (See Deming 1986, 102ff for further discussion.) Note that we're *not* suggesting micromanagement: Learning what your people do, and coaching them on the basis of that knowledge is very different from telling them when and how to do their work (Drucker 1985).

If you really want to know what's going on, test with your staff.

As a manager, you've probably heard time and again that "A good manager delegates." Certainly, you'll have to delegate most of your group's work, and you will probably not be able to play a major contributing role on any project. However, if you don't work on projects, you'll lose many of your technical skills over time, you will not see the real problems that your testers are coping with, and you will find it harder to judge the quality of your staff's work. Participation in the project may not be practical, but in assigning priorities to your own time, you might consider carefully the possibility that active participation in at least one project at a time is important enough to merit a high priority.

You'll lose credibility with your staff if you can't even install or run the software they're testing. We urge you to also reproduce several of the bugs being reported against the product. Give yourself enough background in the product that your staff can talk with you about it intelligently.

Don't expect people to handle multiple projects efficiently.

If you have more projects than testers, you'll be tempted to assign several projects to each tester. Beware of two problems:

- Some people will accept multiple assignments but in a given week (or month) they'll only work on one of those assignments. The other products languish in the background.

- The tester who works actively on all assigned projects fritters time away on administrative overhead. Ultimately, you get someone on several projects, going to lots of meetings, spending a lot of time catching up (reread his notes, check the latest bugs in the database, read reports on new features, reading lots of email, and so on) on each project, and getting very little done on any of them (DeMarco and Lister 1999).

Build your testing staff's domain expertise.

The effectiveness of your staff will sharply increase as they learn more about the external facts that constrain the design of the product, how people use (or will use) products like this one, what problems will matter to them, how the competition solves their problems, and what has been written about using this type of product.

You can build this expertise in several ways:

- Read magazines and books that were written for people like your customers.

- Go to classes (preferably, go to classes taught by people other than your company's employees) taught to customers on how to use products like the one under development.

- Go to classes that teach the underlying subject matter of the product. For example, if you sell a real estate program, study to become a real estate broker, a mortgage broker, or an appraiser.

- Work at your customers' sites. You might do this on a loaner basis (for example, maybe your company will lend you to an important customer for a few weeks during their installation and training on the software) or a part-time basis (make sure you have your company's permission).

- Sell your software or your competitor's software. For example, while working as a software development manager at a consumer software company, one of us, Kaner, learned more about his product's market by selling software at a leading retail store for six months of Saturdays. The publisher and the retailer both knew his goals and encouraged him in this work.

- Answer your company's technical support hotline calls for a few hours per week. Initially, you'll need coaching from a tech support staff member. Eventually, you'll get good at it, and you'll learn a lot (if you take the work seriously, ask questions, and research some of the complaints that you hear).

Build your testing staff's expertise in the relevant technology.

As our hardware and software environments get more complex, more of the problems with our applications will be interaction problems between our application and another application, a remote server, or some other software or hardware that is out of the application developer's immediate control. Nguyen (2000) introduces Web application testers to testing for these types of interaction problems. To be successful at it, you have to know a lot about the other hardware and software. (He provides useful introductory material.)

Additionally, your group will benefit if some of your staff understand the technology of the programmers. For example, it will be helpful if some members of your testing group know a lot about the component library used by the programmers and how to write programs to test the components through their APIs (application programmer interfaces).

Work actively on skills improvement.

You don't just say, "Today I will master cause-effect graphing." If a technique of bug hunting, bug reporting, or bug evaluation is worth learning, you'll probably have to learn several subtasks and practice them several times. It is difficult to improve your skills as technology changes, the competitive market changes, the development tools change, and products come at you from all sides. Even though it is not easy, you must do this work to stay up to date, and it is extremely helpful as a basis for contributing strong value to your company.

Review technical support logs.

To gain insight into the types of problems that will show up once this program is installed and supposed to be working, read through your company's customer complaint records (the phone records and the letters and emails sent to your company by your customers). Ask yourself what you could have done to make a given type of call less likely. Ask yourself what types of tests would be useful to uncover generic problems like this, if there are any, in the software under test.

Help new testers succeed.

When you bring someone into your group, take a few steps to make their first weeks successful:

■ Choose a place (office or cubicle) for the tester and set it up (with two computers and other hardware and software as needed, plus necessary company and project documentation) before he arrives.

- Plan to spend at least a day's worth of meetings with the new employee. Take him around the department, introduce him to everyone he'll work with, talk with him about your hopes and expectations for him.

- Assign the tester a mentor. The mentor shows the new tester around, is available to answer questions, looks at the work the tester is doing and makes suggestions, treats the tester to lunch a few times, and is generally helpful. The mentor has no supervisory authority over the tester and does not report anything about the new staff member to you unless a serious problem occurs. Some companies assign mentors from outside the new employee's department (a tester's mentor might be a programmer or a marketer, for example). The advantage of this is that it fosters communication between departments. The disadvantage is that the mentor might not be able to coach the tester on the technical details of his work.

Have new testers check the documentation against the software.

A *new tester* is someone who is new to this project. He may or may not be experienced in testing other software.

One way to familiarize a new tester with your product is to have him test the manual and the online help against the behavior of the software. By the end of this type of testing, he'll have seen all parts of the program.

It's a worthwhile task to thoroughly test the manual and the online help. Users go to these when they need authoritative information about the software and when they're having problems. Also, in a mass-market product, the documentation probably creates a warranty that the product will behave as described. This type of warranty, based on an actual written statement by the manufacturer, cannot be disclaimed (gotten rid of) by the type of boilerplate contracts used by software companies. Anything the documentation says can be used as evidence to support a claim that the product is defective (Kaner 1995b and Kaner and Pels 1998).

The tester should check every statement of fact (anything that can be proved true or false) with tests of the program. Also, the tester should test any inferences he thinks might reasonably be drawn from the documentation. This provides good training for the new tester and an opportunity to find important bugs (Pettichord 2001b).

Familiarize new testers with the product through positive testing.

After the tester has worked through the user documentation and come to understand what the product is supposed to do, have him try to use the product in simple, but real-life ways. Have him install the product from scratch, possibly on a new system. Have him list some of the things people would try to do with a product like this and then have him use the product to try to do simple versions of them.

The goal of this is to help the tester understand what is good about the product or the vision of the product. With that understanding, he'll be a more informed and more effective critic when he starts looking for failures rather than successes.

Have novice testers edit old bug reports before writing new ones.

A *novice tester* is new to testing, not just new to your project. He has to learn the basic skills of testing, not just how to test this product.

One way to coach a new tester is to have him retest old bugs and write up (for your inspection) an alternately worded report that would have been more effective. This probably involves rewording and follow-up testing (looking for more serious problems related to this one or looking for a broader range of circumstances under which the reported problem appears). Give the tester feedback on tone, clarity, and creativity in follow-up testing.

When you are satisfied that the new tester can write reasonable reports, let him write up new bugs. Until the tester earns your approval, perhaps you should not allow him to write new reports.

Have new testers retest old bugs before testing for new bugs.

A useful way to familiarize new testers with the bugs in the database is to have them retest old bugs. We use three classes of tasks. Each of these can help teach the tester about the product, how it can fail, how it can be tested, and what's in the database.

Replicate currently open bugs. For each bug tested, the tester reports that the bug can still be replicated. He notes with this report the date, the current build ID for the software, and the hardware and software configuration he tested with. Alternatively, the tester might report that the bug is not reproducible and give the same date, build, and configuration information.

Retest fixed bugs. For selected bugs, the tester checks whether bugs that were once fixed have since been broken. These bugs are probably closed. In most companies, no entry goes into the record unless the bug has reappeared, in which case (depending on company policy) the tester will reopen and update the existing bug report or will file a new report that cross-references back to the old one but describes the current misbehavior.

Retest resolved bugs that aren't yet closed. The bug has come back—fixed, deferred, or nonreproducible—or has been rejected in some other way. The tester who reported the bug will retest it and might close it. Have the new tester investigate the bug, too. After his investigation, have him talk with the person who reported and retested the bug. That tester, and you, can give the new tester feedback on his approach, his troubleshooting tactics, and his basis for deciding how much time and effort to invest in retesting a given bug. When you are satisfied that he has an appropriate level of judgment and troubleshooting skill, let him close reports.

Don't put novice testers on nearly finished projects.

If you have to add staff to a project that is getting close to done, don't assign a novice. Assign someone who knows a lot about testing. The experienced tester already knows how to read test matrices, boundary charts, and the rest of the usual test documentation (or can learn this quickly). All you have to tell him is what to test, not how to do every test. He will need time to learn about the product, but he can become productive without using up too much of your time or your staff's time.

The novice, however, needs much more of your instruction on how to test. Some test groups spend enormous amounts of time writing step-by-step testing instructions, for use by novices. We think these groups would be better served by spending that time on finding bugs and getting them fixed. We also think that the novices who use such instructions are likely to miss a lot of bugs, because they don't know the range of defects to look for and no simply written set of instructions can convey the necessary range of observational and interpretive skills.

Do hire novices when you have time to train them or when you have tasks for them that take you very little time to prepare and delegate.

Don't hire novices when you cannot afford the attention to train them. Don't structure your test design and documentation activity in a way that squanders substantial amounts of senior tester time in the service of facilitating mediocre work by newcomers.

The morale of your staff is an important asset.

As Napoleon put it, "Morale is to the physical as three is to one."

Staff who believe that their work is important, that they can accomplish their tasks if they apply themselves, and that their accomplishments will be valued, can make remarkable accomplishments. As their manager, you're the most important guardian of your staff's morale:

- Treat them with courtesy and in a respectful manner.
- Notice their work.
- Compliment good work, enthusiasm, and honest effort.
- If your staff are working late, work late yourself. Not every night, not every weekend day, but often enough that your staff feel as though you're sharing the workload.
- When possible, assign people to tasks and projects that interest them. Encourage them to express their interests and take them into account.
- When a tester is not succeeding at a task, assign someone to assist him, coach him, or if necessary, replace him (and move him to some other task).
- Set up training opportunities. Show that you value the development of skill and professionalism.
- Treat them fairly and require others to treat them fairly.
- Never mislead one of your staff. If you don't know the answer to a question, say so. If you share a hunch about something, be very clear that you're guessing and not speaking from knowledge.
- Never shout at a staff member. Never take advantage of your power to bully someone else.
- Avoid criticizing a staff member in public but do point out errors and problems in private.
- Don't gossip about members of your staff with other members of your staff.

- Never ask a member of your staff for a date and be extremely cautious about asking for or accepting personal favors or gifts, even small gifts. Give more than you get.

Don't let yourself be abused.

Project managers and executives sometimes make unreasonable demands.

You don't have to do what can't be done. Many managers routinely try to pull an extra 10 percent or 20 percent of work from each of their staff, no matter how hard the individual is already working. Don't let yourself be guilt-tripped if you can't do the impossible, nor if you refuse to burn out yourself and your family making the impossible effort.

Software development is not always a 9-to-5 job. You should support your team, and sometimes this might require heavy overtime for a few days or weeks. Sometimes the project manager will need your help to pull the project back on track or to get it finished. By all means, do everything that you reasonably can do, if it will help. But choose your own pace and make your own commitments. Be a volunteer, not a victim.[2]

You don't have to promise the impossible. You don't have to lie. You don't have to cover up problems. In fact, as a tester, the essence of your job is to expose problems and *not* to cover them up. You don't have to, and you never should, compromise your integrity.

Your power comes from having the freedom to say what's so, to the people who need to hear it. If you compromise your reputation for integrity, you'll weaken one of the core supports of your power.

Some employers are unreasonable and abusive, and you can't change them. If the job is intolerable, get your resume on the street and leave when you find a better job.

Don't abuse your staff with overtime.

Many testing groups work chronic overtime. In some companies, testers work on much more extreme schedules than other development groups.

Chronic overtime leads to employee burnout, high turnover, cynicism, politics, and inefficient, sloppy work. We urge you to defend your staff from it.

---

[2]Don't let yourself get caught on a death march. Don't put long hours into a project that is obviously doomed. It helps no one and gradually does you emotional harm. See Yourdon (1997).

Many projects need short bursts of extra help at critical times. This is a normal part of the business. This situation isn't what we're talking about when we refer to abusive overtime. Remember, however, that your staff members each have different limits. Some have family commitments or other commitments that are not very flexible. Deal graciously with the reality of your situation.

Some companies, or some project managers, chronically short-schedule their projects and expect their staffs to make up the difference:

■ Don't write schedules on the assumption that your staff will spend eight hours focused on-task each day. They won't. They can't. They go to meetings and trainings; they write status reports and memos and fill out silly forms from your company's HR department. If you're lucky, they spend six of eight hours per day focused on their official task, working the rest of the time on other things that they have to do.

■ Don't agree to schedules you know are impossible. Instead, estimate as well as you can how long different tasks will take. When faced with a schedule that is shorter than your task list, ask which ones you should do first and which ones should be done if you have time left over. If you face a manager who insists that you do all of them, ask which ones can be done less thoroughly. And, ask for more staff. Sometimes, you'll face an unreasonable executive who insists that you agree to do everything within an impossible time. OK, so maybe you say the words. Remember, however, that the words aren't magical. Reality will roll over your project and your staff like a steamroller, no matter what promises you make. In the face of executives who will not listen to reason, manage your people sensibly, or you'll lose them.

Another cause of chronic overtime is the manager who rewards people for being onsite ("at work"). Someone who is "at work" 80 hours per week might be seen as more dedicated and more deserving than someone else who works 45 hours a week but gets more and better work done. Your challenge is to find a way to make the results of the more efficient employee visible. We can't tell you in a book how to do this. The things we've done that were successful were specific to the individuals (managers and staff).

Two other types of executives will pose overtime-related management challenges for you. One type believes that software scheduling is impossible, that all schedules will slip, and so the best thing to do is to ask for whatever she wants and push everyone as hard as possible. The other type seems to believe that he demonstrates his value to the company by cajoling staff to work as much overtime as possible. We've run into both types. They are hard to reason with because their positions are, in their essence, unreasonable. The good news is that there's a lot of turnover among managers and executives in software companies. Reorganizations will happen. Fools and jerks come and go. Your challenge is to lessen the impact of people like this on your staff.

Don't let your staff be abused.

People sometimes mistreat testers by bullying them, shouting at them, calling them fools and liars, and so on. If you're the test manager and your staff is working on tough projects, you may have to draw some lines. Be prepared to offer private emotional support to your staff and stand up to bullies.

Paired testing can also be a good vehicle for providing testers with mutual support.

In a high-pressure environment, some of your staff will probably do or say regrettable things. Publicly, treat a misbehaving staff member politely. Privately, state clearly to the tester that his conduct was unacceptable. If the misbehavior is a pattern, go through your company's usual disciplinary procedures.

Create training opportunities.

Set up a reading group that meets weekly or twice monthly. The goal is to read a paper or book chapter each week and discuss it (they discuss it; you attend but don't say much). Make this meeting voluntary; no one is compelled to attend. But find a way to reward people who attend regularly and contribute to the meetings. (For example, provide the books to people who have shown that they'll read them.)

Establish lunch-time training meetings (weekly or twice-monthly). Sometimes you give a talk. Sometimes you bring in a guest speaker (perhaps a test manager from another company). You might get someone to agree to do this for free, as long as you'll also talk to their staff. Sometimes one of your staff could make a presentation on a technique or on the challenges of testing a certain type of device or application feature. Sometimes, you could work through an exercise or two, practicing a skill.

If your company reimburses tuition, find out what relevant courses are offered by your local university and what the better software-related courses are online. Similarly, find out what testing (and other relevant) conferences are available and which ones are most applicable to your company's projects. Meet with your staff members individually and offer to help them plan their continuing education. These discussions are excellent opportunities to discuss a tester's longer term goals. (Take these goals into account when you assign the next wave of tasks.) Don't tell someone what courses to take but do point out courses you think are well-taught and relevant to the company's current projects or to the career interests of your staff member.

As a general rule, send staff to courses (especially professional training seminars) and conferences in pairs or triples. They'll talk with each other about what they're learning. Have them make presentations back to you or to the testing group about what they've learned.

Your hiring decisions are your most important decisions.

Hiring the wrong person for the job is one of the worst mistakes you can make as a manager. You'll probably be stuck with that mistake for a long time.

Do everything you can to hire good people.

Hire contractors to give you breathing room during recruiting.

Use temporary help so you can take the time you need to find the right person. Even in companies that severely restrict the use of contractors, this particular use is often favored.

Rarely accept rejects from other groups into testing.

Some people who don't work out well in other groups will do a marvelous job in testing, but not many. The more losers you accept, the more of a "loser" reputation your group will get. Vigorously resist efforts by an executive to give you a rejected staff member who doesn't inspire confidence in you. Even if this "gift" is free (this transfer isn't taking a job away from any of your current staff or a currently open opportunity to hire someone else), your increased head count will haunt you the next time you ask for permission to hire someone. (You just got someone, why do you need even more?) The people around you will also expect your group's capacity to increase in proportion to the increase in your staff size. A new tester attracts new work. If you get new work, but the new tester doesn't do it, everyone else's job just got harder.

Plan in terms of the tasks you need to do in your group and the skills needed to do them.

Don't hire on the basis of simplistic qualifications. The true qualifications of a tester go far beyond having the right degree or having such-and-such years of experience. Hire people who may or may not have the traditional qualifications but who can prove to you that they can do the work.

Staff the testing team with diverse backgrounds.

Don't try to hire a staff of people who all have a B.S. in computer science, two years' experience in testing, experience with a specified automated test tool, and so on. Build a group of people who all have special strengths and who are all very different from each other. We have hired several people who had never done testing but who had other, relevant real-life experience. This can be very successful, if you're bringing skills you need into the group.[3]

We're *not* saying that you should not hire programmers. By all means, do hire programmers. You need them for many tasks. However, you'll have to train them in many nonprogramming areas of knowledge. Your other staff can be nonprogrammers who have many of the areas of nonprogramming knowledge that your programmers don't have. Build a staff whose individual strengths make up for each others' weaknesses.

For example (these examples are all based on successes from our personal experience), imagine bringing in a smart person whose most recent work role

---

[3]Although we cannot always follow his advice, we agree in principle with a comment from one of our reviewers, Rex Black: "When you are doing testing that involves the use of specialized skills, like automated testing and especially performance testing, I believe it is prudent management to make sure that at least two people on your team are competent in those skills."

was as an attorney who can analyze any specification you can give them and is trained as an advocate, a director of sales and marketing (the one we hired trained our staff in new methods of researching and writing bug reports to draw the attention of the marketing department), a hardware repair technician, a librarian (think about testing databases or other information retrieval systems), a programmer, a project manager (of nonsoftware projects), a technical support representative with experience supporting products like the ones you're testing, a translator (especially useful if your company publishes software in many languages), a secretary (think about all the information that you collect, store, and disseminate and all the time management you and your staff have to do), a system administrator who knows networks, or a user of the software you're testing. Any (or many) of the skill sets these people have could benefit your project.

There's a limit on the applicability of this advice. For some products, the tester *must* be able to program. Imagine testing a compiler—to create interesting tests, you have to be able to write code. In some companies, a nonprogramming tester will be treated as a second-class employee no matter how good he is. You have to hire programmers in these cases. Your challenge will be to hire programmers who have diverse backgrounds. In our experience, this is not easy, but it is achievable if you work in a good company, and the industry is not in one of its full-employment boom cycles.

Another diversity issue bears mention. Occasional articles are published about racism and sexism and ageism in the computer industry, and we've seen our share of it. Hiring, training, pay, and promotion preferences that result in groups that are more dominated by white males than they need to be are particularly counter-productive in testing. The broader the range of cultural and experiential backgrounds in your staff, the more ways they'll analyze the software and the more problems they'll find. Diversity is a critical asset in testing, not something to be avoided.

Hire opportunity candidates.

Look in nontraditional places for your staff, especially during a tight labor market. For example, lawyers and accountants have strong analytical skills; surprisingly many will be interested in spending a year (or more) learning how software development is done. Another example is the senior programmer or project manager who just became a single mother, needs to slow her workpace, and can't find support for cutting down her hours in her current job; an offer of a 35-hour position with flexible hours might gain you a staff member with exceptional skills for a year or two. Another example is the retired executive looking for a new, perhaps lower stress, position.

Lesson 237 Hire by consensus.

Let any full-time member of your group and anyone who works closely with your group interview the testing candidate. Let anyone who interviewed the candidate veto him, unless the veto is based on gender, race, age, or some other (unlawful) bias that is irrelevant to the ability of the person to do the job.

It is too easy to dismiss a gut feeling and talk someone out of a veto. However, we've made some bad hiring mistakes, including hiring sexual harassers, by overriding a poorly articulated but strongly felt reaction by one of our staff. Listen carefully and sympathetically to the concerns expressed by one of your staff and honor his veto unless you sense it is based on a discriminatory attitude.

Lesson 238 Hire people who love their work.

Look for enthusiasm and be cautious about people who have a history of issues with past managers. Be especially cautious about people who seem bitter about their past work.

Lesson 239 Hire integrity.

Your department provides controversial information. Your clients' trust is your most important asset. The character of your staff will drive the level of their trust.

Lesson 240 During the interview, have the tester demonstrate the skills you're hiring him for.

For example, if he's an experienced tester, have him write a bug report. (Use an open source program that your company didn't write, to avoid giving the candidate the impression that you're asking for free consulting.) Another example, if you're hiring an automation architect, ask him to analyze a product and its situation and give you a high-level automation plan. (Again, consider using an open source product that is not yours.) Judge him by the questions he asks, the research he does, and the way he puts together the information into an overall approach. The approach doesn't need to be perfect, but it should be sensible and well reasoned. (For more on this, see DeMarco and Lister 1999.)

During the interview, have the tester demonstrate skills he'll actually use on the job over informal aptitude tests.

Several groups do some type of informal aptitude testing, using logic puzzles or numeric puzzles. We don't object to these, but we don't think that they're as informative as some people think they are.

Huge practice effects can be achieved with logic and number puzzles. Kaner used to do them with his daughter when she was about 12. She got pretty good with them. That didn't mean she was smarter, and it didn't make her a better tester. It meant she was better at solving puzzles. These practice effects are the basis of the large industry of test preparation for SAT, LSAT, GRE, and other standardized college admission tests. Practice effects (previous experience) last quite a long time and are more pronounced in speeded tests. They're more pronounced in nonverbal tests and performance tests (Jensen 1980). A person who looks really great on these tests might simply be more familiar with them. A person who looks like a dummy might have no experience solving them but (in our experience) be smart and an excellent tester anyway.

Speed tests select for quick but not necessarily for thorough thinking—mental rabbits. Tortoises sometimes design better products or better strategies for testing products.

When recruiting, ask for work samples.

Not everyone can supply them, but many people can give you samples of code they have written, bug reports they have filed, and papers or reports they have written. People who were laid off or who left a company on good terms can often get permission to share specific, identified pieces of work they have done with potential employers. Other people file reports against open source software and/or write code in their spare time. Never ask for confidential material and make sure that what the person is showing you is not confidential.

Hire quickly after you make up your mind.

Make a high priority of getting the hiring paperwork through your company's channels quickly, or the good candidate will accept another position during your delay.

Put your hiring promises in writing and keep them.

Disputes about whether you actually promised someone something are embittering to the individual who feels shortchanged, alarming to the rest of your staff, and potentially expensive to your credibility. You lose even if you never made the promise. Avoid ambiguity. And never, ever promise something that will be out of your control, such as career path development or promotions.

CHAPTER 10

Your Career in Software Testing

What kind of future can you have in a software testing career? The answer is complex. It's easy to dead-end in testing; you have to manage your career or you might go nowhere. The pay is often lower in testing than in other development positions, but it doesn't have to be if you actively build your skills and pick your employers. Turnover is higher; testers seem to get fired, laid off, or driven out more often than other equally competent developers. Improving your job-hunting and negotiating skills will be valuable.

The suggestions that we provide on job-hunting and negotiation are distinctly American, especially Silicon Valley American. If you're not sure whether our advice applies to your culture, talk with some experienced colleagues.

Some testers think they'll be more attractive job candidates and entitled to more respect if they're certified and more powerful on the job if they're licensed. There are plusses and minuses to certification and licensing. We look at some of each.

Lesson 245

Choose a career track and pursue it.

Two of the common career tracks in testing are technical and managerial.

Some examples of technical jobs within testing (you can go from beginner to expert at any of these) are:

- Automation programmer
- Automation architect
- Performance and scalability tester
- Systems analyst
- User interface and human factors analyst and critic
- Test planner
- Subject matter expert
- Black box tester

Suppose that one of these was your specialty at the end of five years. Our impression is that you would probably have the highest salary and prestige and more employment possibilities if you were an excellent automation architect and the next highest as an excellent automation programmer. Performance and scalability pay well at present, too. Our impression is that you would have the lowest salary if you were an excellent black box manual tester or (depending on the subject matter) a subject matter expert with more knowledge of the subject than of testing techniques.

Here's an interesting conflict of interest. You can make yourself significantly more valuable to your current employer by learning a sufficiently wide range of testing techniques and supplementing them with domain knowledge. You can probably command significantly better pay. However, if you work for a company that shows no loyalty to its staff or you expect to change jobs for some other reason, you'll be better off developing more widely valued skills, even if this is at the expense of your domain knowledge and, therefore, of the effectiveness of your testing for this employer. A useful guiding principle is to identify the skills most needed by your employer (or industry) and acquire them.

Some examples of managerial jobs within testing are:

- Test lead or supervisor
- Test manager
- Director of testing or director of quality
- Internal consultant
- External consultant

You may find promotion opportunities outside of testing. Testers get a broader, and typically shallower, view of the product than the programmers. They often have a product-wide interest, view, and effect. They also interact with managers and senior managers in most other software-related areas of the company. As a result, many skilled test supervisors or managers get the opportunity to train and shift into other management positions, especially the following:

- Program manager or project manager
- Technical support manager
- Product manager (especially for domain experts with technical skills)
- Documentation group manager
- Sales support manager (For high-end products, salespeople are often accompanied by someone who can answer technical questions and develop prototype applications of the product with the customer.)

Another track followed by some testers is process management, including:

- Software metrics specialist
- Software process improvement specialist

We recommend that you approach process management with caution. These positions aren't directly tied to the development or profitability of any product. In some companies, therefore, these positions are more vulnerable to layoffs. Additionally, in some companies, these positions are staffed by underqualified people. We recommend that you gain a thorough grounding in mathematical statistics and measurement theory (read and understand Zuse, 1997 and Austin, 1996) before accepting a position as a metrics specialist. We recommend that you work in at least two, and preferably three, areas (such as testing, programming, and marketing) before taking a position as a process improvement specialist.

Testers' incomes can be higher than programmers' incomes.

Traditionally, testers have made less money than comparably experienced programmers. That's not true in all companies, and some people say that testers have been gaining on programmers over the past few years.

Pay comparisons are more complex. During the dot-boom (1998–2000), salaries were up for all types of software jobs. In many companies, experienced software test automation architects made more than experienced programmers. Experienced black box testers who only did manual testing did not fare as well. During the dot-bomb (2000–2001), salaries have been dropping, and we suspect that average rates for black box manual testers are dropping faster.

Our impression is that testers who have specialized technical skills are often more prized (and harder to find) than testers with managerial skills, who are in turn more prized than black box testers and less experienced test automators.

Feel free to change your track and pursue something else.

You are not locked into testing. You are not locked into a management role or position. You are not locked into any company, any track, or any job.

Businesses have cycles. We've been through tight software job markets and open ones, booms, and contractions. When the job market is open, and employers are desperate, you can make bold moves relatively easily. Even when the job market is tight, however, lots of opportunities are available for people who prepare themselves.

For example, if you want to move out of testing into programming, take courses. If your schedule at work makes it impossible to take courses at a university or university extension (sometimes called professional studies) program, take a self-paced course over the Net or study from one of the book-and-course-on-CD packages. After you gain basic skill in a relevant programming language, offer to do some work, *on your time,* for one of the programming teams. You might get some resistance from your test manager. We suggest that you find a way to reassure him that you will work 40 hours per week on testing. Your time beyond the 40 hours should be respected as your own. (If you can't get that much of an accommodation, and you want to shift into programming or any new track, you might have to find a transitional job somewhere else.)

Whatever path you take, pursue it actively.

This is *your* career. Your company or your manager might be willing to help you do career planning, and they might be good at it. Or not. If you have a direction, and the skills and determination to back it up, your company is more likely to pay for classes and to let you try new things.

Some companies will pay for your courses, some won't. We encourage you to think that you're building *your* career. Take what you need and what interests you. If you have to spend money, treat this as an investment. As you gain new skills, you'll become more valuable either to your company or to your next company (one that values you more highly).

Some companies will let you accept projects with another group as a full-time or part-time assignment. Others won't, or they'll hold you to a full-time load in testing along with a part-time load in the other group. This second case is the more common. Be prepared to work overtime to make the transition. If you can't work overtime (perhaps family responsibilities require you to be home), you might still find time to take self-paced courses and work on nonemployer projects (such as developing open source software) at night. (Be careful to keep your night-time hobby separate from your work. For example, if you write some open source code at home and then do some testing or polishing at work, your employer will probably gain ownership of it. Be careful, too, not to create anything that might compete with any of your employer's products.)

Extend your career beyond software testing.

Many of the happiest and most successful people in software testing move in and out of the field.

Spending your time finding and criticizing other people's mistakes gets old. Try something else. Build skills in another area of software development. Make your own mistakes. Then if you feel like it, come back to do testing again. This will give you more perspective, flexibility, job security, market appeal, better insight into projects' challenges and constraints, more credibility with other members of the development team, and probably a higher salary.

People who manage more than one function are often paid on a different, and higher, scale than the managers of either function alone. Managers who are seen as multifunctional are prized in many companies.

Extend your career beyond your company.

It's *your* career. If your company goes bust tomorrow or lays you off, you're still there, and your career is still there. (You just have to find a new job, and you can often find one that is better than the one you just left.) There's a large community of software testers and an even larger community of software developers. We write, we meet, we argue, we teach each other a great deal, we give each other advice, and we find each other new jobs.

You can get involved in the community in lots of different ways. Go to software testing or software development conferences. Join and participate in the local chapter of the Association for Computing Machinery, the American Society for Quality, the Human Factors and Ergonomics Society, or any other professional society that values software quality. Join the software-test-discuss mailing list (www.testingfaqs.org/swtest-discuss.html) and participate when you have something worth saying. If you agree with the statement of context-driven testing principles at the end of this book, sign up (www.context-driven-software.com) and join our mailing list. Read Agre (2001) for advice on networking.

Conferences are for conferring.

When you attend a conference on software testing or software development, don't just sit in the sessions and listen to the speakers. Do a lot (or at least some) of that. But spend a lot of time meeting with other people at the conference to *discuss* what was presented or what is happening in the field.

If you don't know many people at the conference, meet some. When you go to lunch, sit with people you don't know, listen, and identify people who are interesting and knowledgeable. Take other opportunities to identify interesting people. Then invite them to coffee, or ask whether you can buy them breakfast. When you meet with them, ask them about what they do and about sessions that they've been to. What have they found interesting? Over time (it takes more than one conference), you'll make a group of friends whom you meet mainly at conferences, whom you keep up-to-date with via the Net, whom you attend sessions with, and maybe whom you'll write papers or present panels with. This is how the three of us met.

Not everyone gets sent to conferences by their company. Tell your manager well before the conference that you want to attend a specific conference. Better notice will increase your chance of attending. After you have attended a conference or two, apply to be a speaker. If you're accepted, your company will be more likely to send you, and (assuming you do a good job) you'll gain respect and goodwill within and outside your company.

Lots of other companies are as screwed up as yours.

Many testers are aghast at the bugs in their products and the confusion in their company. This isn't an unusual situation, even in good companies. Testers see what's going wrong, and it looks screwed up. This isn't always fun.

Statistically, you might be in the worst 10 percent. But, probably not—those companies don't even have testers. Networking with testers at other companies may help you get some perspective.

If you don't like your company, look for a different job.

It's usually a good idea to keep your current job; it's almost always easier to get a good job when you're employed than when you're not. Don't post your resume on the Internet, unless you want your boss to eventually see it. Deal with a small number of recruiters and only ones who agree to check with you each time they want to send your resume somewhere.

After interviewing with other companies, you might accept a new position, or you might decide that the company you're with isn't so bad. Deciding to keep the job you have can be a perfectly reasonable and successful outcome of a job search.

If the job you have is so toxic that it poisons how you think about yourself and how you talk about yourself in interviews, you might be better off quitting, taking some time off, and then looking for a new job. An alternative to quitting a toxic company, especially if you can't afford to quit, is to decide that you'll do your work with integrity (honesty, not thoroughness) whatever the deadlines and constraints are, or that you'll find other ways to improve your respect for yourself on the job. Take classes at night if you can. Get extra sleep if you can. The goal is to put yourself into a good mental state, so that you can present yourself to your next potential employer most effectively.

Be prepared in case you have to bet your job (and lose).

One of us, Kaner, always had his ear to the job market, and usually had his resume circulating whenever he worked in a testing group. This isn't because he wanted to switch jobs all the time. It was defensive. He was often in situations that required a controversial stand. Knowing that he had an up-to-date resume, that he had good relationships with a few excellent recruiters, and that he understood what types of openings were out there, with whom, and what they paid, gave him confidence that if he had to find a new job, he could get one reasonably quickly. Knowing *that*, he could afford to take some risks that he might otherwise not have taken.

Build and maintain a list of companies where you'd like to work.

It's pretty easy to find out about companies, especially using the Web, conferences, and networking. Think about places you'd like to work. Meet people who work there. Talk to them.

Build a portfolio.

It's very handy to have a collection of code, documents, and other work samples that demonstrate your competence. You can use it to show off your competence in ways that other job-seekers cannot. Building it, however, is a challenge.

In most companies, your work is proprietary—owned by the company and secret. However, you might create some documents or write some code that is not particularly sensitive. Or, you might create some work products that are sensitive today but not considered sensitive five years later. These are candidates for your portfolio. Some managers will readily grant you the right to use nonsensitive materials, but others will be much more reluctant. Your best opportunities to get permission to use materials that you created at a company might be:

- When you've been laid off, and your manager or Human Resources representative is explaining your termination benefits. If you have specific work samples in hand, they might be glad to sign a document that says that you may show these (named) samples to prospective employers or clients, for the purpose of obtaining work. Get a signature, not just verbal permission.

- Six months to a year after you've left the company, if your former boss is still at the company, and you get along well.

- For use as examples at a conference. If you have permission to disclose a secret to the public at a conference, and you do disclose the secret, you don't need further permission to disclose it again. The secret is no longer a secret.

If you develop software or write papers on your own time, using your own resources, using no company resources whatsoever, and if the material that you develop isn't directly related to your tasks at the company, you probably own what you wrote, and you can probably use it freely. You might have rights to your work under a much broader range of circumstances. The details depend on your contract with your employer and the laws that govern that contract.

Lesson 257 Use your resume as a sales tool.

Your resume excludes you from consideration for some jobs and includes you for others. Your goal is to write a resume that appeals to the right submarket.

- If you're interested in significantly different types of work, write a few different resumes. Focus them differently, to highlight the skills, interests, and background that put you in the best light. Make sure that your descriptions of your background and achievements are compatible across the various versions of your resume (always assume that your employer will eventually see all of your resumes).

- Prepare a historical resume. A historical resume describes your experience in chronological order, from job to job, highlighting your achievements at each job. Some recruiters (and a few employers) prefer functional resumes, which describe your experience from skill to skill, mentioning the company at which you developed the skill as a detail item. There's nothing wrong with functional resumes, but they're used by some people to exaggerate their experience or to hide periods of unemployment. As a result, some hiring managers (us, for example) insist on developing a historical profile of job candidates. If you don't have it in writing, we go through the tedium of asking for the details over the phone or in the face-to-face interview. If you have it in writing, then during a phone interview that focuses on your history, offer to fax the manager a chronological version of your resume. Some managers will be strongly impressed by your preparation and thoughtfulness. Some hiring managers will ignore job candidates who only supply function resumes, unless the candidates' skills are an exceptional fit for the job and their claims are credible.

- Prepare a functional or buzzword resume. Some companies scan resumes into computers or have resumes reviewed quickly by people who don't understand the position that you're applying for. If you want to work for one of those companies, you have to put the right buzz words or phrases into the resume. Functional resumes are good for this. Alternatively, in a historical resume, consider adding a section titled "Key Words: For Computerized Searches" and then list every programming language application, significant skill, and so on in one paragraph. Just name the names, explain nothing.

■ Never exaggerate your background, skill, or experience. Your credibility is one of your major assets. If anyone strongly suspects that you exaggerated or lied on your resume, you won't be hired. People will also see your resume even after you are. Two years after you've been on the job, a manager from another group (or a new manager of yours) might review your resume and see that you claimed expertise in something that you clearly don't know. This manager might not talk with you about this, but he'll probably talk with other managers. It won't help your career.

Lesson 258 Get an inside referral.

Many companies give bonuses to their employees for referring candidates who get hired. Take advantage of this. Use a current employee of your target company to refer you. That way you'll also have a way to get information about the company from the inside and probably a way to get valuable feedback during the interview and negotiation process. It's worked for us.

Lesson 259 Research salary data.

It's easy to get realistic salary expectations from databases like www.salary.com. Know this information and walk into the interview prepared.

Lesson 260 If you're answering an advertisement, tailor your answer to the advertisement.

If an advertisement lists several requirements, respond to them. Point out the ones that you meet and the ones on the list that you don't meet but really want to learn.

Lesson 261 Take advantage of opportunities to interview.

As you (or recruiters) circulate your resume, you may be offered opportunities to interview for a job that you wouldn't expect to accept. The job may not pay well enough, it may be located somewhere you don't want to live, or you may not be impressed with it for some other reason. Regardless, consider accepting the interview opportunity and pursue the interview with the same enthusiasm as you would for a job you really want. The interview is a chance to practice your interview skills in a nonthreatening, but realistic setting.

You'll have the opportunity to practice answering interview questions and hear new questions that you weren't prepared in advance to answer. If you're new or inexperienced at job hunting, you'll be nervous during your initial interviews. After you've participated in several job interviews, you'll have a better idea of what to expect and be more comfortable with the process. Interviews for jobs you don't expect to accept, even if they're offered to you, still help you develop interview experience and confidence.

You may also find that the job is one you'd be willing to accept after all, or the company may have other open positions you'd prefer.

Learn about companies when you apply for jobs with them.

Lesson 262

If you're unemployed and sending out a lot of resumes, you don't have time to research every company. So don't. But when you see a particularly interesting position, you can do a huge amount of research on the Internet for free and a bunch more for a few extra dollars. Go to the company's Web site, read their stuff, download any demo software they provide, and look for information about the programming tools they use. Use search engines. If it's publicly held, go to sites that give investor information and ask questions. The more you know, the more tailored you can make your cover letter.

As soon as you learn that a company (that you're interested in) is interested in you, you should research the company. The more you know, the more effective you'll be in your discussions with them.

If someone does call you for an interview over the phone, ask for information.

- Ask for product literature or literature that describes the company.
- Ask for demonstration copies of software they publish or ask what tools they use to develop and test their software and what types of applications they create.
- Ask where to find other information about the company.

If they send you anything, make sure to read it before your face-to-face interview.

Interviewers want to know whether you want to work at their company and why. Many hiring managers will prefer someone who is eager for the job and enthusiastic about what the job can offer, but only adequately qualified, over someone who is supremely qualified but not so excited. The excited staffer can learn the job and will be more fun to have around. (She'll probably work harder, too.) Simply saying "Oooh, oooh, I am so excited!" is less convincing than showing that you have read about the company and that you're seriously interested in the company's products. Work (in this case research) speaks louder than words.

Ask questions during job interviews.

It's also a good idea to ask questions during an interview (phone or face to face), although you probably don't want to ask too many questions of one person, and you should pick appropriate questions for different people. Here are some examples of questions that often yield interesting answers:

- What kinds of products and services does your company provide?
- Can I see a demonstration of the key product?
- What is special about your products and services? What are the key strengths and weaknesses?
- How did you develop the main product? What were the key development tradeoffs?
- Who are your customers?
- Who is your competition?
- How do you learn about your customers?
- How do you learn about your customers' satisfaction with the overall product, with the design, and with the defects?
- Describe your organization chart (where you are on it, and where I would be on it).
- What is it like to work here?
- What do you do? What kinds of products and services do you (the individual whom you're talking with) provide?
- Can I see some examples?
- Where do you fit in the product development process?
- What do you like about your job?
- What would you like to change?
- How do you make time for your family?
- How much control do you have over your own work?
- Who designs the tests that you run? Who runs the tests that you design?

- Tell me about your test design process.

- Can I see some test plans and test cases?

- How do you feel about your pay, boss, colleagues?

- What courses or conferences did you take last year?

- What other training have you received?

- How do you learn new things?

- Describe three key things that you learned last year.

Keep your eyes and ears open during face-to-face interviews.

- Are the interviewers tired?

- Do the interviewers and other staff speak positively about their work?

- Is there a good sense of morale and team community?

- How is their furniture? How much are they investing in the comfort and productivity of their engineering staff? How does the furniture compare to the managers' or executives' furniture?

- How much space, equipment, and light do working testers get and how much do higher ranking staff get?

- Look for mismatches between claims regarding working conditions and the actual conditions. For example, some companies make a big deal in their ads about a 4-day, 10-hour-per-day work week, but they expect a lot of work on the other three days (the ones you're supposed to have off). Mismatches like this create resentment and an unpleasant environment. They're also early warnings of potential ethical problems of the company's management; if they aren't speaking straight about their basic expectations, what else aren't they speaking straight about?

Lesson 264 · Negotiate your position.

We can only scratch the surface of negotiating in this book. Negotiating is a skill. You have to practice it. Practice with friends and practice with potential employers. (You'll lose a few potential jobs, but you'll learn from your mistakes.)

The more informed you are during a negotiation, the more effective you are as a negotiator. Here's the key information:

- Knowing what you want.

- Knowing what they want.

- Knowing what they think of themselves.

- Knowing how they will present themselves as potential employers.
- Knowing what your alternatives are; what is your best alternative to this job?

Having alternatives is very important in a negotiation. If you're employed, your easiest alternative is to keep your current job and wait until a better one shows up. This is the key reason that people who have a job find it easier to get good jobs than people who don't. People who are unemployed rarely have as credible and obvious an alternative as someone with a job. They're often desperate, and even if they aren't, they're seen as people who need a job soon or they'll run out of savings (and become desperate). As a result, companies often feel that they can offer less money and make fewer other promises to someone who doesn't have a job. If you're unemployed, don't slow down your job search when you make contact with a good-looking company. Speed it up. Find another good-looking company. Whether or not you let each company know about the other (be careful about naming one company to the other, some people feel this is a breach of confidentiality), you will negotiate differently because you will know that you have alternatives. The confidence this gives you will affect how you present yourself.

Here are some issues to raise and consider during negotiation:

- Early in the interview, talk about what you want (nonmonetary issues) and what excites you. If they're excited about your interests, they'll run the interviews (and the rest of the negotiations) in a way that is more intended to persuade you to join the company.
- Refuse to provide previous salary information. Politely reject queries about your salary expectations until after the employer is excited about you. It often helps to explain that your last salary is irrelevant to this position because it was for a different position. What you want is a fair rate for *this* job. Then ask what the pay scale is for this job. Some interviewers will tell you. Others will refuse, and then you get to say, "Let's talk about the money later, after we understand the responsibilities and the opportunities."
- Be enthusiastic but don't be over-eager.
- Speak about their product in their vocabulary.
- Find and point out ways in which you can help them. Make proposals, show examples of your thinking.
- Let them know that you want the job. (In some cultures, it is more appropriate to say that the job is very interesting and seems very desirable but important to avoid saying that you want the job until you're ready to accept it.)

- If you aren't fully qualified for this job, but you want it, talk frankly about it as a stretch opportunity. A stretch opportunity is a challenge, something you haven't done before, something you'll have to develop new skills and knowledge to do, but something that you want to do. Let them see how they could make you happy with this job, how it fits your interests and goals, and how you could grow into the job.

- Keep your eye out for intimidating negotiating styles from the potential employer's staff.

Remember that during the interviews and the negotiations, the company's managers are on their best behavior. They won't get nicer, less intimidating, more honest, or more considerate after you start working at the company.

Some good books on negotiation are Chapman (1996), Fisher and Ertel (1995), Fisher et al. (1991), Freund (1992), Miller (1998), O'Malley (1998), and Tarrant (1997). For general advice on negotiation, we particularly like Freund.

Be cautious about Human Resources.

Human resource people don't make hiring decisions, although they often do decide which resumes the hiring managers get to see. Functional managers (like the testing or development manager) decide who ultimately gets hired. Negotiate with the decision maker, not with Human Resources.

Learn Perl.

Perl is a handy scripting language, and many of the programmers in your company know it, too. (So you can ask them for advice if you get stuck.) You can write a lot of utility programs with Perl. For example, you can analyze log files, feed data to devices, or design some automated tests and feed data to them. The more you use the language, the more new ideas you'll have about how else to use it. (Note: If Perl is not the scripting language of choice in your company, use the language that is, or use the one that you like best. Python and Ruby are often-mentioned alternatives. We're suggesting that if you don't know where to start and don't have a reason to start with a different language, start with Perl.) For more information on scripting languages, check out www.softpanorama.org/Scripting/index.shtml.

Learn Java or C++.

If you have the opportunity to actively apply what you learn, such as by writing your own test tools, learn the primary development language in your company and practice with it. The better you get, the more options you'll have within your company and for your next job.

Download demo copies of testing tools and try them out.

You might have to do this at home, on your own time. We suggest that you get familiar with tools that your company doesn't use (yet). Your company might not want to pay you for this research or have you do this work instead of your main projects.

After you know what's out there and how well it works, you might convince your company to buy and start using the tool. If it's a good one, people will appreciate your recommendation. After a few good recommendations, people might start looking to you as the group tools researcher.

Whether or not your current employer appreciates you staying up to date with testing tools, this knowledge will help you when you interview with potential employers.

Improve your writing skills.

Much of your job involves writing reports and memos to persuade other people to do things. The better you write, the more effective your reports. Take courses in technical and persuasive writing and find other ways to practice and improve your writing.

Improve your public speaking skills.

You can take courses in public speaking at many universities and community colleges. Also, consider joining an organization called *Toastmasters* (www.toastmasters.org). This group provides a safe, encouraging environment for learning and practicing public speaking skills. Many Toastmasters clubs are good places to network; you may be surprised to learn who else is in the room (executives, managers, other engineers, and so on).

Think about getting certified.

Kaner is an American Society for Quality-Certified Quality Engineer (CQE). The Quality Assurance Institute offers certifications in software testing and software quality. The British Computer Society is developing a new certification scheme for testers. You can get certified by other groups as well.

Is it worth it?

Our impression is that the certification exams aren't all that difficult to pass. The questions are often fairly predictable. If you take an exam-focused review course, you'll probably pass the exam. Some groups post sample questions on the Net from time to time. From what we've seen, exams are typically multiple-choice and sometimes open-book. They often test your knowledge of vocabulary and of relatively simple concepts and basic skills. The fact that someone is certified doesn't mean that he's an expert.

Many of the people who get certified do so after taking a series of courses, not just the review course. They use preparation for certification as an opportunity to extend their education. In our experience, these people value their certification and feel that they gained a lot from the process.

Certification can be useful on a resume. It tells your prospective employer that you're serious enough about the field to take enough continuing education to be able to pass a certification exam. This differentiates you from most of the rest of the people applying for any testing job. However, if you're certified (but a nonprogrammer) and someone else isn't certified but can program, don't be surprised if you're not the one who gets the test automation job. Your certification can carry you only so far.

On balance, we think the software testing and software quality certification efforts have been beneficial to the profession. They've encouraged many people to study classic books and papers in the field, learn new techniques, and increase their sophistication in dealing with software quality-related issues.

We are not endorsing the bodies of knowledge or the perspectives of the certifiers. We have differences of opinion with them, but they're entitled to present their views and to qualify people as being knowledgeable in their approaches. The essential difference between certification (which we do not object to) and licensing (which we do object to) is that the certification is more humble. You can practice the craft whether or not you're certified. You can choose the certification that seems most useful or most sensible to you. It is an educational vehicle and not a regulatory vehicle (see Lesson 273, "A warning about the efforts to license software engineers").

We should raise one concern. If you get certified and you're an independent consultant or independent contractor, be cautious about how you market your services. If you present yourself as being certified in Quality Engineering (or some other specialty), you can be held to have promised that you have a certain level of expertise and that you will perform your services up to the level that one should expect from someone who has that level of expertise. If you do a poor job, it will be easier for your customers to sue you for negligence or malpractice (Kaner 1996a). Therefore, even if you are certified, you might not choose to market yourself that way.

If you can get a black belt in only two weeks, avoid fights.

People can make money in the certification business—from review courses, study guides, and tapes and from the exam itself. Many people have a vested interest in certification, that has little to do with your success as an engineer.

Some certifications seem overblown to us. We regard with suspicion any program's claim that they can make you a master or an expert or a black belt in a couple of weeks.

It takes a long time in martial arts to gain a black belt. The first milestone is often the yellow belt, which your instructor will give you when she thinks you're finally more of a danger to others than to yourself. Even this usually takes a lot longer than two weeks.

Maybe a discipline is so simple that you can master it in two weeks; if so, by all means, take your black belt. But don't get into any fights.

A warning about the efforts to license software engineers.

Should software engineers (including testers) be licensed? Other kinds of engineers are licensed, maybe we should, too.

A license to practice engineering is granted by the government. In the United States, you get licensed by state governments, so if you practice in two states, you get two licenses. Licensed professionals are expected to live up to a code of ethics and can be sued for malpractice.

Efforts are underway to require that software engineers be licensed. These efforts are succeeding in Texas, British Columbia, and Ontario. For a current status report, see the Construx Web page on Software Engineering Professionalism, www.construx.com/profession/home.htm. Mead (2001) makes a thoughtful argument in favor of licensing.

An organization, the Software Engineering Coordinating Committee (SWECC), has been developing the Software Engineering Body of

Knowledge (SWEBOK). SWECC was a joint committee of the Institute for Electrical and Electronics Engineers Computer Society (IEEECS) and the Association for Computing Machinery (ACM). The goal of the SWEBOK project was to build consensus around a statement of knowledge that all software engineers should know.

The ACM does not support licensing of software engineers and, therefore, withdrew in June 2000 from the SWEBOK efforts and from the SWECC.

> ACM's position is that our state of knowledge and practice in software engineering is too immature to warrant licensing. Moreover, [the ACM] Council felt licensing would be ineffective in providing assurances about software quality and reliability. . . . [T]he Council further concluded that the framework of a licensed professional engineer, originally developed for civil engineers, does not match the professional industrial practice of software engineering. Such licensing practices would give false assurances of competence even if the body of knowledge were mature; and would preclude many of the most qualified software engineers from becoming licensed . . . . Because SWECC has become so closely identified with licensing of software engineers under a professional engineer model, the ACM Council decided to withdraw from SWECC. (ACM 2000)

The SWEBOK is an important aspect of the licensing movement. SWEBOK should be of interest to you because software testing is one of the areas of SWEBOK, and software quality is another. You can download it from www.swebok.org.

To get your license as a software engineer, you would have to pass an exam. The exam would have to be based on the knowledge and practices that are widely accepted in the field. When licensed, you could be sued for malpractice. A professional commits malpractice if she causes harm to her clients (for example, clients are injured physically, their property is damaged, or they lose money) because she did not exercise the skill or apply the knowledge of a reasonable member of her profession. If SWEBOK is accepted as the Software Engineering Body of Knowledge, legislators, exam creators, judges, lawyers, juries, and newspaper reporters will refer to SWEBOK when they want to understand the standards that define what software engineers should know and should do.

We've made pointed criticisms of statements in SWEBOK in the preface and in Chapter 6, "Documenting Testing." We're not alone. For a broader negative evaluation, see Notkin et al.'s (2000) report to the ACM Council.

The Software Engineering Body of Knowledge (IEEE Computer Society, Trial version 0.95) states in its preface that:

The purpose of this Guide is to provide a consensually validated characterization of the bounds of the software engineering discipline and to provide a topical access to the Body of Knowledge supporting that discipline. . . . The emphasis on engineering practice leads the Guide toward a strong relationship with the normative literature. Most of the computer science, information technology and software engineering literature provides information useful to software engineers, but a relatively small portion is normative. A normative document prescribes what an engineer should do in a specified situation rather than providing information that might be helpful. The normative literature is validated by consensus formed among practitioners and is concentrated in standards and related documents. From the beginning, the SWEBOK project was conceived as having a strong relationship to the normative literature of software engineering. . . . Ultimately, we hope that software engineering practice standards will contain principles traceable to the SWEBOK Guide.

SWEBOK's preface defines consensus:

By consensus, we mean the only practical method for legitimizing a statement of this kind is through broad participation and agreement by all significant sectors of the relevant community.

It is inconceivable to us that a document that has been abandoned by the main society of computing professionals in the United States could be considered a consensus document. In our view, many of the normative statements in SWEBOK do not describe what a reasonable engineer would do in a specified situation.

We think it's dangerous to treat SWEBOK as though it were a consensus document. If SWEBOK is taken as describing the standard of care and knowledge of the profession, what happens to the software engineer on the failing project who did not follow the approaches recommended in SWEBOK? Such a failure could be interpreted as malpractice, even if the engineer applied practices that were in fact more appropriate under the circumstances.

Who decides that failure to apply SWEBOK in a given case is malpractice? Not other engineers. The decision makers are judges, juries, lawyers, and insurance companies—people with little or no engineering experience. Their decision will have enormous influence in the field.

What should we expect as results if we give nonengineers a body of knowledge that prescribes norms that aren't currently followed, that are (in our experience with many large and small software companies) neither treated as authoritative nor even referenced or read by most practitioners, and that often seem to be backed by no more empirical evidence of their merit than a tally of votes of that tiny fraction of the field who participated in a particular standards creation effort? Our expectation is that the malpractice verdicts will be randomly related to the quality of decision-making by the engineers in question.

Courts in the United States have consistently refused to entertain lawsuits for computer-related malpractice because software development and software engineering aren't professions, and you cannot sue someone for professional negligence (malpractice) if they aren't a member of a profession (Kaner 1996a). (A few court decisions have been made since 1996, but they confirm Kaner's summary. For example, the most recent court decision on computer-related malpractice is *Heidtman Steel Products, Inc. v. Compuware Corp.*, 1999. This decision rejected a malpractice lawsuit and provided an extensive list of previous rejections.) Until we have broad and genuine agreement in the field on the skills and decision-making processes that lead to appropriate choices of practices, we think it would be reckless to declare the field a profession and to throw the membership of the field to the mercy of the malpractice-law legal system.

By the way, professional negligence insurance for software engineers isn't very expensive today, because you are so unlikely to be successfully sued for professional negligence. In fields that face significant malpractice litigation, insurance premiums are in the thousands, sometimes in the tens of thousands of dollars per year. Many states require licensed professionals to carry malpractice insurance if they practice their profession in that state. How much do you want to have to spend on insurance in order to be allowed to practice as an independent contractor or consultant?

Our statements about malpractice are sometimes misinterpreted as efforts to protect engineers who do bad work. We would like to clear that up. We are passionate about software quality. We strongly favor laws that hold developers, including development companies, accountable for bad work. All three of us have actively opposed the Uniform Computer Information Transactions Act because it protects software developers and vendors from liability for their defective products. Kaner's book on software consumer protection, *Bad Software*, was reviewed by Ralph Nader as "a how-to-book for consumer protection in the Information Age" (Kaner and Pels 1998, back cover).

We don't oppose the licensing of software engineers because we think that malpractice suits are a bad idea in principle. Under the right circumstances, malpractice suits are excellent tools for policing the competence of a profession. Unfortunately, those circumstances don't apply to software today, and nothing that we can wish or say will make that problem go away.

We do favor tighter standards for software. As a very simple example, we favor a disclosure requirement.

A software vendor (developer, publisher, or reseller) should be required to tell the software customer about every defect in the product that is known to the vendor at the time the product is delivered to the customer. The vendor should be responsible to the customer for any losses caused by defects that were known about but not disclosed to the customer in a way that a typical customer of this product could understand.

We think that this modest requirement would have a significant impact on the quality of products in the marketplace.

We favor legal standards that are tied to damage and losses caused by the defects of the product and the erroneous (false) claims by the vendor. If you impose accountability for bad results, people will fix their processes to yield better results. A few years down *that* road, and we might well achieve general acceptance on a set of engineering practices. At that time, it would be appropriate to rethink the issue of professionalization.

CHAPTER 11

Planning the Testing Strategy

The test plan is the set of ideas that guides your test process. We use the term *test strategy* to refer to the set of ideas that guides your test *design*, throughout the project. Test strategy is an important part of a good test plan. It is the connection between your testing and your mission. The textbooks have plenty to say about the logistics and work products of testing, but not so much about strategy, so that will be our focus in this chapter.

Three basic questions to ask about test strategy are "why bother?", "who cares?", and "how much?"

Lesson 274

Ultimately, there is only one reason you test: Something important might go wrong. Your test process exists to identify, investigate, and report the risks that the product may fail. That's why you need to ask three questions, repeatedly, about your test strategy:

- *Why bother?* Testing is expensive. Don't include activities in your strategy unless they address a risk that matters enough to spend time testing.

- *Who cares?* Reasons to test are not laws of nature; they're rooted in the feelings and values of people who matter. Don't include activities in your strategy unless they serve somebody's interest.

■ *How much?* Some strategies are much easier to say than do. "We will test all combinations of printer features" is one short sentence that launches a thousand tests (or a hundred thousand). How much of that are you really going to do?

There are many possible test strategies.

Test strategy is a set of choices. You can have many choices. Here are several alternative strategies:

■ We will release the product to friendly users after a brief internal review to find any truly glaring problems. The friendly users will put the product into service and tell us about any changes they'd like us to make.

■ We will define use cases in the form of sequences of user interactions with the product that represent, altogether, all the ways we expect normal people to use the product. We will augment that with stress testing and abnormal use testing (invalid data and error conditions). Our top priority is finding fundamental deviations from specified behavior, but we're also concerned with ways in which this program might violate user expectations. Reliability is a concern, but we haven't yet decided how best to evaluate that.

■ We will perform parallel exploratory testing and automated regression test development and execution. The exploratory testing will be risk-based, and allocated to coverage areas as needed. We'll revisit the allocation each week. The automated regression testing will focus on validating basic functions (capability testing) to provide an early warning system about major functional failures. We will also be alert to opportunities for high-volume random testing.

Each of the preceding is a strategy. Notice that they're each different. Each has a different emphasis. Each tells a little story about how we're going to test. Good test strategies tell compelling stories that explain and justify the testing to be done. Just as there are many stories that can be told, there are many possible test strategies.

Note that each of the strategies is rather generic. On a real project, we would make use of our specific knowledge of the product to design more targeted test strategies. Still, even these generic paragraphs show that test strategy is more than a list of test techniques, yet less than a full-blown test plan.

Lesson 276
The real test plan is the set of ideas that guides your test process.

Your test plan is *whatever ideas guide what you do*. That you have such ideas is important. Whether and how you document those ideas is an entirely separate issue.

Whenever you hear the argument that it's important to create documentation for what you intend to do, remember the missing adjective between "create" and "documentation": Should it be good or poor documentation? Most people would agree that it's important *not* to create *poor* documentation. The problem is: Good documentation is hard to write. It's expensive and hard to maintain.

There's a lot of testing literature that says, in essence "you can't do testing well without a written test plan." In our experience, the main positive effect of that advice has been better job security for the paper and toner manufacturers. There are too many badly written plans. And we've seen a lot of good testing done without following written plans. It's time for better advice.

Don't confuse the contents of your plan with the means by which you communicate and manage the plan. You have many options other than a formal written treatise: an oral plan, a plan on a whiteboard, a one-page plan, a series of emails, a set of outlines, or an issue list. Do what fulfills the mission.

Lesson 277
Design your test plan to fit your context.

One way to visualize the test planning situation is shown in Figure 11.1. This is the Satisfice Context Model. The five bubbles on the points of the star represent what you're given: resources and constraints. The center of the star represents your choices. The object of planning is to make choices about test process that allow you to test within the constraints of the project environment, while exploiting your resources, enabling you to achieve your mission.

The five givens are:

- *Development.* The system that produces the product you will test. How do you receive the product? How testable is it?
- *Requirements.* The criteria for a successful product. What are the product risks? Whose opinion about quality matters?

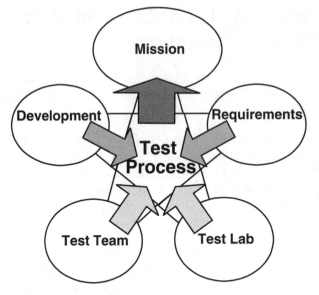

Figure 11.1 Satisfice Context Model.

- *Test team.* The people available to test the product. Do you have the right staff? Are they up to speed on the technology?

- *Test lab.* The systems, tools, and materials that allow you to do your job. Do you have the right equipment? Is your bug-tracking system in good order?

- *Mission.* The problems you must solve to be seen as successful by your clients. Find important bugs fast? Produce an accurate assessment of quality?

You may be able to negotiate for a better set of givens. You might hire staff or convince the programmers to make a more testable product. However, you can't expect much control over any of that. Your control comes in how you respond to your situation: What are your strategy, logistics, and work products going to be?

Use the test plan to express choices about strategy, logistics, and work products.

A good test plan, whether documented or not, expresses a set of choices about the test process. Three major categories describe the choices you must make:

- *Strategy.* How will you cover the product to find important problems fast? What specifically will you test? What techniques will you use to create tests? How will you recognize bugs when they occur? The test strategy specifies the relationship between the test project and the test mission.

- *Logistics.* How will you apply resources to fulfill the test strategy? Who will test? When will they test? What do you need to be successful?

- *Work Products.* How will your work be presented to your clients? How will you track bugs? What test documentation will you create? What reports will you make?

If you don't make these choices explicitly in the test plan, you make them implicitly by some other means. You don't have the option of not choosing, unless you just refuse to test.

Don't let logistics and work products blind you to strategy.

Strategy is often lost in the glare of the components of the test plan. We've seen test plan documents that give ample details of the schedule and the team and the test documentation to be produced, yet say nearly nothing about how the product will be tested. This seems backward. It implies there's nothing to testing, other than putting a tester in front of a keyboard at the right time and place. Don't expect your coworkers to respect what you do as a tester if you don't tell them about it.

How to lie with test cases.

If you take all the briefcases in your company and pile them up, you don't know anything about the value of what's inside them. If you have 37 briefcases, and they jointly weigh 384 pounds, what does that say about the future of the company? Nothing. Yet, the contents of those briefcases might have a lot to do with your future. The only way you can settle the issue is to open the briefcases and sort through the content.

Test cases are like briefcases. Counting them without regard to content tells you nothing. Calculating the ratio of passes to fails tells you nothing: Is a 90 percent passing rate good or horrible? No one can know without intimate knowledge of the contents of the tests. Calculating the ratio of implemented cases to planned cases tells you nothing; maybe the hardest were postponed to the end, and the last 10 percent of the cases will take 50 percent of the time to implement. Or maybe the number of planned cases is totally inadequate to cover the risks that matter.

Sometimes test managers agree with us about this but feel that they have no alternative. Well, there is an alternative: nothing. Consider that it may be better to know little and deal with that reality, than to know little and pretend you know a lot. There's another alternative: Talk about risks and coverage. In other words, examine and discuss the content of your tests.[1]

Testers who use unqualified, unexplained test case metrics to convey the extent and completeness of testing to their clients are, intentionally or not, *deceiving* them.

Lesson 281 Your test strategy is more than your tests.

Your strategy contains the reasoning behind the testing that you do. When asked about your test strategy, it may seem that the best answer is to point to your tests and say, "These 500 tests are my strategy for testing this product." Well, that may be an accurate answer, but it's not very helpful. It's information overload, and it tells nothing about how well those tests fulfill your mission. Provide information that helps: Summarize the techniques and motivations that produced your tests.

Lesson 282 Your test strategy explains your testing.

When you have a clear strategy in mind, and you test in accordance with that strategy, you can explain your test process quickly and convincingly to anyone who asks. That wins support for your test process from the rest of the

---

[1]Johanna Rothman feels that our position on this is too extreme. She writes, "Another alternative you have is to discuss what these numbers mean. For example, when your test pass ratio falls from 98% to 30% and you're at the beginning of the project, should you worry? Most likely not. But, if you're a week before Beta, or worse, product ship, you should probably worry. Why? At the beginning of the project, you don't expect to run many of the tests. At the end of the project, you expect to run most of, if not all, the tests. You can use the numbers to discuss the problem of why your expectations are not being met. Maybe you don't have enough people to run through all the tests, or enough people to write the bug reports, or enough people to verify the fixed bugs. You can use these numbers to explain your concerns."

Jeff Bleiberg writes, "Typically, there is a need to provide visibility into the testing process. This can be done with metrics. But I've found no matter how 'robust' and 'self-explanatory' I think the metrics are, people will misinterpret them. So, one of my rules is that I never distribute reports, I conduct status meetings in which I discuss the metrics and their meaning."

team. When you aren't clear on your test strategy, your explanations are more likely to sound confused and unconvincing.

A good test strategy is:

- *Product-specific.* Whatever good a generic test strategy may be, a strategy that is specific to the product and technology at hand will be that much better.

- *Risk-focused.* Show how the test process will address the things that matter most. Connect the test process to your mission on this project.

- *Diversified.* In most situations, a diversified strategy is better than a monolithic strategy. A diversified strategy is one that includes a variety of different test techniques or approaches. Problems that sneak past one test approach may well be captured by another approach.

- *Practical.* You must be able to perform the strategy. Don't suggest a test strategy that is far beyond the capabilities of the project.

Lesson 283 **Apply diverse half-measures.**

A less thorough, more diversified test strategy is better than a more thorough, less diverse strategy. In other words, it's better to do more different kinds of testing to a pretty good level, than to do one or two kinds of testing perfectly. We call this the principle of *diverse half-measures*.

This strategic principle derives from the structured complexity of software products. When you test, you are sampling a complex space. No single test technique will sample this space in a way that finds all important problems quickly. Any given test technique may find a lot of bugs at first, but the find-rate curve will flatten out. If you switch to a technique that is sensitive to a different kind of problem, your find rate may well climb again. In terms of overall bug-finding productivity, perform each technique to the point of sufficiently diminished returns and switch to a new technique.

Diversification has another purpose that is rooted in a puzzle: How is it possible to test a product for months and ship it, only for your users to discover, on the very next day, big problems that you didn't know about? A few things could cause this situation. A major cause is tunnel vision. It wasn't that you didn't test enough; it was that you didn't perform the right *kind* of test. We've seen cases where a company ran hundreds of thousands of test cases and still missed simple obvious problems, because they ran an insufficient variety of tests.

To ensure diversity, use the five-fold testing system (the classification system presented in Chapter 3, "Testing Techniques") to select techniques from all five categories. Diversify to maximize the find rate. Diversify to minimize the chances of overlooking an important problem.

Cultivate the raw materials of powerful test strategies.

Your test strategy is made possible by the resources available to perform it. Throughout the project, and across all projects, cultivate these resources so that you maximize your strategic options. Some of these resources are:

- Your skill in each test technique.
- Your knowledge of the underlying technologies of the product.
- Friends with special testing or technical skills.
- Repositories of raw test data.
- A variety of test platforms, including multiple operating systems and hardware configurations.
- A variety of test tools.
- Actual user data.
- Testability functions built into the product (*e.g.* log files, assertions, and test menus)

Your first strategy on a project is always wrong.

Strategy should evolve as you continue to learn about the product and its failure patterns. We recommend your strategy be based on risk. That leaves you with a problem: *You don't know what the risks are.* At the start of the project, all you have are rumors about where the good bugs hang out. Educated guesses, if you're lucky. Your strategy at the start of the project is therefore likely to suffer from at least one of two problems: not focused on risk or focused on areas that seem like risks but aren't.

You can solve this problem by not prematurely committing to one and only one test strategy. Let your strategy evolve as you learn more about the product, as you see where its weaknesses are, and as new ways to test it occur to you.

Project lifecycles like the V-Model expect you to know what your strategy should be right at the start of the project. Because you'd have to be not only a genius, but a wealthy mind-reading genius, to get your strategy right the first time, we think the V-Model is a poor way to organize a project. If you're stuck with the V-Model, consider developing a test plan early and then sneaking new and better tests in later, after everyone has stopped paying attention to the documentation and is just trying to ship a good product on time.

At every phase of the project, ask yourself "what can I test now and how can I test it?"

We sometimes see projects that take a project phase, such as system integration, and declare that only certain kinds of testing, such as requirements-based testing, are permissible during that phase. This is as puzzling as the prohibition against wearing white after Labor Day. Why follow such general and sweeping rules?

The project phase when you test and the architectural level at which you test (unit, subsystem, or system) are considerations for your test strategy, but are not the dominant considerations. We recommend simply asking yourself, at any point in the project, "What can I test, here and now, and how can I test it well?"

Don't assume that certain techniques are useful only at certain times. Let your test strategy be opportunistic. At all times, test whatever is worth testing and use whatever test techniques serve your clients best.

Test to the maturity of the product.

Although generic project phase test strategies are inadequate, it makes good sense to test differently depending on how mature the product is.

- *Early in the project, test sympathetically.* Early in the project, the product doesn't work very well, and you don't know very much about it. Harsh tests at this stage are unnecessary for the most part, because even simple tests will find bugs. Also, the programmers, who know that the product is immature, are nervous about testers scowling too hard at their baby. What the programmers want to know is whether the features, as they get implemented, are basically operational.

- *In the middle of the project, test aggressively.* As the product comes together and the major features are implemented and shaken down, simple tests lose their effectiveness. The programmers also feel more confident in the product. They move from feature design and implementation to full-time bug fixing. This is the time to use more demanding and complex tests. Mine flaky parts of the product for all they're worth. Find and report as many bugs as you can. Build a backlog of bugs for the developers to work through.

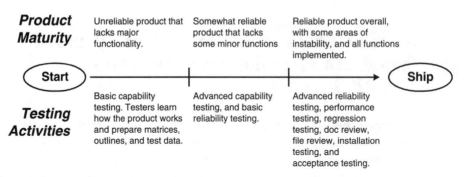

Figure 11.2 Product cycle.

- *Near the end of the project, test diversely.* It's harder to find bugs in a mature product, so you have to get more creative. This is the time to push the diversity of your testing to the limit of your imagination and the support management will give you. Use helpers, automation, special testing events (bug finding parties or bug bounties), heuristics, beta testers— anything and everything. If you do this well, your bug find rate will look a lot like the ideal curve in the diagram. Push it high through aggressive testing and keep it high by diversifying and rediversifying your tests until you simply run out of ideas for new and better tests.

- *In the final days, test meticulously.* Making a mistake in the final days can cost your company dearly. As the ship date nears, the focus of testing

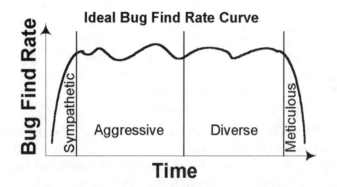

Figure 11.3 The ideal result of sustained, aggressive testing.

should become more defensive. Test each change carefully. Check that all the files to be released are the correct version. Use pair testing to provide two more eyes for each test.

The overall goal is to continually adjust the strategy as the product improves, so that the find rate of important bugs is strong throughout the project.

Use test levels to simplify discussions of test complexity.

To simplify communication about the test complexity in the strategy, many test projects have found it helpful to distinguish levels of testing. Lower levels are simpler tests, less powerful tests. Higher levels are more complex, more powerful tests. This can simplify the discussion of test strategy by providing a shorthand for talking about classes of testing. Here's one example of a test level hierarchy:

■ *Level 0, Smoke Testing.* Simple tests that show the product is ready for independent testing; a sanity check. If level 0 tests fail, send it back to the programmers.

■ *Level 1, Capability Testing.* Tests that verify the capability of each function of the product. The goal is to make sure each function is capable of performing its task. Convoluted scenarios, challenging data, and function interactions are avoided at this level.

■ *Level 2, Function Testing.* Tests that examine both the capability and basic reliability of each individual function and subfunction of the product. Data coverage and complex test result evaluation methods are of interest. Use boundary, stress, and error handling tests; avoid convoluted scenarios and function interactions.

■ *Level 3, Complex Testing.* Tests that involve interactions and flow of control among groups of functions to form complex scenarios. The focus of evaluation is expanded and may include performance assessment, compatibility, resource contention, memory leaks, long-term reliability, or other types of quality criteria that become testable when the product is more mature.

Each of these levels may correspond to a number of different test techniques or combinations of techniques. The overall theme is to start testing broadly and sympathetically, then move into depth and deviousness as the product matures. Performing level 3 tests on a very early build of the product, without first performing level 1 and 2 tests, will probably lead to very annoyed programmers. More likely, you won't be able to run those tests.

Lesson 289

Test the gray box.

Even though you probably don't have full knowledge of the internals of the product you test, a test strategy based partly on internals is a powerful idea. We call this gray box testing. The concept is simple: If you know something about how the product works on the inside, you can test it better from the outside. This is not to be confused with white box testing, which attempts to cover the internals of the product in detail. In gray box mode, you are testing from the outside of the product, just as you do with black box, but your testing choices are informed by your knowledge of how the underlying components operate and interact.

Gray box testing is especially important with Web and Internet applications, because the Internet is built around loosely integrated components that connect via relatively well-defined interfaces. Unless you understand the architecture of the Net, your testing will be skin deep. Hung Nguyen's *Testing Applications on the Web* (2000) is a good example of gray box test strategy applied to the Web.

Lesson 290

Beware of ancestor worship when reusing test materials.

When reusing a test or any test material, don't treat it as a black box. Get to know it. Study it. Figure out why it is designed the way it is. In many cases, archival test material is of such poor quality that it would be much better not to reuse it. The tendency of many testers is to trust old test materials just because they *are* old and probably mysterious. We've repeatedly discovered ancient tests being routinely executed long after (in some cases years after) they became obsolete. We've seen smart skilled testers unquestioningly follow tests written by far less skilled testers. This is the dark side of reuse.

One test lab we know has a standing rule "always test with a Compaq Presario, because they are notoriously incompatible." The odd thing is, that rule was written in 1996. Is it still valid today? Has anyone revisited this issue? Does anyone dare question the authority of the Ancient Ones who wrote the rule?

If you feel attracted to the idea of writing tests that will be reused, ask yourself how people will know what your tests mean, why they exist, and when they should be retired or reinvented. Otherwise, there's a good chance that your clients will treat your work as a magical totem, rather than use your tests as you intended.

Two testers testing the same thing are probably not duplicating efforts.

Some testers wring their hands about the possibility of duplicated effort. Relax. Don't worry about people overlapping on the same test tasks or testing the same product in the same way. Duplicated test effort is not the same thing as duplicated tests. Two testers testing the same thing have a fair likelihood of finding different problems. That's because the testers are probably not running the same tests. Even when they think they are running the same tests, there is bound to be some variation between them. Besides, one tester may notice a problem that another tester overlooked. It's very common.

Duplicated test effort is almost never a waste. The real question is not waste, but whether one part of the product deserves to be double-teamed.

Design your test strategy in response to project factors as well as product risks.

A good strategy is shaped not only by product risks, but also by factors within the project. Here are some project-based strategic principles:

- *Don't lose bugs in the cracks between testers.* Unless you apply diverse half-measures or overlapping testing assignments, you face a real risk of not testing something because it lies on the boundary between the assignments of two testers (or teams).

- *Frequently test what you're asked to test.* You're testing on behalf of many clients. What do they think you should test? Find out and make sure you're doing at least some of it.

- *Occasionally test what you're asked not to test.* Sometimes you're asked not to test certain parts of the product. This can be a delicate matter, and we can't tell you what to do. However, sometimes the things you're asked not to test are the things that need it most.

- *Test the confusion and conflict.* Like coder; like code. Wherever there is confusion and conflict, bugs will thrive. If the programmer seems not quite sure what a feature is supposed to do, test it. If he's new to the technology, test it. If two programmers are building units that interface with each other, test the interface. You won't be disappointed.

- *Don't beat a dead feature.* When it's clear that a feature seems full of bugs, don't continue to test it unless you check in with the developer. It may be a bad build or a bad configuration. Also, if a component is so bad that it's going to be replaced rather than revised, any bugs you find will be summarily closed, so don't bother testing.

- *More change means more testing.* Theoretically, the tiniest change in the product can create large and nonlocal effects. That means any change can potentially invalidate all the testing you've ever done on the product. In reality, most changes have a fairly localized effect. However, it is certainly true that you must follow the changes with your testing. The more change in the product, the more testing you must do. This becomes a big deal in the end game of a project.

Treat test cycles as the heartbeat of the test process.

You provide your testing in cycles. Test cycles begin with a build and end with one of two things: the next build or a determination that further testing is unwarranted. Your test strategy is made concrete in the test cycles. Plan your test cycles to get the best information to your clients as soon as you possibly can. Here's one way to organize a test cycle:

1. *Receive the product.* Make sure you get the right build.

2. *Configure your test system.* Clean your test system. Restore the disk image to a pristine state or completely uninstall the previous version of the product.

3. *Verify testability.* Is this a good build? Is it worth your time to test? Start by running smoke tests: simple tests that demonstrate that each major function is present and basically operational.

4. *Determine what is new or changed.* What new code has been written that extends or modifies the capabilities of the product?

5. *Determine what bugs have been fixed.* Also look for problems that have been rejected and respond accordingly.

6. *Test fixes.* Test fixes first while they're still fresh in the minds of the programmers. If fixes fail, they want to know quickly.

7. *Test new or changed areas.* The next hottest topic in the programmers' minds is probably new code.

8. *Test other areas (remember, higher risk stuff first).* Now test everything else (that matters), until time runs out or you've tested it enough. If you have automated regression tests, run them.

9. *Report results.* Results should be reported periodically, at least once a day, throughout the test cycle.

How To Evolve a Context-Driven Test Plan

This guide will assist you with your test planning. Remember, the real test plan is the set of ideas that actually guides your testing. We've designed the guide to be helpful whether or not you are writing a test plan *document*.

This is not a template. It's not a form to be filled out. It's a set of ideas meant to jog your thinking, so you'll be less likely to forget something important. We use terse language and descriptions that may not be suited to a novice tester. This guide is designed more to support an experienced tester or test lead.

Following are seven task themes. Visit the themes in any order. In fact, jump freely from one to the other. Just realize that the quality of your test plan is related to how well you've performed tasks and considered issues like the ones documented here. The *Status Check* sections will help you decide when you have a good enough plan, but we recommend revisiting and revising your plan (at least in your head) throughout the project.

1. Monitor major test planning challenges.

Look for risks, roadblocks, or other challenges that will impact the time, effort, or feasibility of planning a practical and effective test strategy. Get a sense for the overall scope of the planning effort. Monitor these issues throughout the project.

STATUS CHECK

❑ Are any product quality standards especially critical to achieve or difficult to measure?

❑ Is the product complex or hard to learn?

❑ Will testers require special training or tools?

❑ Is any part of the test platform difficult to obtain or configure?

❑ Will you test unintegrated or semioperable product components?

❑ Are there any particular testability problems?

❑ Does the project team lack experience with the product design, technology, or user base?

❑ Does testing have to start soon?

❑ Is any information needed for planning not yet available?

❑ Are you unable to review a version of the product to be tested (even a demo, prototype, or old version)?

❑ Is adequate testing staff difficult to hire or organize?

❑ Must you adhere to an unfamiliar test methodology?

❑ Are project plans made without regard to testing needs?

❑ Is the plan subject to lengthy negotiation or approval?

❑ Are you remote from your clients?

❑ Are project plans changing frequently?

❑ Will the plan be subject to audit?

❑ Are your clients unsure of what they want from you?

2. Clarify your mission.

Any or all of the goals in this section may be part of your testing mission. Some are more important than others. Based on your knowledge of the project, rank these goals. For any that apply, discover any specific success metrics by which you'll be judged.

MISSION ELEMENTS TO CONSIDER

❏ Find important problems fast.

❏ Perform a comprehensive quality assessment.

❏ Certify product quality to a specific standard.

❏ Minimize testing time or cost.

❏ Maximize testing efficiency.

❏ Advise clients on improving quality or testability.

❏ Advise clients on how to test.

❏ Make sure that the test process is fully accountable.

❏ Rigorously follow certain methods or instructions.

❏ Satisfy particular stakeholders.

POSSIBLE WORK PRODUCTS

❏ Brief email outlining your mission.

❏ One-page test project charter.

STATUS CHECK

❏ Do you know who your clients are?

❏ Do the people who matter agree on your mission?

❏ Is your mission sufficiently clear that you can base your planning on it?

3. Analyze the product.

Get to know the product and the underlying technology. Learn how the product will be used. Steep yourself in it. As you progress through the project, your testing will become better because you will be more of a product expert.

WHAT TO ANALYZE

❑ Users (who they are and what they do)

❑ Structure (code, files, etc.)

❑ Functions (what the product does)

❑ Data (input, output, states, etc.)

❑ Platforms (external hardware and software)

❑ Operations (what product's used for)

WAYS TO ANALYZE

❑ Perform exploratory testing.

❑ Review product and project documentation.

❑ Interview designers and users.

❑ Compare with similar products.

POSSIBLE WORK PRODUCTS

❑ Test coverage outline.

❑ Annotated specifications.

❑ Product issue list.

STATUS CHECK

❑ Do designers approve of the product coverage outline?

❑ Do designers think you understand the product?

❑ Can you visualize the product and predict behavior?

❑ Are you able to produce test data (input and results)?

❑ Can you configure and operate the product?

❑ Do you understand how the product will be used?

❑ Are you aware of gaps or inconsistencies in the design?

❑ Have you found implicit specifications as well as explicit?

4. Analyze product risk.

How might this product fail in a way that matters? At first you'll have a general idea, at best. As you progress through the project, your test strategy and your testing will become better because you'll learn more about the failure dynamics of the product.

WHAT TO ANALYZE

❑ Threats (challenging situations and data)

❑ Vulnerabilities (where it's likely to fail)

❑ Failure modes (possible kinds of problems)

❑ Victim impact (how problems matter)

WAYS TO ANALYZE

❑ Review requirements and specifications.

❑ Review actual failures.

❑ Interview designers and users.

❑ Review product against risk heuristics and quality criteria categories.

❑ Identify general fault and failure patterns.

POSSIBLE WORK PRODUCTS

❑ Component/risk matrix.

❑ Risk list.

STATUS CHECK

❑ Do the designers and users concur with the risk analysis?

❑ Will you be able to detect all significant kinds of problems, should they occur during testing?

❑ Do you know where to focus testing effort for maximum effectiveness?

❑ Can the designers do anything to make important problems easier to detect, or less likely to occur?

❑ How will you discover if your risk analysis is accurate?

5. Design the test strategy.

What can you do to test rapidly and effectively based on the best information you have about the product? By all means make the best decisions you can, up front, but let your strategy improve throughout the project.

CONSIDER TECHNIQUES FROM FIVE PERSPECTIVES

❑ Tester-focused techniques.

❑ Coverage-focused techniques (both structural and functional).

❑ Problem-focused techniques.

❑ Activity-focused techniques.

❑ Evaluation-focused techniques.

WAYS TO PLAN

❑ Match techniques to risks and product areas.

❑ Visualize specific and practical techniques.

❑ Diversify your strategy to minimize the chance of missing important problems.

❑ Look for ways automation could allow you to expand your strategy.

❑ Don't over plan. Let testers use their brains.

POSSIBLE WORK PRODUCTS

❑ Itemized statement of each test strategy chosen and how it will be applied.

❑ Risk/task matrix.

❑ List of issues or challenges inherent in the chosen strategies.

❑ Advisory of poorly covered parts of the product.

❑ Test cases (only if required).

STATUS CHECK

❑ Do your clients concur with the test strategy?

❑ Is everything in the test strategy necessary?

❑ Can you actually carry out this strategy?

❑ Is the test strategy too generic; could it just as easily apply to any product?

❑ Is there any category of important problem that you know you are not testing for?

❑ Has the strategy made use of available resources and helpers?

6. Plan logistics.

How will you implement your strategy? Your test strategy is profoundly affected by logistical constraints or mandates. Try to negotiate for the resources you need and exploit whatever you have.

LOGISTICAL AREAS
- ❏ Test effort estimation and scheduling.
- ❏ Testability advocacy.
- ❏ Test team staffing (right skills).
- ❏ Tester training and supervision.
- ❏ Tester task assignments.
- ❏ Product information gathering and management.
- ❏ Project meetings, communication, and coordination.
- ❏ Relations with all other project functions, including development.
- ❏ Test platform acquisition and configuration.
- ❏ Agreements and protocols.
- ❏ Test tools and automation.
- ❏ Stubbing and simulation needs.
- ❏ Test suite management and maintenance.
- ❏ Build and transmittal protocol.
- ❏ Test cycle administration.
- ❏ Bug reporting system and protocol.
- ❏ Test status reporting protocol.
- ❏ Code freeze and incremental testing.
- ❏ Pressure management in the end game.
- ❏ Sign-off protocol.
- ❏ Evaluation of test effectiveness.

POSSIBLE WORK PRODUCTS
- ❏ Issues list.
- ❏ Project risk analysis.
- ❏ Responsibility matrix.
- ❏ Test schedule.

STATUS CHECK

❏ Do the logistics of the project support the test strategy?

❏ Are there any problems that block testing?

❏ Are the logistics and strategy adaptable in the face of foreseeable problems?

❏ Can you start testing now and sort out the rest of the issues later?

7. Share the plan.

You are not alone. The test process must serve the project. So, involve the project in your test planning process. You don't have to be grandiose about it. At least chat with key members of the team to get their perspective and implicit consent to pursue your plan.

WAYS TO SHARE

❏ Engage designers and stakeholders in the test planning process.

❏ Actively solicit opinions about the test plan.

❏ Do everything possible to help the developers succeed.

❏ Help the developers understand how what they do impacts testing.

❏ Talk to technical writers and technical support people about sharing quality information.

❏ Get designers and developers to review and approve reference materials.

❏ Record and track agreements.

❏ Get people to review the plan in pieces.

❏ Improve reviewability by minimizing unnecessary text in test plan documents.

GOALS

❏ Common understanding of the test process.

❏ Common commitment to the test process.

❏ Reasonable participation in the test process.

❏ Management has reasonable expectations about the test process.

STATUS CHECK

❏ Is the project team paying attention to the test plan?

❏ Does the project team, especially first-line management, understand the role of the test team?

❏ Does the project team feel that the test team has the best interests of the project at heart?

❏ Is there an adversarial or constructive relationship between the test team and the rest of the project?

❏ Does anyone feel that the testers are "off on a tangent" rather than focused on important testing?

How Good Is This Test Plan?

The answer to the question, "How good is this test plan?" can be given only with reference to an idea of what a test plan should be. Although a number of public standards specify test plan document formats, they provide little basis for distinguishing a better plan from a worse plan. This model identifies basic concepts, functions that a test plan serves, criteria that a test plan should satisfy, and some heuristics to assist in determining whether the criteria are satisfied with respect to the functions.

Terms and Concepts

- *Test plan.* The test plan is the set of ideas that guide or represent the test process. Often those ideas are only partially documented, spread across multiple documents, and subject to change as the project evolves.

- *Test plan document.* A test plan document is any document intended to convey test plan ideas. However, test plan documents are not the only source of information about the test plan. Test plan information is also contained in the oral tradition of the project and the culture of the company.

- *Test strategy.* The test strategy specifies the relationship between the test project and the test mission. The strategy deals with what will be tested and how. Test strategy is distinct from the logistics of implementing the strategy.

- *Test logistics.* The means by which the test strategy is implemented and results delivered. Test logistics includes details such as who, where, and when the testing is done and the supporting materials to be used.

- *Test process.* Process has many meanings. In this document, we use the word to mean how the testing actually unfolds (as opposed to how it's supposed to unfold or how documents might say that it's unfolding).

The Functions of a Test Plan

Test plan functions are what a test plan is supposed to help us do. Following is a list of functions served by an ideal test plan. However, a test plan document may address only a subset of these functions. The rest are handled in other documents or managed directly by the test manager or individual tester without the support of any document. Thus, a test plan should be judged only with regard to those functions that it intends to serve or are insufficiently served by other means.

- Support the development of a quality assessment that enables wise and timely product decisions.

- Describe and justify the test strategy in relation to product requirements and product risk. Promote awareness of the benefits and limitations of the test strategy.

- Describe and justify any special requirements or entry criteria that must be met in order for the test project to proceed, as well as any exit or process for determining when to stop testing.

- Support the initiation and organization of the test project, including preparations, staffing, delegation of responsibilities, facility acquisition, task planning, and scheduling.

- Support daily management and evaluation of the test project and test strategy.

- Support effective coordination, collaboration, and other relations among members of the test team and between the test team and the rest of the project.

- Identify and manage any risks or issues that may impact the project.

- Specify the deliverables of the test project and the delivery process.

- Record historical information in support of process audits, process improvement, and future test projects.

Test Plan Quality Criteria

How well does the test plan serve its various functions? This list of criteria may help you think about that:

- *Usefulness.* Will the test plan effectively serve its intended functions?

- *Accuracy.* Is the test plan document accurate with respect to any statements of fact?

- *Efficiency.* Does it make efficient use of available resources?

- *Adaptability.* Will it tolerate reasonable change and unpredictability in the project?

- *Clarity.* Is the test plan self-consistent and sufficiently unambiguous?

- *Usability.* Is the test plan document concise, maintainable, and helpfully organized?

- *Compliance.* Does the test plan meet externally imposed requirements?

- *Foundation.* Is the test plan the product of an effective test planning process?

- *Feasibility.* Is the test plan within the capability of the organization that must use it?

Test Plan Heuristics

To evaluate a test plan, consider how it fulfills its functions and how it meets the quality criteria. To do that, we suggest applying the following heuristics. A heuristic is a rule of thumb or educated guess. None of the heuristics in our list is equally important in every situation, and some may not apply at all in your situation. Each heuristic is described in terms of a general rule, and a brief basis for that rule. The basis is intended to help determine when and where a heuristic applies.

HEURISTIC	BASIS FOR HEURISTIC
1. *Important problems fast.* Testing should be optimized to find important problems fast, rather than attempting to find all problems with equal urgency.	Fixes may be difficult and time-consuming. They may introduce new problems. Therefore, finding problems as soon as possible will give the team the best chance of fixing them safely.
2. *Focus on risk.* Test strategy should focus most effort on areas of potential technical risk, while still putting some effort into low-risk areas just in case the risk analysis is wrong.	Complete testing is impossible, and we can never know if our perception of technical risk is completely accurate.
3. *Maximize diversity.* Test strategy should be diversified in terms of test techniques and perspectives. Methods of evaluating test coverage should take into account multiple dimensions of coverage, including structural, functional, data, platform, operations, and requirements.	No single test technique can reveal all important problems in a linear fashion. We can never know for sure if we have found all the problems that matter. Diversification minimizes the risk that the test strategy will be blind to certain kinds of problems.
4. *Avoid overscripting.* Avoid pre-specifying tests in detail unless there is a specific and compelling reason to do so. The test strategy should incorporate reasonable variation and make use of the tester's ability to use situational reasoning to focus on important, but unanticipated problems.	A rigid test strategy may make it more likely that a particular subset of problems will be uncovered, but in a complex system, it reduces the likelihood that all important problems will be uncovered. Reasonable variability in testing, such as that which results from interactive, exploratory testing, increases incidental test coverage, without substantially sacrificing essential coverage.

HEURISTIC	BASIC FOR HEURISTIC
5. *Test to the intent.* It is important to test against implied requirements—the full extent of what the requirements mean, not just what they say. Why does each requirement matter? Find out. Test the spirit, not just the letter.	Testing only against explicit written requirements will not reveal all important problems, because defined requirements are generally incomplete, and natural language is inherently ambiguous. Many requirements probably aren't written down.
6. *We are not alone.* The test plan should promote collaboration with all other functions of the project, especially programming, technical support, and technical writing. Whenever possible, testers should also collaborate with actual customers and users, in order to better understand their requirements.	Other teams and stakeholders often have information about product problems or potential problems that can be of use to the test team. Their perspective may help the testers make a better analysis of risk. Testers may also have information that is of use to them.
7. *Promote testability.* Consult with programmers to help them build a more testable product.	The likelihood that a test strategy will serve its purpose is profoundly affected by the testability of the product.
8. *Test plans aren't generic.* A test plan should highlight the nonroutine, project-specific aspects of the test strategy and test project.	Every software project worth doing involves special technical challenges that a good test effort must address. A generic test plan indicates a weak test planning process.
9. *Content or nothing.* A test plan document should avoid any unnecessary text. Do not state the obvious. Make every sentence count. If you have different audiences, consider preparing different versions of the plan for each audience.	Any text that looks unnecessary or seems obvious will reduce the probability that any of the document will be read. Readers will assume they already understand what the document contains.
10. *Don't program people.* The test project should use humans for what humans do well and use automation for what automation does well. Manual testing should allow for improvisation and on-the-spot critical thinking, while automated testing should be used for tests that require high repeatability, high speed, and no judgment.	Many test projects suffer under the false belief that human testers are effective when they use exactingly specified test scripts or that test automation duplicates the value of human cognition in the test execution process. Manual and automated testing are not two forms of the same thing. They are two entirely different classes of test technique.

	HEURISTIC	**BASIC FOR HEURISTIC**
11.	*The test schedule depends.* The test schedule should be represented and justified in such a way as to highlight any dependencies on the progress of development, the testability of the product, time required to report problems, and the project team's assessment of risk.	A monolithic test schedule in a test plan often indicates the false belief that testing is an independent activity. The test schedule can stand alone only to the extent that the product is highly testable, development is complete, and the test process is not interrupted by the frequent need to report problems.
12.	*Avoid the bottleneck.* The test process should be kept off the critical path to the extent possible. This can be done by testing in parallel with development work and finding problems worth fixing faster than the programmers fix them.	This is important in order to deflect pressure to truncate the test process.
13.	*Rapid feedback.* The feedback loop between testers and programmers should be as tight as possible. Test cycles should be designed to provide rapid feedback to programmers about recent additions and changes they have made before a full regression test is commenced. Whenever possible, testers and programmers should work physically near each other.	This is important in order to maximize the efficiency and speed of quality improvement. It also helps keep testing off the critical path.
14.	*Testers aren't the only testers.* The test project should employ channels of information about quality other than formal testing in order to help evaluate and adjust the test project. Examples of these channels are inspections, field testing, or informal testing by people outside of the test team.	By examining product quality information gathered through various means beyond the test team, blind spots in the formal test strategy can be uncovered.
15.	*Review documentation.* All archival test documentation should be reviewed by someone other than the person who wrote it. The review process used should be commensurate with the criticality of the document.	Tunnel vision is the great occupational hazard of testing. Review not only helps to reveal blind spots in test design, but it can also help promote dialog and peer education about test practices.

The Context-Driven Approach to Software Testing

We belong to a group of people who are sometimes called the *context-driven school* of software testing. After several years (on and off), we have finally developed a statement of principles that, we believe, captures the community of views among the loose collection of people who provide intellectual leadership to this school.

This book, *Lessons Learned in Software Testing,* presents a large set of examples of context-driven thinking and interpretation of our experience in software development. Along with the book, we have created a web site, context-driven-testing.com, to further the development of the school.

If you read the principles and illustrations below and decide that you want to identify yourself as part of the school, visit context-driven-testing.com and join the community.

The Seven Basic Principles of the Context-Driven School

1. The value of any practice depends on its context.
2. There are good practices in context, but there are no best practices.
3. People, working together, are the most important part of any project's context.
4. Projects unfold over time in ways that are often not predictable.

5. The product is a solution. If the problem isn't solved, the product doesn't work.

6. Good software testing is a challenging intellectual process.

7. Only through judgment and skill, exercised cooperatively throughout the entire project, are we able to do the right things at the right times to effectively test our products.

Illustrations of the Principles in Action:

- Testing groups exist to provide testing-related services. They do not run the development project; they serve the project.

- Testing is done on behalf of stakeholders in the service of developing, qualifying, debugging, investigating, or selling a product. Entirely different testing strategies could be appropriate for these different objectives.

- It is entirely proper for different test groups to have different missions. A core practice in the service of one mission might be irrelevant or counter-productive in the service of another.

- Metrics that are not valid are dangerous.

- The essential value of any test case lies in its ability to provide information (*i.e.,* to reduce uncertainty).

- All oracles are fallible. Even if the product appears to pass your test, it might well have failed it in ways that you (or the automated test program) were not monitoring.

- Automated testing is not automatic manual testing: It's nonsensical to talk about automated tests as if they were automated human testing.

- Different types of defects will be revealed by different types of tests—tests should become more challenging or should focus on different risks as the program becomes more stable.

- Test artifacts are worthwhile to the degree that they satisfy their stakeholders' relevant requirements.

An Example

Consider two projects. One is developing the control software for an airplane. What *"correct behavior"* means is a highly technical and mathematical subject. FAA regulations must be followed. Anything you do—

or don't do—would be evidence in a lawsuit 20 years from now. The development staff share an engineering culture that values caution, precision, repeatability, and double-checking everyone's work.

Another project is developing a word processor that is to be used over the web. "Correct behavior" is whatever woos a vast and inarticulate audience of Microsoft Word users over to your software. There are no regulatory requirements that matter (other than those governing public stock offerings). Time to market matters—20 months from now, it will all be over, for good or ill. The development staff decidedly do *not* come from an engineering culture and attempts to talk in a way normal for the first culture will cause them to refer to you as "damage to be routed around."

Testing practices appropriate to the first project will fail in the second. Practices appropriate to the second project would be criminally negligent in the first.

Members of the Context-Driven School

If you agree with these principles and you want to be identified as a member of this school, please email us at context@satisfice.com.

■ The following published authors have identified themselves as agreeing with these principles:

Cem Kaner

James Bach

Bret Pettichord

Anna S. W. Allison

Ståle Amland

Bernie Berger

Jaya R. Carl

Ross Collard

Christopher Denardis

Marge Farrell

Erick Griffin

Sam Guckenheimer

Elisabeth Hendrickson

Kathy Iberle

Bob Johnson

Karen Johnson

Mark Johnson

Alan A. Jorgensen, Ph.D.

Brian Marick

Patricia A. McQuaid, Ph.D.

Alan Myrvold

Noel Nyman

Pat McGee

Johanna Rothman

Jane Stepak

Paul Szymkowiak

Andy Tinkham

Steve Tolman

Bibliography

-A-

Agre, Phil. 2001. Networking on the Network. Available at dlis.gseis.ucla.edu/people/pagre/network.html.

Amland, Ståle. 1999. Risk Based Testing and Metrics. Available at www .amland.no/Word%20Documents/EuroSTAR%20'99%20Paper.doc.

Asböck, Stefan. 2000. *load testing for eConfidence*. Lexington, MA: Segue Software, Inc. Available via www.segue.com.

Association for Computing Machinery. 2000. A Summary of the ACM Position on Software Engineering as a Licensed Engineering Profession. Available at www.acm.org/serving/se_policy/selep_main.html.

Austin, Robert. 1996. *Measuring and Managing Performance in Organizations.* New York: Dorset House Publishing.

-B-

Bach, James, 1999a. Reframing Requirements Analysis. *IEEE Computer* 32:6. 113–114.

Bach, James, 1999b. A Low Tech Testing Dashboard. Available at /www .satisfice.com/presentations/dashboard.pdf.

Bach, James, 1999c. James Bach on Risk-Based Testing. STQE Magazine. vol. 1 #6.

Baron, Jonathan. 1994. *Thinking and Deciding.* Cambridge: Cambridge University Press.

Beck, Kent, 1999. *Extreme Programming Explained.* Reading, Massachusetts: Addison-Wesley.

Beck, Kent, M. Beedle, A. van Bennekum, A. Cockburn, W. Cunningham, M. Fowler, J. Grenning, J. Highsmith, A. Hunt, R. Jeffries, J. Kern, B. Marick. R. C. Martin, S. Mellor, K. Schwaber, J. Sutherland, D. Thomas. 2001. *Manifesto for Agile Software Development* [online]. Available at www.agilealliance.org/.

Beizer, Boris. 1990. *Software Testing Techniques, 2nd edition.* Boston: International Thompson Computer Press.

Bender, Richard A. 1991. Requirements-based Testing, *Quality Assurance Institute Journal,* 27–32.

Black, Rex. 1999. *Managing the Testing Process.* Redmond, Washington: Microsoft Press.

Booth, Wayne C., Gregory G. Colomb, and Joseph M. Williams. 1995. *The Craft of Research.* Chicago: University of Chicago Press.

Brooks, Frederick P. 1995. *The Mythical Man-Month: Anniversary Edition with Four New Chapters.* Reading Massachusetts: Addison-Wesley.

Brown, John Seely and Paul Duguid. 2000. *The Social Life of Information.* Boston: Harvard Business School Press.

Buwalda, Hans and Maartje Kasdorp. 1999. Getting Automated Testing Under Control, *Software Testing & Quality Engineering,* November 1999.

-C-

Chapman, Jack. 1996. *Negotiating Your Salary: How to Make $1000 a Minute, 3rd edition.* Berkeley: Ten Speed Press.

Cohen, Daniel M., Siddhartha R. Dalal, Jesse Parelius, and Gardner C. Patton. 1996. The Combinatorial Design Approach to Automatic Test Generation. *IEEE Software,* Volume 13#5, September. Available at www.argreenhouse.com/papers/gcp/AETGissre96.shtml.

Cohen, D. M., S. R. Dalal, M. L. Fredman, and G. C. Patton. 1997. The AETG System: An Approach to Testing Based on Combinatorial Design. IEEE Transactions on Software Engineering. Vol 23#7, July. Available at www.argreenhouse.com/papers/gcp/AETGieee97.shtml.

Cohen, Noam. 2000. Building a Testpoint Framework. *Dr. Dobbs Journal.* March 2000.

Collard, Ross. 1999. Deriving Test Cases from Use Cases. *Software Testing & Quality Engineering,* July–August.

Collard, Ross. Forthcoming. *Software Testing & QA Techniques* (a multivolume series). (Some of this material is available in the course notes he hands out to his students.)

Constantine, Larry L. 1995. *Constantine on Peopleware.* Yourdon Press.

Construx 2001. Software Engineering Professionalism Web site. Available at www.construx.com/profession/home.htm.

-D-

Daconta, Michael C., Eric Monk, J. Paul Keller, and Keith Bohnenberger. 2000. *Java Pitfalls: Time-Saving Solutions and Workarounds to Improve Programs.* New York: John Wiley & Sons.

de Bono, Edward. 1970. *Lateral Thinking: Creativity Step by Step.* New York: Harper and Row.

DeMarco, Tom. 1997. *The Deadline.* New York: Dorset House Publishing.

DeMarco, Tom and Timothy Lister. 1999. *Peopleware: Productive Projects and Teams,* 2nd *edition.* New York: Dorset House Publishing.

Deming, W. Edwards. 1986. *Out of the Crisis.* Cambridge, Massachusetts: MIT Press.

DeNardis, Chris, 2000. Perspectives of a Test Manager. *STQE Magazine* 2: 5. Available at www.stickyminds.com/sitewide.asp?sid=194646&sqry=%2AJ%28MIXED%29%2AR%28relevance%29%2AK%28simplesite%29%2AF%28Perspectives+from+a+Test+Manager%29%2A&sidx=0&sopp=10&ObjectId=1976&Function=DETAILBROWSE&ObjectType=ART.

DiMaggio, Len. 2000. Looking Under The Hood. *STQE Magazine.* January.

Dörner, Dietrich. 1996. *The Logic of Failure.* Trans. Rita Kimber and Robert Kimber. New York: Metropolitan Books. Originally published in 1989.

Drucker, Peter. 1985. *The Effective Executive.* Harper Colophon.

Dustin, Elfriede, Jeff Rashka, and John Paul. 1999. *Automated Software Testing.* Reading, Massachusetts: Addison-Wesley.

Dwyer, Graham and Graham Freeburn. Business Object Scenarios: a fifth-generation approach to automated testing. In Fewster and Graham (1999).

-E-

Elmendorf, William R., 1973. *Cause-Effect Graphs in Functional Testing* Technical Report TR-00.2487, IBM Systems Development Division, Poughkeepsie, N.Y.

-F-

Fewster, Mark and Dorothy Graham. 1999. *Software Test Automation: Effective Use of Text Execution Tools.* Reading, Massachusetts: Addison-Wesley.

Feynman, Richard. 1989. *What Do You Care What Other People Think: Further Adventures of a Curious Character.* New York: Bantam Books.

Fisher, R. and D. Ertel. 1995. *Getting Ready to Negotiate: The Getting to Yes Workbook.*

Fisher, Roger, William Ury and Bruce Patton. 1991. *Getting to Yes.* Boston: Houghton Mifflin Co.

Freund, James C. 1992. *Smart Negotiating: How to Make Good Deals in the Real World.* Simon and Schuster.

-G-

Gause, Donald C. and Gerald M. Weinberg. 1989. *Exploring Requirements: Quality Before Design.* New York: Dorset House Publishing.

Gilb, Tom. 1997. *Evo: The Evolutionary Project Managers Handbook.* Available at /www.result-planning.com/, click on Download Center. If this document is not available, check for related material at www.stsc.hill.af.mil/swtesting/gilb.asp.

Glaser, Barney G. and Anselm L. Strauss. 1999. *The Discovery of Grounded Theory: Strategies for Qualitative Research.* New York: Aldine de Gruyter.

-H-

Heidtman Steel Products, Inc. v. Compuware Corp. 1999 U.S. Dist. Lexis 21700, U.S. District Court, N.D. Ohio.

Hendrickson, Elisabeth. 1999. Making the Right Choice: The Features You Need in a GUI Test Automation Tool. *STQE Magazine*, May. Available at www.qualitytree.com/feature/mtrc.pdf.

Hendrickson, Elisabeth. 2001a. Better Testing, Worse Quality? Available at www.qualitytree.com/feature/btwq.pdf.

Hendrickson, Elisabeth. 2001b. Bug Hunting: Going on a Software Safari. *Proceedings of the Software Testing Analysis & Review Conference* (STAR East). Orlando, Florida: May.

Hendrickson, Elisabeth. Undated. Architecture Reverse Engineering. Available at www.testing.com/test-patterns/patterns/Architecture-Reverse-Engineering.pdf.

Hendrickson, Elisabeth. Forthcoming. *Bug Hunting.* New York: Dorset House Publishing. (Some of this material is available in the course notes she hands to students in her course on *Bug Hunting.)*

Hoffman, Douglas. 1999a. Cost Benefits Analysis of Test Automation, *Proceedings of the Software Testing Analysis & Review Conference* (STAR East). Orlando, Florida: May.

Hoffman, Douglas. 1999b. Test Automation Architectures: Planning for Test Automation. *Proceedings of the International Software Quality Week.* San Francisco, May.

Hoffman, Douglas. 2000. The Darker Side of Metrics. Proceedings of the *Pacific Northwest Software Quality Conference*, October 17–18. Portland, Oregon.

Houlihan, Paul. 2001. Targeted Software Fault Insertion, *Proceedings of the Software Testing Analysis & Review Conference* (STAR East) Orlando, Florida: May. Available at www.mango.com/technology.

Humphrey, Watts S. 1990. *Managing the Software Process.* Reading, Massachusetts: Addison-Wesley.

Humphrey, Watts S. 1997. *Managing Technical People.* Reading, Massachusetts: Addison-Wesley.

Hutchins, Edwin. 1995. *Cognition in the Wild.* Cambridge, Massachusetts: MIT Press.

-I-

IEEE Computer Society. 2001. *Software Engineering Body of Knowledge, trial version 0.95.* Available at www.swebok.org/documents/stoneman095/Trial_Version_0_95.pdf.

InstallShield Corporation. 1999. *Creating a Project with the NetInstall Spy.* Available at http://support.installshield.com/reference/netinstall/UG/ugchapter3.pdf.

-J-

Jacobson, Ivar. 1992. *Object-Oriented Software Engineering.* Wokingham: Addison-Wesley.

Jeffries, Ron, Ann Anderson, and Chet Hendrickson. 2000. *Extreme Programming Installed.* Reading, Massachusetts: Addison-Wesley.

Jensen, Arthur Robert. 1980. *Bias in Mental Testing.* Free Press.

Johnson, Karen. 2001. Mining Gold from Server Logs. *STQE Magazine.* January.

Jorgensen, Paul C. 1995. Software Testing: A Craftsman's Approach. Boca Raton, Florida: CRC Press.

-K-

Kaner, Cem. 1995a. Software Negligence and Testing Coverage. *Software QA Quarterly* volume 2, number 2: 18. Available at http://kaner.com/coverage.htm.

Kaner, Cem. 1995b. Liability for Defective Documentation. *Software QA Quarterly*, volume 2, number 3: 8. Available at www.kaner.com/baddocs.htm.

Kaner, Cem. 1996a. Computer Malpractice, *Software QA*, volume 3, number 4: 23. Available at www.badsoftware.com/malprac.htm.

Kaner, Cem. 1996b. *Negotiating Testing Resources*. Available at www.kaner .com/negotiate.htm.

Kaner, Cem. 1998a. *Avoiding Shelfware: A Manager's View of Automated GUI Testing*. Available at www.kaner.com/pdfs/shelfwar.pdf.

Kaner, Cem. 1998b. Liability for Product Incompatibility. *Software QA Magazine*, September.

Kaner, Cem. 2000a. Measurement of the Extent of Testing. Available at www.kaner.com/pnsqc.html.

Kaner, Cem. 2000b. Architectures of Test Automation. Available at http://kaner.com/testarch.html.

Kaner, Cem, James Bach, Hung Quoc. Nguyen, Jack Falk, and Bob Johnson. 2002. *Testing Computer Software, 3rd edition, Volume 1*. Forthcoming.

Kaner, Cem, Jack Falk, and Hong Nguyen. 1993. *Testing Computer Software, 2nd edition, 1999 reprint*. New York: John Wiley & Sons.

Kaner, Cem, Elisabeth Hendrickson and Jennifer Smith-Brock. 2000. Managing the Proportion of Testers to (Other) Developers. *Proceedings of the International Software Quality Week*. San Francisco.

Kaner, Cem and David Pels. 1997. *Article 2B and Software Customer Dissatisfaction*. Available at www.badsoftware.com/stats.htm.

Kaner, Cem and David Pels. 1998. *Bad Software*. New York: John Wiley & Sons.

Kaner, Cem and John R. Vokey. 1984. A Better Random Number Generator for Apple's Floating Point BASIC. *Micro*, June, 26–35. Available at www.kaner.com/random.html.

Kaplan, Robert S. and David P. Norton. 1996. *The Balanced Scorecard: Translating Strategy into Action*. Cambridge, Massachusetts: Harvard Business School Press.

Koslowski, Barbara. 1996. *Theory and Evidence: The Development of Scientific Reasoning*. Cambridge, Massachusetts: MIT Press.

Kruchten, Philippe. 2000. *The Rational Unified Process, an Introduction, 2nd edition*. Reading, Massachusetts: Addison-Wesley.

-L-

Lakatos, Imre. 1976. *Proofs and Refutations: The Logic of Mathematical Discovery*. Cambridge, Massachusetts: Cambridge University Press.

Lawrence, Brian and Bob Johnson. 1998. *A Product Life Cycle (PLC) Model*. Available at www.coyotevalley.com/plc/builder.htm.

Lebow, Rob. 1990. *A Journey Into the Heroic Environment*. Rocklin, California: Prima Publishing.

Levy, David A. 1997. *Tools of Critical Thinking: Metathoughts for Psychology*. Boston: Allyn and Bacon.

Linz, Tilo and Matthias Daigl. 1998a. GUI Testing Made Painless: Implementation and Results of the ESSI PIE 24306. Available at www.imbus.de/forschung/pie24306/gui_test_made_painless.html.

Linz, Tilo and Matthias Daigl. 1998b. How to Automate Testing of Graphical User Interfaces. Available at www.imbus.de/forschung/pie24306/gui/aquis-full_paper-1.3.html.

-M-

Marick, Brian. 1995. *The Craft of Software Testing.* Upper Saddle River, New Jersey: Prentice Hall.

Marick, Brian. 1998. When Should a Test be Automated? Available at www.testing.com/writings/automate.pdf.

Marick, Brian. 1999. How to Misuse Code Coverage. Available at www.testing.com/writings/coverage.pdf.

Marick, Brian. 2000. Using Ring Buffer Logging to Help Find Bugs. Available at http://visibleworkings.com/trace/Documentation/ring-buffer.pdf.

Marick, Brian. Undated. How Many Bugs Do Regression Tests Find? Available at www.testingcraft.com/regression-test-bugs.html.

Mead, Nancy. 2001. Issues in Licensing and Certification of Software Engineers. July 23. Available at www.sei.cmu.edu/staff/nrm/license.html.

Michalko, Michael. 1991. *Thinkertoys: A Handbook of Business Creativity.* Berkeley, California: Ten Speed Press.

Miller, L. J. 1998. Get More Money on Your Next Job: 25 Proven Strategies for Getting More Money, Better Benefits, & Greater Job Security. McGraw-Hill Professional Publishing.

-N-

Nguyen, Hung Quoc. 2000. *Testing Applications on the Web.* New York: John Wiley & Sons.

Norman, Donald A. 1993. *Things that make us smart: Defending human attributes in the age of the machine.* Reading, Massachusetts: Addison-Wesley.

Notkin, David A., Michael Gorlick, and Mary Shaw. 2000. An Assessment of Software Engineering Body of Knowledge Efforts: A Report to the ACM Council. Available at www.acm.org/serving/se_policy/bok_assessment.pdf.

Nyman, Noel. 2000. Using Monkey Test Tools, *Software Testing & Quality Engineering,* January.

-O-

Olve, Nils-Goran, Jan Roy, and Magnus Wetter. 1999. *Performance Drivers: A Practical Guide to Using the Balanced Scorecard.* New York: John Wiley & Sons.

O'Malley, Michael. 1998. *Are You Paid What You're Worth?* Broadway Books.

Ostrand, Thomas J. and Marc J. Balcer. 1988. The Category-Partition Method for Specifying and Generating Functional Tests. *Communications of the ACM.* Volume 31 #6: 676–686. June.

-P-

Park, S. K. and K. W. Miller. 1988. Random Number Generators: Good ones are hard to find. *Communications of the ACM,* October, volume 31, issue 10, 1192–1201.

Pettichord, Bret. 1996. Success with Test Automation. *Proceedings of the International Software Quality Week.* San Francisco, California: May 1996. Available at www.io.com/~wazmo/succpap.htm.

Pettichord, Bret. 1999. Seven Steps to Test Automation Success. *Proceedings of the Software Testing Analysis & Review Conference* (STAR West). San Jose, California. November. Available at www.io.com/~wazmo/papers/seven_steps.html.

Pettichord, Bret. 2000a. Beyond the Bug Battle, *Proceedings of the Software Testing Analysis & Review Conference* (STAR East). Orlando, Florida: May.

Pettichord, Bret. 2000b. Testers and Developers Think Differently. *Software Testing & Quality Engineering.* January. Available at www.io.com/~wazmo/papers/testers_and_developers.pdf.

Pettichord, Bret. 2001a. Hey Vendors, Give Us Real Scripting Languages. *Stickyminds.com.* Available at http://stickyminds.com/sitewide.asp?sid= 409206&sqry=%2AJ%28MIXED%29%2AR%28createdate%29%2AK% 28simplesite%29%2AF%28scripting+languages%29%2A&sidx=0&sopp= 10&ObjectId=2326&Function=DETAILBROWSE&ObjectType=COL.

Pettichord, Bret. 2001b. What you don't know may help you. *Stickyminds.com.* July. Available at www.stickyminds.com/sitewide.asp?ObjectId=2629& ObjectType=COL&Function=edetail.

Pettichord, Bret. 2001c. Let observation be your crystal ball. *Stickyminds.com,* May. Available at www.stickyminds.com/sitewide.asp?ObjectId=2498& ObjectType=COL&Function=edetail.

Polya, George. 1957. *How to Solve It.* Princeton: Princeton University Press.

Popper, Karl. 1989. *Conjectures and Refutations: The Growth of Scientific Knowledge.* London: Routledge.

PowerQuest Corporation. 2001. *Drive Image.* Available at www.powerquest .com/driveimage/.

-R-

Rational Software Corporation. 2001. *Rational Purify for Unix*. Available at www.rational.com/products/purify_unix/index.jsp.

Rational Software Corporation. 2001. *Rational Test Foundation for Windows 2000.* Available at www.rational.com/products/testfoundation/ w2k_ds.jsp.

Robinson, Harry. 1999. Finite State Model-Based Testing on a Shoestring. Star West 1999. Available at www.geocities.com/model_based_testing/ shoestring.htm.

-S-

Schneier, Bruce. 2000a. Computer Security: Will We Ever Learn? *Crypto-Gram*, May 15. Available at www.counterpane.com/crypto-gram-0005.html.

Schneier, Bruce. 2000b. *Secrets & Lies*. New York: John Wiley & Sons.

Simmonds, Erik. 2000. When Will We Be Done Testing? Software Defect Arrival. Proceedings of the Pacific Northwest Software Quality Conference, October 17–18. Portland, Oregon.

Sims, Henry P. Jr. and Charles C. Manz. 1996. *Company of Heroes*. New York: John Wiley & Sons.

Solow, Daniel. 1990. *How to Read and Do Proofs*. New York: John Wiley & Sons.

Strauss, Anselm and Juliet Corbin, eds. 1997. *Grounded Theory in Practice*. Thousand Oaks: SAGE Publications.

Strauss, Anselm and Juliet Corbin. 1998. *Basics of Qualitative Research, 2nd edition*. Thousand Oaks: SAGE Publications.

Sweeney, Mary R. 2001. *Automation Testing Using Visual Basic*. Berkeley, CA: Apress.

-T-

Tarrant, John J. 1997. *Perks & Parachutes: Negotiating Your Best Possible Employment Deal, from Salary and Bonus to Benefits and Protection*. Times Books.

Telles, Matt and Yuan Hsieh. 2001. *The Science of Debugging*. Scottsdale, Arizona: Coriolis.

Tukey, John W. 1977. *Exploratory Data Analysis*. Reading, Massachusetts: Addison-Wesley.

-W-

Webster, Bruce. 1995. *Pitfalls of Object-Oriented Development*. M&T Books.

Weick, Karl E. 1995. *Sensemaking in Organizations*. Thousand Oaks: SAGE Publications.

Weinberg, Gerald M. 1992. *Quality Software Management, Volume 1: Systems Thinking.* New York: Dorset House Publishing.

Weinberg, Gerald M. 1997a. *Quality Software Management, Volume 2: First-Order Measurement.* New York: Dorset House Publishing.

Weinberg, Gerald M. 1997b. *Quality Software Management, Volume 3: Congruent Action.* New York: Dorset House Publishing.

Weinberg, Gerald M. 1997c. *Quality Software Management, Volume 4: Anticipating Change.* New York: Dorset House Publishing.

Weinberg, Gerald M. 1998. *The Psychology of Computer Programming, Silver Anniversary Edition.* New York: Dorset House Publishing.

Weinberg, Gerald M. 2001. *An Introduction to General Systems Thinking: Silver Anniversary Edition.* New York: Dorset House Publishing.

Whittaker, James and Alan Jorgensen. 1999. Why Software Fails. ACM Software Engineering Notes, July. Available at http://se.fit.edu/papers/SwFails.pdf.

Whittaker, James and Alan Jorgensen. 2000. How to Break Software. Proceedings of the Software Testing Analysis & Review Conference, May. Orlando, Florida.

Whittaker, James. 2002. *How to Break Software.* Reading, Massachusetts: Addison-Wesley.

Wiegers, Karl E. 1996. *Creating a Software Engineering Culture.* New York: Dorset House Publishing.

Worrall, John and Gregory Currie, eds. 1978. *The methodology of scientific research programmes.* Cambridge, Massachusetts: Cambridge University Press.

Wurman, Richard Saul. 1991. *Follow the Yellow Brick Road: Learning to Give, Take, and Use Instructions.* New York: Bantam Books.

-Y-

Yourdon, Edward. 1997. *Death March: The Complete Software Developer's Guide to Surviving 'Mission Impossible' Projects.* Indianapolis, Indiana: Prentice Hall Computer Books.

-Z-

Zuse, Horst. 1997. *A Framework of Software Measurement.* Walter de Gruyter, Inc.

Index

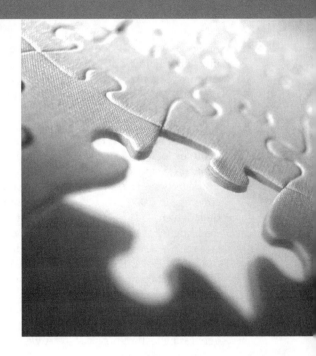